Mackintosh's
The Government and
Politics of Britain

Peter G. Richards

Hutchinson

London   Melbourne   Sydney   Auckland   Johannesburg

Hutchinson & Co. (Publishers) Ltd

An imprint of the Hutchinson Publishing Group

17–21 Conway Street, London W1P 6JD
and 51 Washington Street, Dover, New Hampshire 03820, USA

Hutchinson Group (Australia) Pty Ltd
16–22 Church Street, Hawthorn, Melbourne, Victoria 3122

Hutchinson Group (NZ) Ltd
32–34 View Road, PO Box 40–086, Glenfield, Auckland 10

Hutchinson Group (SA) (Pty) Ltd
PO Box 337, Bergvlei 2012, South Africa

First published 1970   Reprinted 1978, 1979
Second edition 1971   Fifth edition 1982
Third edition 1974   Reprinted 1982, 1983
Reprinted 1975   Sixth edition 1984
Fourth edition 1977   Reprinted 1985

Set in Times

Printed and bound in Great Britain by
Anchor Brendon Ltd,
Tiptree, Essex

British Library Cataloguing in Publication Data
Mackintosh, John P.
    Mackintosh's The government and politics of Britain — 6th ed
    1. Great Britain — Politics and government — 1964-
    I. Title   II. Richards, Peter G.
    III. Mackintosh, John P. Government and politics of Britain
    320.941   JN231

Library of Congress Cataloging in Publication Data
Mackintosh, John Pitcairn 1929-
    Mackintosh's The government and politics of Britain.
    Rev. ed. of The government and politics of Britain.
    5th ed. 1981.
    Includes index.
    1. Great Britain—Politics and government—1945-
I. Richards, Peter G. II. Mackintosh, John Pitcairn, 1929-.
The government and politics of Britain.
III. Title.
JN231.M32 198lb 320.941   84–4480

ISBN   0   09   156281   3

Contents

Preface to the fifth edition   8

Preface to the sixth edition   9

Preface   10

1 **Describing the British Constitution**   11

2 **The Westminster model**   16

3 **Forces of change**   23

4 **British government today**   36

5 **Political leadership – producing a Prime Minister**   45
   The process of selection within the parties – The
   role of the Crown – The causes and effects of the
   two-party system –
   The reasons for changes in voting behaviour –
   The character of
   British political leadership

6 **Political leadership – the strength of the Prime**
   Minister   62
   Party loyalty, the whips and patronage – Support
   of his colleagues, the Cabinet and the civil
   service – Right to choose the date of general elections

6   *Contents*

7   **Political leadership – the limitations on the Prime
    Minister's power**   75
    Limitations of party loyalty and Cabinet control –
    The party outside Parliament as a constraint –
    Governing through the House of Commons –
    Governing through the civil service – Relations
    with the pressure groups – The mass media

8   **Political leadership – can the Prime Minister be
    sacked?**   97
    Strength of a Labour leader – Strength of a
    Conservative leader

9   **The leadership and its relations with the
    electorate; the state and the citizen**   103
    Politicians and the public – Parties and electors –
    Contacts through officials and pressure groups –
    Opinion polls – By-elections – Referenda –
    Personal contacts – The public's reactions to
    politics – Direct action – Why do people obey the
    government? – Personal freedom – The place of
    the courts – Public inquiries and administrative
    tribunals – The ombudsman – Enforcing the law:
    the army and the police

10 **Governing through Parliament**   142
    The role of Parliament – How the executive
    gained control of Parliament – The legislative
    process – Authorizing public expenditure and
    taxation – Pressing the government from the

floor of the House – Pressing the government:
upstairs and informal methods – Standing and select
committees – Televising the House of Commons –
The House of Lords – The influence of Parliament

11 Governing through the Whitehall departments   179
A highly centralized country – The convention of
ministerial responsibility – The Northcote–
Trevelyan principles – Departmental
organization and the Treasury – Criticisms of the
civil service: its relations with ministers –
Criticisms of the civil service: its administrative
methods – The civil service and Parliament – The
case for political advice

12 Government outside Whitehall   198
The nationalized industries – Local government:
its structure and weaknesses – Regionalism and
devolution – Northern Ireland

**13 The direction of change: the attitudes of the
parties**   225
Away from the Westminster model towards
what? – The political parties and the community
– The Labour Party – The Conservative Party –
The SDP, Liberals and Nationalists –
Conclusion: no clear direction

Further reading   247
Index   249

Preface to the fifth edition

The early death of John P. Mackintosh in 1978 at the age of 48 was a great loss to Parliament, to public life and to the study of British politics. *The Government and Politics of Great Britain* has been one of the most successful student textbooks on this subject because the author had intimate personal experience of the subject. Indeed, it was his life. At the time of his death the book had already passed through four editions. Now a new one is needed which I have been asked to prepare.

It is important that the analysis of British government should keep pace with events. The fifth edition of *The Government and Politics of Great Britain* covers developments as far as the start of 1981. Thus the new material describes the unusual unofficial coalition basis of the parliamentary support for the Callaghan Government (1977–9), the circumstances of the 1979 Conservative victory and the subsequent tensions within the Labour Party. A few sections have been rewritten, notably those on referenda, local government and regional government, and the whole text has been thoroughly revised. To prevent the book becoming much longer, some material relating to events which occurred twenty or more years ago has been excised. An attempt has been made to sustain the style and the argument of the original work. This task has been eased because, on almost all matters, my approach is very similar to that of John Mackintosh.

Peter G. Richards
University of Southampton
January 1981

Preface to the sixth edition

The past three years have seen major changes in the shape of British
politics. Since the end of the last war there has been a remarkable
amount of agreement between the two major parties on matters of
basic policy – on defence, foreign affairs and the welfare state. That
consensus has now ended. Indeed, it is now misleading to speak of
a two-party system. Parliament is still dominated by two parties but,
viewed in the terms of the choice of electors, there is essentially a
three-way split in opinion: the weight of Conservative and Labour
representation in the House of Commons is but the result of a quirk
of our electoral system. The Labour Party has been in turmoil over
internal arguments and has undertaken great changes in its
constitutional arrangements. Through alterations in personnel and
attitudes, the Conservative Party led by Margaret Thatcher is very
different from the Conservative Party of Harold Macmillan. In
Parliament the backbenchers have managed to secure wider
opportunities to exercise initiative.

Perhaps the greatest change of all is the nature of political debate.
Inflation and the balance of payments are no longer crucial factors.
Unemployment has soared to levels unknown for half a century but
somehow has not had a major impact on the public mind, at least
at the general election. The following pages describe and assess
these developments. Meanwhile, the future remains an exciting
enigma. Some argue that British politics is entering a new age of
certainty and stability; some feel that further great upheavals lie not
too far ahead.

Peter G. Richards
University of Southampton
October 1983

Preface

This book was suggested to me by Professor W.A. Robson, and I am most grateful to him and to Hutchinson University Library for giving me this opportunity. The opportunity came towards the end of the 1966–70 Parliament when I had had time to acquire some general views as to how British government works. The book is not intended to provide a factual guide – many of these already exist – nor is it to lead the student towards the more detailed studies that have been written about specialized aspects or our government and politics. The book is an interpretation, an extended essay trying to explain how the system works and what it looks like to someone in one of the best spectator seats. As such I have referred to those major controversies which need to be dealt with in order to establish or explain my views, but academic or political controversies which have no bearing on my theme are not mentioned.

I must thank Miss Louise McAdam for her great kindness and incredible accuracy and speed in typing the book, and my wife and family for putting up with me during the period when it was being written. I dedicate it to my daughter Deirdre Victoria Una whose birth occurred to cheer me up and speed the writing of the last chapter.

John P. Mackintosh
House of Commons
April 1970

1 Describing the British Constitution

It is often said that Britain has an unwritten constitution, but this is true only in the sense that rules guiding the system are not set out in a single document with a special procedure required for amending these rules, as was done in the United States. But a great number of these rules are written and embodied in Acts of Parliament such as the Representation of the People Act 1948, which prescribes the arrangements for holding elections, or the Parliament Acts of 1911 and 1949 which set out some of the relations between the House of Lords and the House of Commons. Other aspects of the system which are not laws but are established practices (such as the convention that the Queen asks the leader of the majority party after an election to form a government) are written down in many books on British politics. It is not illegal to break these established practices but if a serious attempt to avoid them occurred, it would indicate that profound changes were taking place in the whole system. Again, there is another category of practices, examples being the way the Cabinet is organized or parliamentary candidates selected, which are neither law nor established conventions but are simply convenient methods of procedure whose change would involve no major shake-up in the process of government. It might even be some time before such changes were noticed.

The difficulty in producing an accurate and comprehensive account of these laws, conventions and practices is partly that they are scattered over the history of the country from the Habeas Corpus Act of 1679, which prevents people being held in prison without trial, and the convention that the Queen will not veto legislation, which has been built up since 1708, to recent changes in parliamentary procedure dealing with the control of public expenditure. In part, the difficulty is that situations which call for the application of certain conventions may be few and far between. Thus, how far a convention would apply today may not be absolutely clear, while some conventions (such as 'the collective responsibility of ministers') may have changed their actual content or meaning though the words used remain the same. As a result, to try and describe the British Constitution is like trying to explain the working of an ancient university with its old statutes, more recent regulations, traditions begun for one purpose but still useful for another where new students and teachers are continually altering current practice.

There is yet a further problem in that so many developments of all kinds in Britain and in the rest of the world have some effect on the working of the institutions that it is hard to know where to stop the account. For example, changes in voters' attitudes are likely, in time, to alter the responses of the political parties and to have an influence on the kind of people who are prepared to go into politics. In 1955, a combination of forces inside and outside Parliament led to the end of the BBC's monopoly of broadcasting and the creation of commercial television which has probably had some effect on the public's responses. On the other hand, Acts of Parliament insisting on political balance in television have meant that the public receives much of its political news without the slant and editorializing which is normal in newspapers. At a different level, British membership of the Common Market has already altered the tax system and has begun to change the methods by which agriculture is supported. Further afield, a wave of isolationism in the United States and the withdrawal of her forces in Europe could force Britain to return to conscription and to forge closer defence links with her European partners.

It is because of the ancient origins of many of the laws and conventions of the constitution that books on British government often start with an historical section. However, it is not essential to go far back into history because most of the conventions, practices and maxims which have been inherited either date from the late nineteenth century or were in operation then. Also it is important not just to list the various acts or to describe how Parliament or the civil service developed, but to show their interconnections. Each part of the machinery of government can only be understood in terms of the other cog wheels with which it must intermesh and many of the maxims or descriptions are only meaningful if they can be seen in relation to the whole system in operation at the time when the conventions became established.

It so happens that the pattern of government which evolved in

Britain between 1870 and 1914 was regarded then (and by many since then) with particular satisfaction. Not only were a large number of books written about it, but most of the commentators assumed that there could scarcely be any improvement. There were several reasons for the belief that the system prevailing at that time was close to perfection. In those years Britain was particularly powerful and successful, the dominating mood being one of confidence that progress would continue and that Britain's peculiar and powerful position in the world would always remain. Looking back, it seemed clear to the Victorians that Britain had been through the social and political phases or overcome the difficulties then besetting most other nations. Personal liberty and equality before the law had been established. A respected monarchy gave continuity and an aura of authority to the government, yet all personal or arbitrary rule had been eliminated. The aristocracy had never been marched to the guillotine, yet their powers had been tempered and shared with the other classes in the community. As late as the 1860s, there had been serious worries that any move towards democracy would introduce class warfare and political instability but, by the 1880s, these fears had faded. It was accepted that Britain had managed, apparently with unique success, to combine a proper degree of governmental authority with responsiveness to popular opinion, that patriotism, property and stability had been fortified rather than endangered by bringing all sections of the population into a continuing debate about public policy.

Exemplifying this self-confidence, late nineteenth-century historians tended to regard all aspects of British history as stages in an inevitable march towards this happy conclusion. They thought they had discovered that the Anglo-Saxon tribes, even before coming to Britain, had always proceeded by open decisions at 'folk moots' and that these albeit rudimentary democratic practices had tempered the Norman autocracy introduced into England after 1066. Any further attempts at despotic rule were countered by baronial revolts which forced respect for basic liberties upon recalcitrant sovereigns. These concessions and rights were embodied in Magna Carta. Then the practices of presenting grievances, of agreeing to grants of taxation and of making proclamations clarifying ancient custom, were all brought together in periodic Parliaments dating from the time of Simon de Montfort and Edward I. The Lancastrian kings, it was alleged, were involved in a 'constitutional experiment' of rule with Parliament, while even the Tudor despotism only served to confirm these trends, since Parliament was used to carry through the Reformation and to show patriotic support for Queen Elizabeth. From this point of view, Charles I may have had a tragic history but he was guilty of attempting to halt the country's steady progress towards constitutional monarchy and the emergence of the House of Commons as an essential partner in government. Charles II and James II had the same failings and the English genius for non-violent progress was revealed when the latter monarch was allowed to escape. A new monarch was installed and what these historians dubbed as 'the Glorious Revolution of 1688' established simply that Parliament could not be set aside or overruled. Next, it was argued that the late seventeenth century saw the invention of the two-party system, the descendants of the Roundheads and Cavaliers becoming the Whigs and Tories who were content to fight it out at the hustings and in the House of Commons. According to this version of British history, George III's great error was to try and restore a measure of personal rule but luckily this was abandoned by his successors. The Reform Bill of 1832 created a uniform right to vote for men of property who were thus brought into the political system without any sharp break with tradition. Then the Reform Acts of 1867 and 1884 carried the process further and gave all established male householders a voice and a vote.

This, known as 'the Whig theory of history', viewed the system of government in practice in Britain between 1880 and 1914 as virtually the last word. The pattern then established was regarded as not only the culmination of fifteen hundred years of progress but was itself so simple, so logical, so effective and satisfactory, that the accounts of it had great force. These accounts filled the books and the minds of students of British government long after much had changed and were still regarded as largely correct until the 1940s. Thus the conventions and practices of the late Victorian period were not considered as merely true for that time, they were regarded as proper or normal. When further changes occurred, they were noticed with reluctance and tended to be regarded as departures from the norm, the main features of this system, which may be called 'the Westminster model', still dominating the textbooks in use after the Second World War. It then became the basis of the constitutions which were carefully written up for emergent nations of the Commonwealth on the grounds that if this system was the most advanced yet produced, why not hand it on in its complete form to the new states of Africa and Asia? Also, nationalist leaders who learnt their politics in Britain or from British books and teachers were so convinced by the merits of the system that they would settle for nothing less. Any adaptations to meet special historical or social conditions in their countries would have been regarded as insulting, as suggestions that they were not capable of the most advanced form of democracy.

Because of the strength of this tradition, to understand the meaning and original relevance of much that is said about current British government and politics, it is worth considering 'the Westminster model' as it was supposed to work at the end of the last century. Those describing it at the time neglected to note that a is always the case, social, political and legal conditions were changing. They did not think they were writing about a stage but an end-product and thus their account may not have been true of any one precise moment, since practices they thought essential may have been declining and trends they had failed to notice may have been starting. But the account was broadly correct for the 1880–1914 period and relevant for this book in that it explains what is still for many British politicians and informed observers, the proper state of affairs and the values and attitudes which continue to underlie many of the maxims used to describe the British political system.

2 The Westminster model

The key feature of the British system of the 1880–1914 period, according to its exponents, was the Cabinet. This body of some sixteen senior political leaders, presided over by the Prime Minister, had two functions. On the one hand, the Cabinet governed the country and on the other, it sat in, led, was maintained, criticized and influenced by the House of Commons. As Bagehot put it in 1865, the 'Cabinet is a combining committee – a *hyphen* which joins, a *buckle* which fastens, the legislative part of the state to the executive part of the state'. In the Cabinet, which operated totally informally without officials present or minutes taken, all the major policy issues were thrashed out. The Prime Minister might, like Peel or Gladstone, have a commanding presence or, like Lord Aberdeen, might act essentially as a chairman taking no major part in discussions himself. While Prime Ministers advised the Crown as to who should be appointed to the Cabinet, the House of Commons played a background role in the selection. Some men had such a reputation that they could not be omitted and, conversely, to be a failure in the House was a serious disqualification for high office. Also, leaving a powerful man on the backbenches might expose the Cabinet to dangerous attacks. Most of those likely to be appointed were men of wealth, usually with a considerable social or commercial reputation which gave them a position which was not solely derived from politics. For these reasons, the relationship between the Prime Minister and his colleagues was said to be that of a *primus inter pares*; he could lead and suggest but his fellow ministers had to be persuaded. Sacking ministers was scarcely proper but they were usually ready to resign if they had major doubts on policy issues, though no Prime Minister or Cabinet wanted to face the parliamentary problems that would be created by pointed criticisms from ex-ministers.

The source of the Cabinet's strength and its ultimate responsiveness to criticism came alike from the ministers' position in the House of Commons. There they normally enjoyed the support of a majority held together by party loyalty. MPs were returned at elections largely because of their views which indicated the party they supported, though many MPs had a personal hold on their constituencies. Once in the House, they wanted to see the leaders of their party succeed and were likely, other things being equal, to provide the Cabinet.with fairly steady support. On the other hand, if the policies of the government failed, if it seemed to run counter to the principles espoused by its followers or if the Opposition seemed to be winning the argument, MPs might become restive and vote against their own leaders. The Cabinet, sensing such dangers, could then agree to modify its policies. Thus ministers enjoyed considerable power in the House so long as their policies were successful and were arousing both public acclaim and the enthusiasm of their own supporters. But a dispirited leadership, external setbacks, an impression of incompetence or of internal disagreements could lead to heavy pressure on the government to change its policies. If this yielded no results, the Commons might go on to dismiss a government, a general election only being necessary if the Parliament was near the end of its life or if MPs were not prepared to support another combination of ministers.

Because of the pressure of the House of Commons, all administration had to be handled by ministers answerable to Parliament. In the early nineteenth century, some administrative functions had been allocated to commissioners or boards (e.g. the administration of the Poor Law) simply because it was feared that the monarch might use appointments to such posts as a method of influencing the House of Commons. After the 1830s, these fears ceased and Parliament began to insist on its right to question all policies. MPs demanded that every aspect of central government should be allocated to one or other minister who could then be held responsible for all the actions of his department. This was the doctrine of 'ministerial responsibility' which had reality in two senses. First, the departments were small enough for the minister to have seen and to have endorsed every decision likely to arouse outside comment and, second, if there was comment, the House of Commons would insist on holding the minister personally responsible. A further doctrine of 'collective responsibility' arose also in the face of parliamentary pressure. Ministers found that they had to support each other, for if one of them voiced doubts, it made the position of the entire Cabinet too precarious. This convention was reasonable in that all major decisons were taken collectively by the Cabinet.

Little was said about the process of administration because it was relatively simple. If the Cabinet proposed something and the House of Commons agreed, then the senior civil servants had merely to write the appropriate letters. There was no problem of the relations between officials and ministers as the distinction between political decisions and the execution of policy was so clear. Civil servants were, after the reforms of 1870, all recruited by open competition, the administrative class from the universities, the executive class from those who had completed a full school education and the clerical grade from those with a suitable, more elementary education. The civil service was not supposed to have views on politics or on policy issues or to have contact with outside interests. They were protected from parliamentary criticism and were allowed to serve one government after another on the assumption that they loyally carried out whatever policy was determined by the Cabinet. The small amount of local, as opposed to central, administration was placed in the hands of elected county and borough councils.

The primary tasks of the House of Commons in this period have been explained; each party evolved a leadership which it supported while the House as a whole commented on and criticized the performance of those leaders who were in office at that time. The House exercised these functions through the traditional forms of the power to legislate, to grant money and to debate. The process of legislation was designed to let the House know what the Cabinet or the private members sponsoring the bill intended (first reading), to give MPs ample time to debate the principles involved (second reading), to amend the proposal in detail (Committee of the whole House) and to have a look at the final result (third reading). In financial matters, the House worked on the same annual programme as the government. It scrutinized civil and defence estimates in the spring, and could amend or alter them. Then from April to July both the detailed expenditure proposals and the methods of raising revenue were debated and determined. In the autumn, the Public Accounts Committee (set up in 1860) scrutinized the accounts for the previous year to see that every penny had been spent as authorized by Parliament. The responsibility for raising the money and watching over its expenditure within the government lay with the Treasury which thus acquired a central and commanding position inside the government. Finally, with the Commons controlling the use of two or three days' time each week and with the government reluctant to close or curtail debate (powers to do so were taken in 1882), there was little need for a special question time or methods of getting at ministers. The House could and did debate any issue as it arose, private members could call for papers (that is, for official documents), they could propose select committees of investigation, move and carry bills and go on and on talking about the Cabinet's proposals until they had arrived at a conclusion. Ministers had to attend the House on every sitting day and explain and defend their policies with the Prime Minister (if he was in the Commons) acting as Leader of the House and chief spokesman for the Cabinet.

The House of Lords was of secondary importance but it had powers to amend and reject bills passed by the Commons though its leaders usually accepted that a measure clearly demanded by that House and by the country had to be passed. If the mass of peers looked like holding out against the Commons on a serious issue, the Cabinet could in the last resort ask the Crown to create sufficient peers to alter the balance. The Lords could also do much useful tidying up of legislation and its members contained sufficient men of talent to provide about a third of the ministers in nineteenth-century cabinets.

In such a system, there was little room for royal initiative. The Crown provided an impartial or non-political focus of loyalty, an embodiment of national feeling. The political functions of the Crown were to provide continuity, particularly when a Cabinet was defeated either in the Commons or at a general election. Then the king or queen had the task of initiating consultations to find out which new leader was most likely to command the confidence of the majority in the Commons. In nine cases out of ten, the answer was obvious and in the tenth was soon established. Apart from this, the Crown could, under very special circumstances, refuse to grant a dissolution (if it was thought that the existing House of Commons was ready to maintain another Prime Minister without an election being held). The sovereign could also, as Bagehot put it, insist on being consulted and then encourage or warn ministers but, in the last resort, the views of the Cabinet had to prevail.

Little was said in most descriptions of the Westminster model about the electorate or the electoral system. There were discussions of the transferable vote or proportional representation (tried in a limited form in certain three-member seats after 1867) but on the whole it was accepted that either single- or double-member seats (which largely disappeared after 1884) were an adequate way of allowing public opinion to express itself. There was also little emphasis on the party machines outside Parliament for these were only growing up in the 1880s. In general, it was still assumed that elections were for the purpose of choosing a House of Commons and were not a means of selecting a government. Thus the laws designed to diminish the influence of money in elections set limits not on expenditure in the national campaigns but on the costs of standing in individual constituencies. Party leaders did, from the 1870s, tour the country and candidates explained which principles they favoured. General and even by-elections were contested with considerable partisanship creating, on occasion, great excitement. Under these circumstances, a division into two wide-ranging groups or parties was accepted as natural and proper. This led the satirist W. S. Gilbert to inquire:

How Nature always does contrive
That every boy and every gal,
That's born into the world alive,
Is either a little Liberal,
Or else a little Conservative!

The great virtues of this model were its efficiency and beneficial effect on the community. The interdependence of the Cabinet and the Commons meant that when the country and MPs agreed that action was needed, the Cabinet's powers could be enormously augmented. When the political leadership began to falter, it could at once be checked, stopped, questioned, made to provide full explanations and then, if necessary, altered or dismissed. The good effect was that the system emphasized government by discussion, by argument with the assumption that the best case wins in the end. No single class swamped Parliament. The aristocracy were most numerous but even the landed interest could be defeated by an unanswerable argument, as happened when Peel felt he had to reply to the case put by the Anti-Corn Law League in the House. Such a system drew the ablest and those most desirous of serving their country into politics. It provided a great public spectacle and educated the entire community by exposing the facts and the arguments. The nightly battles in the chamber attracted the attention of all who were interested in current affairs and in the great moral and political issues of the day.

Because, in this way, power lay in the interaction of the Commons and the Cabinet, anyone with a case or a special interest concentrated on the Commons. The Anti-Slavery Society, the Anti-Corn Law League and the factory reformers all sought to penetrate the House while the railway companies and the churches had their backbench spokesmen. But there were other interests involved and because landed and industrial wealth could clash, there was little evidence of the 'haves' uniting to exploit the 'have nots'. After Parliament had reached its decision, the administration of the laws was entrusted to a small group of non-political, upper middle-class but highly able officials, their actions being given extra authority by the fact that they were technically acting in the name of a king or queen revered as the figurehead and exemplar of the nation.

One reason for the strength of this system was that while this fairly simple pattern of administration remained constant, any social and political changes, such as the further development of an urbanized, industrialized society and of demands for a wider distribution of political power, could easily be accommodated by a refashioning of the institutions of control. As a result of such pressures, the Commons found its membership broadened, the constituencies reformed, party organizations outside Parliament established, the Crown and the Lords relegated and the civil service reorganized to permit control through the relevant minister.

Although scarcely the product of conscious planning, the enthusiasm for representative institutions was such that the gradual growth of the administration was matched, for most of the period, by the increasing watchfulness of politicians and effectiveness of the House of Commons. It is true, as a general proposition, that systems of control must alter and adapt to follow changes in the system they are trying to monitor. The act of checking by a legislature must be based on relevant information of what ministers and officials are doing and must come at the moment when decisions are still open to influence. In this, the House of Commons was reasonably successful in the last decades of the nineteenth century and up to 1914.

One of the main problems of recent years has been that while the pattern of government has been adapted at an ever-increasing pace to the needs of society, including, for instance, the administration of hospitals, the stimulation of decaying industries, the promotion of tourism, the preservation of the countryside and so on, little has been done to adapt the machinery of control to keep pace with this new network of government. This is because the British have been prepared to tackle practical problems of administration and management but, since the Westminster model was supposed to be the most advanced method of democratic control, there was thought to be no need for equivalent alterations in its form or approach. A further reason is that the late nineteenth-century enthusiasm for democratic control has waned but no other coherent political philosophy has taken its place.

3 Forces of change

Since the 1880–1914 period, the organization of life in Britain and the factors in society affecting the political superstructure have been altering very rapidly. Even in the period when the Westminster model was supposed to have been working perfectly, there were many changes, but these were barely noticed since they could all be described by the same maxims and, if any comment was necessary, they could be regarded simply as extensions of the right to vote or as improvements in administrative methods.

But the changes taking place were significant and their effects cumulative and lasting. The change that led to the most far-reaching consequences was the rapid move towards a mass electorate. Before 1832 it is hard to estimate the number of voters but there were probably some 500,000. With the first Reform Act of that year, the vote was given to men only on a restrictive property qualification and in 1867 it was extended to all male householders in borough constituencies. In 1884 the same general principle was applied to the county seats. The 1918 Act enfranchised all men over 21 and all women over 30, the younger women being included in 1928. Finally, in 1969 the age for voting was lowered to 18.

The effects of this mass electorate were pervasive, altering the whole political life of Britain and deeply affecting the institutional structure. It was assumed that because the Westminster model was essentially democratic, this vast increase in the electorate could be accommodated without any profound changes, but this was not true. For instance, a mass electorate, averaging 65,000 voters in each constituency, has totally altered the relationship between the MP and his constituents. Before 1867 and even up to 1884, many candidates could hope to speak personally to most of the electors during an election campaign but soon after this ceased to be possible. When the voters, instead of choosing someone they knew and trusted as their representative, began to focus on what was happening in Parliament, this magnified the role of the press. The papers concentrated less on the local MP than on the issues and on the leaders in Parliament. So the mass electorate began to look past the member they voted for directly to the men who were governing the country or leading the opposition.

Year	Electorate	Central government gross income (£ million)
1833	717,224	50
1868	2,225,692	71
1886	4,937,204	88
1900	6,730,935	140
1918	21,392,322	889
1945	33,240,000	3,401
1966	35,964,684	9,144
1982	42,000,000	84,896

Facing this new situation, the senior politicians found that general elections were becoming too important to leave local contests merely to anyone who happened to be interested in that constituency. So long as this had been the case, some constituencies were contested but others went by default. To remedy this, the Conservatives built up, and the Liberals adopted, organizations which linked the constituencies and these in time hardened into party machines which in their turn affected the working of the political system. The party organizations were composed of associations of enthusiasts in the constituencies who could be asked to put pressure on the local MP if he was proving troublesome at Westminster. They also retained a degree of independence in their selection of candidates and were thus in a position to affect the kind of members being returned to Parliament. On the other hand, the national gatherings of these local associations can show some life of their own and have, on occasion, tried to influence the government's choice of policies or personnel. While the main source of a politician's power has remained his standing in the parliamentary party, popularity among constituency activists as revealed at the annual conferences or, in the case of the Labour Party, in the votes for the National Executive, has assumed some importance.

With a mass electorate who could only be reached through

meetings or the press (later through television), the party leaders began to campaign outside their constituencies by touring the country elaborating their policies. Either by virtue of the criticisms of the existing government or directly because of the proposals put forward, these campaigns set out programmes of action to which the political leaders became committed. At the same time as the transition to a mass electorate, the political philosophy of the electorate changed as new voters were brought into the system and began to put forward demands which had not hitherto been voiced, at least by those who had had votes. The small, largely propertied electorate of the 1850s and 1860s had accepted that the government's task was confined to foreign affairs, defence, internal law and order and raising the very limited amount of money needed to pay for these services. A certain degree of regulation of social and industrial practices was also possible, such as specifying a minimum age for children or maximum hours for women who were working in difficult conditions, and some elementary services could be provided, such as free primary education. But it was not thought proper to extend regulations to cover the hours of work of adult men; they were best left to look after themselves – a view taken by the Trades Union Congress until the late 1880s. Nor was it considered proper or possible for the government to act in any way which influenced the activity of industry or the rates of wages that were paid. When Keir Hardie was elected in 1892 as the first independent Labour member he was deeply offended, not so much by political attacks, as by the assumption on all sides that unemployment and poverty were not issues which should concern Parliament.

But with the growth of a mass electorate, voters gradually came to expect more from the political machine, the politicians soon sensing and responding to these demands. First there was the call for legal protection for trade unions, then for regulation of hours of work in dangerous trades and then a demand for relief for the unemployed, for the indigent in old age and for those who fell sick or were injured at work. These demands began in the 1890s and then flourished after 1906 with the passage of the first spate of interventionist legislation, a further milestone being marked by the bitterly contested Budget introduced by Lloyd George in 1909. This was the first Budget which proposed to use taxation as a means of social policy, taking money from one section of the community to give it to another, thus opening up a whole new vista of governmental activity for the mass electorate to demand and for political leaders to offer.

The First World War saw a great increase in the government's activities, with intervention in industry, food rationing, the conscription of manpower and the expenditure of vast sums of money. In the election at the end of the war, the Labour Party emerged as the second largest party in the House of Commons (though it was not recognized as the official Opposition till 1922) with a policy of state ownership of the basic industries and of state action to ensure a reasonable standard of life for all sections of the community, policies which were endorsed by the trade union movement. The predominantly Conservative post-war coalition created a Ministry of Health, which then included housing. This ministry admitted the principle that the government should help to build houses if those provided by private landlords and builders were inadequate.

There was a fierce debate between the Labour and Conservative parties in the 1920s as to how much the government could or should do to revive the basic industries, alleviate unemployment and provide for those in difficulty, though there was little difference between their actual policies when in office. The major changes came in the 1930s after the world-wide slump of 1929–33, the National Government (Conservative in all but name) turning to aid industry by pushing through reorganizations of the coal, cotton, shipbuilding and steel industries. Britain left the gold standard and abandoned free trade, adopting a system of industrial protection, the government thus becoming steadily more involved in the task of holding the ring for private industry and in creating suitable conditions for private activity.

The Second World War again led to a major increase in the government's activities but this time with more lasting effects. In 1944 a White Paper, *Employment Policy* (Cmnd 6527), for the first time recognized that the government could, by overall management of the economy, ensure full employment and accepted that this was a proper concern for any administration. Earlier in 1942, Sir William (later Lord) Beveridge had published a report which received great publicity. Its principle was that the government should create a pattern of welfare payments (in sickness, injury, accident, unemployment, old age and exceptional circumstances) which were supposed to ensure that no one in the community was ever destitute. The Labour Government, elected at the end of the war in 1945, put all these proposals into force and added a National Health Service paid for by a combination of weekly payments and a contribution from the Treasury. Unlike what happened after the First World War, many wartime controls were retained. This was partly in order to concentrate investment in certain fields, partly to meet balance of payments problems, partly to ensure fairness in time of scarcity and partly because these methods had worked well in the war and seemed compatible with the ideology of the Labour Party. The Attlee Government went on to take the coal, gas and electricity industries, the railways, the Bank of England, and parts of the road haulage and steel industries into public ownership. Certain enterprises ranging from the London Port Authority to the London Passenger Transport Board and the British Broadcasting Corporation had been started or taken over by the state before the war, but the post 1945 series of Nationalization Acts was the first large-scale take-over of sectors of private industry. When the Conservatives came to power in 1951, they accelerated the dismantling of controls begun by the Labour Government in its last years and ended rationing, but of the nationalized industries, only steel was returned to private ownership.

By the end of the 1950s or the early 1960s the government was being asked to do even more in providing higher education, in building motorways, protecting the countryside, stopping the congestion of the cities and supporting the regions of Britain which had lower rates of growth, lower wages and higher rates of unemployment and emigration than the rest of the country. The Conservatives had responded to this shift in mood in their last years of office. Then the Labour Party, returned to power in 1964 (by a six-seat majority) and in 1966 (by a majority of ninety-six), went a stage further by preparing an elaborate National Plan. This failed because the government decided to meet severe balance of payments problems by a policy of deflation. In practice, by the end of the 1960s it was generally accepted that regional imbalance, the prevention of environmental pollution and the preservation of amenities were all tasks for the government.

Thus, in the period under consideration, the demands of a mass electorate, uninhibited by any notions that governmental action was inherently undesirable or inappropriate, all led in the direction of greater government involvement in the life of the community. The number of civil servants in Whitehall, which had stood at 280,000 in 1900, rose to 745,120 in 1975 but had fallen to 648,000 by

1983. At the same time, the civil service's conception of its task altered. In the mid nineteenth century, officials were simply the clerks for the ministers, ministers who could and sometimes did personally dictate every important dispatch or letter leaving their department. By the end of the century some formidable figures were emerging such as Sir Robert Morant and Alfred (later Lord) Milner, who clearly put up suggestions on matters of policy and gave their departments a distinctive outlook. Lloyd George's social reforms required much more positive administration, though after the First World War there was a swing back to the view that civil servants ought not to be actively forming policy – a view which coincided with a somewhat negative or defensive attitude in all aspects of public life. By the 1940s, because of the Second World War and the consequent social reforms and post-war economic problems, officials had to act in a much more positive capacity and it became accepted that a major task for civil servants from the level of assistant secretary upwards was to advise on policy. But the traditionally cautious approach was still common in the early 1960s. Then the Fulton Committee on the Reform of the Civil Service reported in 1968, wanting an even more definite turn towards the concept of civil servants as managers whose skills and inventiveness would have a major effect on the rate of growth of the entire economy.

Thus while the Westminster model was never reconstructed or revised, the continuation of trends such as the extension of the right to vote, the consequent growth of parties, the new demands of the electorate and the complex administration required to fulfil these demands all affected it, introducing new elements and finally altering the balance between the institutions. As regards new elements, the tremendous increase in government intervention in the economy meant that many sectors of private industry formed pressure groups to put their case to the government. At the same time, the growth of a mass electorate and of a fairly rigid party system so reduced the power of the House of Commons, that these pressure groups preferred to deal directly with Whitehall. Under the Westminster model, all direction on matters of policy was supposed to come from politicians so that civil servants in the 1860s and 1870s thought it improper for them to see pressure group representatives – everything had to go through the House of Commons and the appropriate minister. The executive committee of the Trades Union Congress was originally called the

Parliamentary Committee because the point of unions coming together was to press for favourable legislation and this, in turn, meant lobbying Parliament. Likewise the various groups of industrialists dealt primarily with favourable MPs. By the end of the century, this attitude was changing and pressure groups have found it increasingly worthwhile to deal directly with Whitehall. On the civil service side, inhibitions about such contacts have declined and, since the 1940s, it has been accepted that departments should always consult with recognized pressure groups, most items of legislation being worked out in this way before they are ever placed before the legislature. (A fascinating example of the hangover of the old proprieties is that it is thought to be 'unconstitutional' to show the draft of a clause in a bill to the spokesman for a pressure group. They can be told the content of the clause and can bargain as to whether it is acceptable or not, but they are not allowed to see the final wording because of the old conventions of the Westminster model which required that Parliament must be the first to see the actual words of the government's legislative proposals.)

But the cardinal virtue of British government in its classic period had been the delicate balance between authority and popular control, between the Cabinet and the House of Commons. And it was here that the responses to new political demands and to new administrative tasks produced the most important and perhaps least appreciated changes; least appreciated because the words used and the outward forms remained the same. Yet the trends and their effects can be clearly discerned. While governments in the 1850s and 1860s could rely on something approaching a consensus of backbench support and only faced defeat if they seriously antagonized distinct bodies of MPs, by the 1890s the opposition was indulging in systematic attacks and governments had to rely much more exclusively on their own backbenchers. The number of party divisions in the House (defined as cases where nine-tenths of each major party voted together) rose from around 30 per cent in the early 1860s to 60 per cent in the early 1870s to over 90 per cent in the 1890s. Because of this 'state of bloodless civil war', as Lord Salisbury put it, governments were able to command the support of their backbenchers and so assumed control of the House of Commons. This was achieved by stages between 1882 and 1902 when Mr Balfour carried his procedural reforms or 'parliamentary railway timetable', so called because it was possible under his revised Standing Orders to know just what station along the road to enactment any item of legislation would have reached by a given date.

These changes all increased the power of the executive so that by the turn of the century, the government could rely on voting down any undesirable motions in the House. This enabled the government to cut down the flow of information to MPs, stopping, for instance, the nineteenth-century practice of regularly publishing sets of documents (Blue Books) explaining or revealing the recent conduct of foreign policy. Detailed scrutiny of the financial estimates ceased. Question time developed as a less satisfactory substitute for the right to raise debates, whenever a member so desired, on motions to go into committee and on other procedural opportunities. Forty years later, after the Second World War, the limited value of questions began to decline as so many members wanted to intervene in the same period of time that the Speaker decided to limit each member to one supplementary question, and the whole process was speeded up so that any reasonably competent minister has little difficulty in withholding information.

The complexity of legislation and the practice of prior consultation with pressure groups, already referred to, had the same effect as did the very large extension in the Prime Minister's patronage in the form of ministerial appointments. Governments in the 1880s had some thirty-five ministers in the House of Commons. By 1918 the figure had risen to sixty; in 1945 it reached seventy. Legislation limits the number of MPs who may receive ministerial salaries and this restriction does limit the extent of the patronage of the Prime Minister. Nevertheless, the ration of jobs is generous. An act in 1964 increased the maximum from seventy to ninety-one. In 1979, Mrs Thatcher appointed eighty-five MPs to ministerial posts. At the same time, the outlook of members had altered in that many came into politics in order to have some influence on public life and could see no way of achieving their objective unless they held office. Being an MP does not in itself confer sufficient opportunities or satisfaction on the more ambitious and capable members. Also, few MPs have the wealth or social prestige of their nineteenth-century predecessors so that they have fewer satisfying alternatives to the quest for political advancement and ministerial office.

Thus though so many outward features of the Cabinet and of the House of Commons remain the same, the balance between them, which was such a central and admired feature of the Westminster model, has been steadily altered in favour of the executive as a result of the trends that have been described. Whatever is thought of the virtues and failings of British government today, it cannot be denied that relations between the executive and the legislature are quite different from the relations existing a hundred years ago. The capacity of the Commons to remove one government and install another, to amend legislation, to pick off ministers, to extract information and to push the government into changes of policy, has largely disappeared. While this may or may not be a desirable development, the mistake is to go on talking as if these powers existed or, and this is a more sophisticated modern twist, to admit the present situation but then to assert that the use of these powers in the last third of the nineteenth century has been greatly exaggerated or misunderstood; in short, that there has been little change.

The reader may wonder why it is necessary to spend so much time explaining that the Westminster model, the idealized version of British government in the 1880–1914 period, has changed in the last sixty years. This is partly because, as has been explained, its language is still used and misleads current observers and its maxims are still quoted either to cover up or to try to accommodate current practice. But there is a further point. The pace of development of the two sides of government, one being the executive or the administration, and the other the system of supervision or control, seems to alternate. Up till the late eighteenth century, there had been almost no administrative reform, no innovation or renovation in government. The process began in the 1780s under the Younger Pitt at a time when all reform of Parliament or local government was anathema. It was resumed in the 1820s and 1830s, under the influence of Bentham, the radical reformers and the free traders, many of the old cobwebs being swept aside. Administration was grouped in a few departments all under ministerial control, urban local government was reformed, the legal system was tidied up and financial organization was focused on annual accounting of all the money that flowed into and out of one Consolidated Fund.

Political reform was begun in 1832 and accelerated after 1867, the distinctive feature of the late nineteenth century being that, apart from the reorganization of the civil service and its recruitment by open competition (1870), there were no further extensive changes in the practical operation of government. The new departures were not administrative or organizational but political. What was carefully elaborated was the system of popular control based on the moral doctrines of equality of respect for the individual and of the individual's right to make his own judgement of political issues. As Gladstone put it in 1864 when he 'set the Thames on fire', 'I venture to say that every man who is not presumably incapacitated by some consideration of personal unfitness or of political danger, is morally entitled to come within the pale of the Constitution.' This doctrine underlay the extension of the right to vote in 1867 and 1884, the introduction of the secret ballot in 1872, the Corrupt Practices Act of 1883, much of the intense battle over Irish Home Rule and the final adjustment of relations between the House of Commons and the House of Lords in the Parliament Act of 1911.

Since the turn of the century, however, the pendulum has swung the other way and the vast administrative developments noted at the opening of this chapter have altered the whole shape of British government, but there has also been no new political theory and almost no new machinery of scrutiny or control to match the increased scope and power of the executive. Ostensibly Britain still adheres to the democratic doctrines enunciated by the late nineteenth-century liberals, but with flagging conviction. There are strong undercurrents which, though not often brought to the surface in public discussion, run strongly in favour of keeping decisions in the hands of limited groups of experts, men chosen for their knowledge, training or existing authority.

The curious result was that by the 1960s, when it began to be recognized that the system of political control was outdated and when some of the forms of government built into the Westminster model began to prove administratively inadequate, there was no strong ideology to provide guidelines for the necessary reforms. For instance, local government of the old county and borough pattern had become barely capable of carrying on the tasks assigned to it by the central government and demanded by the voters, so the structure had, by common consent, to be changed. But there was no agreement as to whether a reformed system should involve more devolution or more central control, whether it should be based on the doctrine of genuine local democracy or whether the role of elected members should be largely advisory. Similarly the Treasury found the House of Commons' system of annual provision of part of the money needed for government (which the Treasury had abandoned in 1962 in favour of a five-year rolling programme covering the whole of public expenditure) a nuisance and sometimes so misleading to foreign financial circles as to be positively damaging. But this dissatisfaction did not mean that there was any agreement about the nature of a reformed system; that is, whether it should lead to a restoration of the House of Commons' former actual capacity to scrutinize public expenditure or whether this should remain a formality. Again the public sensed that the rôle of backbench MPs had altered to such an extent that reforms of parliamentary procedure were necessary and ministers found some of the older aspects of procedure tedious; but there was no doctrine which gave a ready answer to the fundamental question of what backbench MPs were supposed to do, how much influence they should have or whether the object was to make it easier or harder for the executive to manage the House of Commons.

In all these cases, the governments of the 1960s and 1970s either tended to hand the task over to a royal commission or began piecemeal pragmatic changes in the hope that such difficult and unanswered questions would resolve themselves. Needless to say this did not happen and while most of the value judgements still repeated the old slogans of democratic control, the actual effect of the reforms proposed usually left these issues open.

A good example is the effort to reform local government which was examined by the Mallaby Committee (restricted to staffing) and the Maud Committee (restricted to management), the Redcliffe–Maud Commission (restricted to existing functions of English local government), the Wheatley Commission (same for Scotland), the Seebohm Committee on Local Authority and Allied Personal Services and in two White Papers on Welsh local government and in Green Papers on the administrative reorganization of the Scottish and of the English and Welsh health services. The whole problem of the size of authorities and the degree of devolution was belatedly put to a separate royal commission under Lord Crowther (later, when he died, under Lord Kilbrandon) which reported in late 1973. But in the meantime, the Labour Government published a White Paper (Cmnd 4276) in early 1970 accepting those aspects of the Redcliffe–Maud Report which made for a more efficient pattern of local authorities and which permitted easier and more effective control by the central government.

The Conservative Government elected in 1970 passed the Local Government Act 1972, which made considerable changes in local authority areas but did little to extend the freedom of action of local authorities. This reform ignored entirely the crucial question of local government finance. The subsequent Labour Government appointed a committee to examine this subject: the Report of the Layfield Committee (Cmnd 6433), published in 1976, posed stark alternatives. Did the country want a system of local administration of services which, in essence, was controlled by Whitehall? Or did it want *local* government, a pattern in which local councils were free to exercise considerable discretion over the quality of local services? The government failed to respond to this choice. It was not prepared to offer local authorities much greater freedom to spend money: to do so would undermine the already threatened ability of the Treasury to influence economic policy. Equally, for political reasons, the government could not publicly indicate a preference for greater central control.

In the Commons the Select Committee on Procedure has produced a stream of reports since 1966. Some of the proposals have favoured an increase of backbench influence, particularly by forming specialist or investigatory committees of the kind common in legislatures abroad. Other proposals have been aimed at helping the government to get its business through the House more easily.

On the civil service, a committee was set up in 1966 under Lord Fulton but it was restricted to the 'structure, recruitment and management' of the service so that its report (published in 1968) was not able to deal with the key question of how far and in what way Parliament should supervise the machinery of government and of how far ministers themselves can and should control their departments.

So while governmental systems can always be said to be 'in transition' in that change never stops, British government is in a peculiar state of transition and indecision. The administrative requirements of a government which spends a half of the total gross national product and the demands of an electorate which expects the government to provide a rising standard of living, reasonable social welfare and the preservation of the overall level of amenities, are both being met. In doing so, there has had to be a process of administrative adaptation and development. But while this has been proceeding, there has been confusion, inaction and a drift away from the old principles of democratic scrutiny and supervision whenever that aspect of institutional renewal has come up for decision.

In the next chapter, there is an attempt to give a brief overall picture of the working of the current system of government which is then explained and elaborated in the following chapters; the last chapter returns to this question of attitudes to the institutions of democratic control and to the likely direction that changes might take in the next decade.

4 British government today

In analysing a system of government, the student of politics is seeking to find out who wields power, how the machinery for the exercise of power operates, what are the constraints on those with power and why society is prepared to accept these arrangements. Some, particularly those who exercise considerable power, have tended to cast doubt on the idea that power can be located in this way and it is true that in no political system is there that crock of gold at the end of the politicians' rainbow: untrammelled power. This is the correct comment on the anecdote told by the late Aneurin Bevan in the House of Commons. Explaining his quest for the source of authority in this country, he recounted how his father had said to him, 'You see that man walking along the other side of the street, Aneurin. That's Mr Davies. You should observe him. He's a member of the urban district council and he has power.' So Bevan, in due course, got himself elected to the urban district council and some months later complained to the clerk that he had not found any power. 'Ah,' said the clerk, 'things have changed. Since those days the power has gone to the county council.' On the county council, Bevan was told that 'because of the new local government legislation . . . the power is now with the government and Parliament'. But when he became a backbench opposition MP, he found he was still powerless. 'It is all monopolized by the Treasury Bench over there,' Bevan declared, pointing to the Prime Minister and the other senior ministers.

In fact, Bevan was wrong in several senses. On the one hand, neither the Prime Minister nor the Cabinet has complete power. On the other, in each of the posts Bevan had occupied, he had exercised more power than the average citizen, though Bevan can be excused some frustration as he was at that time occupying one of the least influential positions in British government, that of the rank-and-file elected Member of Parliament. In practice there are several senses in which power can be located in certain persons or institutions.

President Harry Truman had a sign on his desk in the White House, 'The buck stops here', and bucks of different sizes stop at different levels throughout the governmental machine in the sense that at this point a decision has to be taken. But to find out where a governmental decision is taken or what influences have been brought to bear only partly solves the questions, 'Who has power?' and 'How much does he have?' There are two rather different approaches possible. The first deals with what happens if different individuals at the head of institutions want different decisions and concludes that the man or body who triumphs, who wins the vote or gets his ideas or candidate accepted, has most power. The second approach concentrates not on the decision to take a certain line but on whether the objective of the policy is achieved. It is important to distinguish between these two sides of the question. 'Who has power?' as concentration on one rather than the other produces very different answers.

For example, an author who dwells chiefly on the second aspect, on the outcome of policies, is Sir Ian Gilmour in *The Body Politic*. In his chapter on the Prime Minister, he notes that successive governments failed to reform the economy in the 1920s, to strengthen defence policy in the 1930s; refused 'to join the discussions on the European Coal and Steel Community' and 'to join Europe in the 1950s'; failed 'to bring local government into the twentieth century' and 'to reform the trade unions'. He concludes that 'these incidents or evasions do not suggest the presence of great power'. But these failures were due either to lack of solutions, to lack of political will or to positive decisions not to act. They are not guides to the balance of power between the premier and his colleagues or between the Cabinet and Parliament. In terms of estimating which persons or institutions are most powerful within the government, the issue is who decides what the government *tries* to do, irrespective of whether satisfactory or sensible results are achieved.

But this does not mean that there is no connection between the two. To set certain goals and then frequently fail to achieve them does weaken the total position of even the most powerful elements in the political system. It may also cast doubt on the effectiveness of the system itself.

Nevertheless, the first objective for a student of politics is to try and discover where power lies within the system. The task is to set out the principles, methods and machinery according to which a society arranges that some of its members lead, organize and, if necessary, coerce others. The problem in such a study is that there is an endless amount of information which could be deployed. Much of it, however, can be omitted as there are countless almost identical traffic offences, many very similar minor items of legislation and building one school is much like building another. An account that tries to decide which institutions or persons really matter has to look at the rather special cases where there is conflict, where one body has overriden another. When there is no conflict, it is harder to determine where the final decisions are actually made. Moreover, most of the important cases have special features and it is hard to be sure what cases are normal or typical. Facing this difficulty, the only solution is to describe numbers of occasions when the same type of case has occurred so that even though each one is different, some general picture will emerge of how the system operates.

Considered in this way, contemporary British government is highly complex with many power centres, many institutions which cannot be coerced and persons who cannot be removed or pressurized; but the main flow of power is between the leadership and the people. At intervals, at least once every five years, the public choose their leadership, the choice being narrowed down to one man and a number of lieutenants by the two-party system. Directly the choice is made, power within the system concentrates on the Prime Minister, though he may share part of it with one or two senior colleagues and with his Cabinet, this team then dominating British government till the next election. During these years, the chief limitation on the leadership's power is a combination of the Commons, the parties, the civil service and the pressure groups, together with the actual problems to be faced and the reactions of the electorate. In the last resort, what matters to the Prime Minister and the Cabinet is their standing with the public as revealed in the opinion polls, in by-election results and in their general sense of success and popularity or of failure and public disparagement. But in the short run what matters may be, for example, getting an anti-inflation policy to work and obtaining the co-operation of the unions and of management.

The purely political institutions through which the leadership operates have an influence on what is done, but relatively little actual power to stop the Prime Minister and his team once they have made up their minds to act. The chief obstacles, when such decisions have been made, do not lie in Parliament, where the government has an almost watertight grip on the Commons and on a largely subservient House of Lords, or in the civil service which can be ordered and regrouped. The chief obstacles are usually external institutions over which the government has little direct control though resistance by these bodies may encourage opposition in the Commons. Thus in 1975 the Labour Government made an agreement with the Trades Union Congress, the 'social contract', which involved voluntary trade union acceptance of limits on wage claims in return for a variety of social and economic policies of which the TUC approved. The system continued until the autumn of 1978 when it collapsed due to growing opposition from trade unionists. Continued attempts to restrict pay awards in the public services produced strike action. Similarly, Mr Macmillan was able to commit his party to an application to join the Common Market in 1961 despite considerable internal opposition. The ultimate failure when the French veto was applied did not materially alter Mr Macmillan's power as against his colleagues in the Cabinet, his party or the House of Commons. Nor were the voters disappointed, but the effect was to leave the government policyless and dispirited. In 1972, Mr Heath's policy of controlling wages by defeating union claims as they arose was not lost in Parliament (where its legislative counterpart was the Industrial Relations Bill) but was defeated when the government had to face a miners' strike and called an election which it lost.

Nevertheless, within the political machine, the Prime Minister dominates. He chooses his colleagues and while he may be limited by the need to take in certain popular or impressive figures, his own position is almost totally secure and the position of his lieutenants is open to change. They can, with only a few exceptions, be demoted or dismissed. Prime Ministers occupy a lonely pinnacle and if the government's fortunes are low, there will be criticism of their leadership from within the ranks of their party in Parliament. There were serious criticisms of Mr Macmillan in 1963 and attempts to remove Mr Wilson in 1969 but though these attempts came at times of maximum weakness for these two Prime Ministers, in neither case was there any serious chance of success. The Prime Minister is the embodiment of the government in the eyes of the public, appearing in far more news stories than either the Leader of the Opposition or any other member of the Cabinet. He can, to a large extent, manage his own public relations by careful release of news at the appropriate moments. Given success, British Prime Ministers receive great acclaim, though equally they are subject to severe personal attacks if the tide sets against them.

While the Leader of the Opposition derives certain powers from the fact that he or she may become Prime Minister, to be out of office means lack of patronage, lack of any backing from the Whitehall machine and the leader's service to the party is incomplete until victory and office have been achieved. In this situation, the leader has less freedom to choose frontbenchers (in the Labour Party, the key members are chosen by an annual election in the parliamentary party). Attempts to remove the Leader of the Opposition have sometimes been successful, Sir Alec Douglas-Home resigning in 1965, to be succeeded by Mr Heath who, in his turn, was defeated by Mrs Thatcher for the Conservative leadership in 1975.

In the present system, the work of government is performed by the senior civil service in constant co-operation and consultation with the mass of local government councils, public and privately-owned industries and other pressure groups. This complex of organizations cannot be separated easily into public and private sectors and the government's area of influence extends far beyond the bodies which it actually controls by law. But, at the same time, this means that the area of manoeuvre open to any government is limited. It inherits a large number of on-going policies and commitments and a public with certain expectations. Thus public expenditure is planned for five years ahead and departmental sub-heads are fixed for three years ahead. A new government can alter the atmosphere, the context and, to some extent, the priorities but it has no clean slate on which to write. Within these limitations, there has been some controversy about how far the established long-term views of the departments are imposed on ministers, but the minister is not left on his own and defenceless. He can be reinforced by the Prime Minister and the Cabinet. Departmental views and capacity for action may be a limiting factor, but the limits can also come from the politicians. For example, Mr Wilson prevented any serious discussion of devaluation from 1964 to November 1967, although the Treasury was perfectly willing to examine this option and Mr Heath ruled out an incomes policy for two years after the 1970 election.

Governments also operate through Parliament, the chief function of the House of Commons being to support the government of the day, to defend its policies and carry its legislation. Thus the House of Commons is the place where the government explains its policies and intentions and the opposition makes its counter case. Politicians often prefer to make their announcements direct over television to the electorate but, because the enactment of laws still requires passage through the House and MPs can be touchy if they are ignored, there will usually be a ministerial statement in the House.

In the heyday of the Victorian era, Parliament had a certain corporate feeling as against the executive. Backbenchers controlled part of the timetable which enabled them to extract information from the government and to force issues on to the floor of the House. Also, political leaders accepted that government was by discussion in the parliamentary forum with public attention focusing on the House of Commons. Now that the government controls the entire timetable of the House, information can be denied and many ministers prefer not to proceed by means of public discussion but to act first and then explain and defend their policies later. This has reached the extent that some policies have been begun and charges levied from the announcement of the government's intention to act rather than wait till the legislation is passed.

Similarly, the role of the parties outside Parliament has altered. These bodies, especially the Liberal and Labour Parties, do have some identity, some life of their own, particularly when the parties are in opposition and there is some interaction between the ideas of the leadership and the views of the local activists. There has always been a gap between Labour Governments and the National Executive Committee of the party but normally politicians regard the parties as electoral machines and the annual conferences as public relations exercises where the activists are manipulated and the wider electorate impressed by what they see on television.

Thus these intermediary agencies, the civil service, Parliament and the parties do execute the policies and have an effect on the method of work and mode of performance of the political leaders, but the primary relationship is between the leaders and the led, between the Prime Minister, his colleagues and the electorate. If ministers pay attention to pressure groups or to backbench revolts, it is because they suspect that this is evidence of real reactions among the voters. The old assumptions that there is a swing back to the government before an election and that, by and large, the

British electorate is fairly steady in its allegiances, are now less widely held. Declining support for the two main parties, nationalist upsurges in Scotland and Wales and the five to six million votes which went Liberal in 1974, have all shown a new volatility among the electorate which must disturb those in office.

The mass electorate has a short memory, is little interested in foreign affairs and appears to vote more on its overall impression of its own degree of comfort under the government in question. Thus the emphasis in political campaigning has swung from argument over issues to the creation of images, to the capacity of political leaders to gauge and anticipate the mood of the electorate and to deliver the goods in terms of the general standard of living.

Winning and holding power under these circumstances becomes involved with two related problems. The first is that politicians are encouraged to raise unrealistic expectations by which they are later judged. Thus some may advocate increased public expenditure and suggest that it will be painlessly paid for out of 'a higher growth rate' while others argue that taxation can be cut without any diminution in the other benefits enjoyed by the public simply 'by concentrating social aid on those who most need it'. Then there is the second difficulty that the politicians are not in sole control of the process by which the public's expectations are formed. The content of current western industrial civilization as put across by the press and by commercial television suggests that the greatest good in life is increased material standards, increased consumption, increased relaxation, so that criteria are set by which the performance of the Prime Minister and the government of the day are judged. When there is a period of endemic economic difficulties such as over the balance of payments in the 1960s and over inflation in the 1970s, there is an atmosphere of failure about both sets of political leaders and the electorate turns in increasing exasperation from one party to the other, with occasional bursts of support for third parties.

Thus the tone of the current political system is very different from that of the Westminster model. Then Parliament was a genuine intermediary between the people and the political leaders. While Gladstone and Disraeli, Joseph Chamberlain and Randolph Churchill, did appeal directly to the voters and conducted major election campaigns, they had to carry the House of Commons. Moreover the House could and did until the 1880s enforce certain changes (and the belief that this was possible hung on for a generation). Because the political leaders had learned their business in the era of small electorates and in a House with some independence and authority, they saw their task and their relations with the electors in a different light. The Victorian theory of political leadership, given that there was a popular element in the constitution, was that the party spokesmen put forward their own views about the needs of the country. It was improper to search for issues, to put up proposals simply to excite support. The object of political leadership was to take up such problems as forced themselves on the country's attention or needed to be considered (such as Irish grievances or near-eastern foreign policy) even if no one really wanted to think about them. It was also assumed that the electorate had their own independently formulated opinions and that they sat in judgement on their political leaders, in part being educated or convinced by the debates in the Commons and in part giving the leadership their reactions as independent, fair-minded voters.

Nowadays the prevailing tone places less emphasis on discussion and on the judgement of the leadership and of the led. Politicians tend to allege that it is the last year or two before an election that matters and that it is not arguments but subjective impressions that count. They seek to take up issues which will appeal to the public, suppressing aspects which could be awkward, so that while their propaganda has a relationship to the real problems of the country, they do not dwell on issues whose solution may be painful or where no agreed or clear solution is evident.

While this approach has been successful when Prime Ministers have been able to meet the expectations of the voters – and no premiers have received more general acclaim than Macmillan ('Supermac', 'Wondermac') in 1957–60 or Wilson after his 1966 victory – it has also led to great troughs of discontent when governments have not been able to deliver the hoped-for goods. Perhaps because the electorate has been led to expect so much more from government and from the political system at a time when Britain has been adjusting to a new role as a second-level, mainly European power and the economy has had to face a more competitive and exposed position in world trade, there has been considerable alienation and apathy. Because government by argument and open decision has been less practised, because politics has been seen as a problem of management rather than of facing the facts, there have been outbursts of resentment, a tendency by some to turn to protests and to demonstrations in order to obtain results and by others to feel a contempt for politics and a sense of alienation from the whole system.

The next seven chapters consider this present pattern of British government and politics in detail and in the last chapter there is an examination of what views the parties take of possible changes in the pattern of government and of what the outcome is likely to be.

5 Political leadership – producing a Prime Minister

The process of selection within the parties

In Britain, as in most western industrialized countries, there is a slightly ambivalent attitude to political leadership. The Prime Minister is the representative of the country on all critical international occasions and provides a leadership which, besides being of one political character, has a broader national aspect. Usually the Prime Minister runs ahead of his party in the opinion polls in that a larger percentage of people approve of his conduct than say they would vote for his party at an immediate election. There is a sense in which the public, though sceptical and difficult to please, want the Prime Minister to be someone they can admire, someone who will rise above the small change of political conflict, who will conspicuously avoid the failings usually attributed to politicians.

This attitude undoubtedly influences the parties in their choice of a leader but so do other factors. The procedure for selecting a leader in the Labour and Conservative Parties is now carefully set down. The Labour Party in its early years arranged for the annual election of a chairman, later called the leader of the party, though it was rapidly assumed that once he was chosen, there would be automatic re-election unless some section of the party wished to make a serious challenge. Once the leader became Prime Minister, even the formality of annual re-election was dropped. Those entitled to vote were the Labour MPs. If, at the first ballot, no candidate had an overall majority, the one with least votes was eliminated and further ballots were held until somebody had an absolute majority. Candidates could also withdraw between ballots.

The special conference in January 1981 decided that in future the leader and deputy leader should be chosen by an electoral college in which the votes should be allocated as follows – 30 per cent to Labour MPs, 30 per cent to constituency Labour Parties, 40 per cent to trade unions. This arrangement proved very controversial. Some argued that the election should be organized simply on the basis that each individual member of the Labour Party should have a vote; others argued that it was wrong that so much weight should be given to trade union opinion. Since the original purpose of the reform was to allow wider participation in the choice of leader, the decision to give a powerful role to trade unions may seem strange. Who decides how a trade union shall use its vote? There is no uniform answer to this question, but normally a small élite of union leaders decide what to do. Those who belong to this élite are not necessarily members of the Labour Party. A union's general secretary is very influential. The distribution of votes to unions is also open to criticism. The size of a union's vote depends upon the number of its members it registers with the Labour Party as affiliated members: this figure can be more or less than the number of union members who actually pay a political levy to their union. In essence, unions can buy votes. At a Labour Party conference the total of union votes is several times greater than that of the combined votes of local Labour Parties. It has always been the case that the large unions, assuming that they agree among themselves, can control the Labour Party conference. The January 1981 conference made this influence more visible by extending it towards the election of the leader.

It is arguable that the block vote system is undemocratic. Certainly it can lead to peculiar results. Thus the decision in January 1981 did not command majority support. It received 510,000 more votes than an alternative proposal, but the Amalgamated Union of Engineering Workers abstained because it objected to both suggestions. As the AUEW vote is much larger than 510,000, the new arrangement for electing the leader was carried by a minority vote.

The creation of the electoral college did not end constitutional argument within the Labour Party. In February 1983 Mr Shore and Mr Hattersley, respectively Shadow Chancellor and Shadow Home Secretary, announced their support for a campaign to force constituency Labour Parties to hold a ballot of members to decide who the local party should support in leadership elections. The same process should also apply to the selection and re-selection of parliamentary candidates. Those who favoured the formation of an electoral college for the leadership elections had pressed their case in terms of wider participation and intra-party democracy. The 'one member one vote' theme is a logical continuation of this process. Yet those who argue for more democracy expect to gain from the outcome: the advocacy of principles is not disinterested. Before 1981 those who wanted the electoral college thought that the Left-wing of the Labour Party would gain thereby, because the limited group of active members who control most constituency parties are far to the Left of the majority of Labour MPs; the same is also true of some trade unions. Those who now press for 'one member one vote' expect this reform to limit the influence of Left-wing activists by making effective the views of rank-and-file supporters who are more likely to vote for candidates with moderate opinions.

During the 1983 Labour leadership election there was a substantial pressure to widen participation, in particular through ballots of union members. The pressure was largely unsuccessful. Union leaders pleaded that the expense would be prohibitive. In some cases the records of who paid the political levy to the Labour Party may have been incomplete. Further, if executive committees consult the mass membership they are eroding their own power. Such a prospect is even less pleasing when it is feared that the mass membership might come to a different conclusion: sometimes this denial of democracy is justified by the assertion that rank-and-file opinion is swayed by comment in the capitalist press. Yet another obstacle to holding a union ballot is the question of who should be entitled to vote – all union members or only those who pay the political levy. The common-sense answer is that only those who subscribe to the Labour Party should join in the process of choosing its leader. But there are grave legal doubts over whether a union would be justified in discriminating between those of its members who pay the political levy and those who do not. A union is supposed to make its decisions in the interests of all its members. Should not all its members have equal rights? In any case, not all members of union executives are members of the Labour Party, so leaving the decision on which candidate to support to a limited élite does not mean that the choice is limited to Labour Party supporters. The issue is an awkward one for both the Labour Party and the trade union movement. The complex nature of the Labour Party's constitution with provision for affiliated organizations and block votes simply cannot be reconciled with the simple democratic principles of one person one vote and one vote one value.

In the Conservative Party, if the leadership became vacant during a period when the party was in Opposition it was laid down (since

1937) that the new leader should be chosen by a body consisting of all Conservative MPs and Conservative peers, all prospective Conservative candidates and the Executive Committee of the National Union of Conservative Associations.

When the Conservative Party was in office and the leader died or resigned, it was left to the monarch to select a successor. But the monarch clearly had a duty to choose the person with the greatest body of support among Conservative MPs and the Crown's staff arranged for consultations so that this information could be provided. Trouble arose in 1923 over the selection of Baldwin when it was alleged that certain views, particularly those of the dying Bonar Law, the retiring Prime Minister, were misrepresented to the King. In 1957, the Queen was advised to choose Mr Macmillan after a straw poll of the members of the Cabinet had gone to sixteen to one in his favour but there was grumbling that other sections of the party were not adequately represented. This grumbling was much more serious in late 1963 when Mr Macmillan was succeeded by Sir Alec Douglas-Home. In this case there was careful sounding carried out by Lord Dilhorne, the Lord Chancellor, in the Cabinet, by the Chief Whip among MPs, by the Chief Whip in the Lords and by one of the chairmen of the party organization among constituency activists. The outcome was a recommendation in favour of Sir Alec Douglas-Home but there were considerable misgivings, because it was evident that no candidate had had a clear majority and so a process of weighting was adopted. Mr Iain Macleod, one of the minor contenders for the leadership, held that 'the result of the methods used was contradiction and misrepresentation' and he refused to join Sir Alec Douglas-Home's Government.

As a result of this controversy, a new method was adopted in 1965 for use whether the party is in or out of office whereby a ballot is held of all Conservative MPs. To be elected, a candidate must have an overall majority and 15 per cent more votes than his nearest rival. If this is not achieved, a second ballot is held two to four days later for the same or new candidates and an overall majority is sufficient. If no candidate secures such a majority, a third ballot takes place among the top three, with the MPs indicating their first and second preferences which are redistributed to produce one person with an overall majority.

Curiously enough, Sir Alec Douglas-Home did not submit himself to this process when it was adopted in February 1965, so that it was first applied when he chose to resign (see page 95) in July 1965. Mr Heath obtained 150 votes to Mr Maudling's 133 and Mr Powell's 15 so that a second ballot was required, but before this could be held Mr Maudling and Mr Powell retired from the contest, leaving Mr Heath in possession. The same procedure worked smoothly in 1975 when Mrs Thatcher had the most votes in the first ballot which eliminated Mr Heath and then went on to defeat Mr Whitelaw for the leadership.

The choice of party leader is the occasion of maximum power for backbenchers, but these moments arise with decreasing frequency. Conservative MPs still enjoy this right. Liberals and Social Democrats have adopted systems of voting by their mass membership. Labour, as noted above, in 1981 gave its MPs a voice in the election of leader, but their voice is no longer dominant. It is too soon to tell how far the opening up of the selection process will affect the choices made. The obvious prospect is that less attention will be paid to the quality of parliamentary performances and oratorical skill on a public platform and more weight will be attached to opinions on policy and adept appearances on television. The outcome could be less moderate leaders.

In the Labour Party the ideological stance of aspirants for leadership is of great importance. It is often said that Labour likes to be led from left of centre. Certainly this assertion would help to explain the choice of three of the last four Labour leaders, Wilson, Foot and Kinnock. (In 1963 Mr Wilson was thought to be more Left-wing than his rivals, Mr Brown and Mr Callaghan.) The expansion of the electoral college in 1981 to include trade unions and constituency parties must further increase the weight attached to the policies advocated by potential leaders. MPs are interested in winning elections, in the acquisition of power: active party members and enthusiastic trade unionists who attend union conferences are more likely to seek a leader who will be a safe keeper of the party's conscience. So the tendency after 1981 will be to pay less attention to the electorate's wishes and more to what the party enthusiasts desire. Of course, the ideal situation is to find a candidate who commands public respect and confidence and who is also popular with party members. In 1963 Mr Wilson satisfied both these criteria. His successors have been less well placed.

On only one occasion, when Mr Wilson retired in 1976, has Labour had to find a leader when the party was in office. Necessarily in such circumstances the chances of the candidates must be influenced by their status in the government. One would expect a very senior minister to be chosen. This situation helped to lead to the election of Mr Callaghan. It would also render impossible the choice of someone like Mr Kinnock who has no ministerial experience whatever. When the party is deeply troubled and divided there is a natural tendency to prefer a leader who can be expected to heal the wounds and try to build a reunited party: the needs of the party are given preference over any calculation of what may appeal to the voters. Mr Foot was chosen on this basis in 1980 but was less than wholly successful in uniting the party. The electorate were unimpressed partly because of Mr Foot's policies and partly because of his age; to choose a potential Prime Minister who could not hope to achieve that office much before his seventieth birthday did not inspire confidence. After the emphatic rejection of Mr Foot at the 1983 election the mood in the Labour Party demanded a move to a younger generation and helped to secure the choice of Mr Kinnock. Two of his rivals, Mr Heffer and Mr Shore, were thought to be too old while Mr Hattersley and Mr Shore were felt to be too moderate or Right-wing in their general attitudes.

The Labour Party, but not the Conservative Party, elects a deputy leader. However, the deputy is unlikely to become leader. Only once since 1945 has the deputy attained the top post. Mr Foot did so in 1980 and this exception to the general rule is unlikely to encourage a repetition. Why are deputies passed over? Perhaps, like Mr Morrison, they are felt to be too old. More often they are thought to be too Right-wing, e.g. Mr Brown, Mr Jenkins and Mr Healey. It is also the case that a deputy tends to be associated with the leader, so that to choose a deputy is an unexciting choice which surrenders some possibility of exploring new avenues and alternative policies. As noted above, the Conservatives do not formally choose a deputy, but Mr Whitelaw was accepted as *de facto* deputy to Mr Heath and also to Mrs Thatcher: his loyalty and close association with Mr Heath helped to secure his defeat by Mrs Thatcher in the 1975 Conservative leadership election.

The post of deputy leader is still very important. The occupant can have an important influence on policy and colour the image that a party presents to the public. In 1981 Mr Healey defeated Mr Benn for the job of deputy leader by a tiny margin. Had Mr Benn won he would have played a major role in the 1983 election campaign; as it was he was kept away from the centre of attention in his Bristol constituency. If Mr Benn had been more prominent, the Labour Party would have presented a more Left-wing image to the electorate which could not have been helpful to Labour's fortunes. In 1983 the Labour Party realized that it needed to project a vision of a 'broad church' to strengthen its appeal to the electorate; thus it chose a Right-wing deputy leader and Mr Hattersley defeated Mr Meacher by a comfortable margin of roughly 2 to 1.

A further problem for the Labour Party is the possibility that the new electoral college system could produce a leader who was not greatly respected by Labour MPs either because of his policies, the quality of his parliamentary performance or, indeed, because of personal characteristics. MPs know their fellow MPs more intimately than those outside Parliament although, admittedly, gossip column writers are fairly uninhibited. Yet if, for whatever reason, Labour MPs find they have a leader imposed on them that they do not want, then further tension in the party cannot be avoided.

The role of the Crown

It is as well to dispose of any doubts about the role of the Crown in this process. Because the Labour Party's rules obliged them to meet and elect a leader in the event of any vacancy, no question of royal influence could arise. But during the period when the Conservative Party in office preferred an informal system of soundings, the result of which was conveyed to the Crown, it was inevitable that those who disliked the outcome would, at times, suggest that the monarch's own views had played a part. This point was made, for instance, when George V sent for Mr Baldwin rather than Lord Curzon in 1923, though more emphasis was placed on possible misrepresentations of advice by those around the King. George V, himself, may have thought that to have a Prime Minister in the House of Lords would create difficulties, but in fact the advice reaching the King was quite decisively in favour of Baldwin. In rather different circumstances, George V was criticized (by Herbert Morrison and later by Professor Moodie in *Political Studies*, February 1957) for asking Ramsay MacDonald to lead a national government after he had tendered his resignation as Prime Minister in 1931.

This case arose because, although the Labour Party had a machinery for electing a leader, MacDonald was deserting his party without even informing them of the fact. Thus Labour MPs were not in a position to meet and elect someone (presumably Arthur Henderson) as leader as they were unaware of the situation. Faced with the resignation of the Prime Minister who was not asking for a general election, the King quite properly turned to the leaders of the other two parties, Mr Baldwin and Mr Samuel. They both said they were prepared to serve in a national government under Mr MacDonald and advised the King to put the proposition to MacDonald. The critics have argued that the King should have summoned other senior Labour Privy Councillors to find out how many of the Labour Party were likely to follow MacDonald. But to have done so would have opened the King to the charge of intriguing behind the back of the man who was still the accredited leader of the Labour Party. Moreover the King's task was (and still is in such situations) to find the strongest government available in the existing House of Commons. The Conservative and Liberal leaders in 1931 had a majority between them and the addition of MacDonald, however few his Labour supporters, could only add strength to the combination, so that George V acted perfectly properly on this occasion.

The suggestion that the Crown had a preference was made in a few quarters in 1957 after the selection of Macmillan and in 1963 after the choice of Douglas-Home; Mr Paul Johnson in the *New Statesman* of 24 January 1964 argued that if, in any sense, the advice given contained an element of doubt, the Queen would be bound to prefer the 'genuine Tory' – Mr Macmillan or Sir Alec Douglas-Home – to Mr Butler. The only difficulty about this point of view is that in each case there is absolutely no supporting evidence. When the advice about the state of feeling in the Conservative Party reached the Palace, it was couched in an unequivocal form and the Queen had no choice unless she was prepared to doubt the word of the senior statesman (in the latter case her Prime Minister) who conveyed the advice.

There is, therefore, no scope for royal influence on the choice of Prime Ministers given the normal alternation of parties. Even in exceptional cases, such as 1931, where the two-party system has temporarily broken down, or in February 1974, when no party had clearly won the election, the Crown operates on the advice of the existing party leaders. It is true that if no party has an overall majority in the Commons, there may be dispute about the proper course of action. A Prime Minister is entitled to ask for a dissolution of Parliament and such a request will always be granted. But does such a right extend to a party leader without a firm majority in the Commons who is invited to try to form a Cabinet? This issue can provoke complex constitutional argument. The development of a multi-party system with the probability of coalition government and the possibility of fluid coalitions does potentially make the task of the Crown more awkward and controversial.

The causes and effects of the two-party system

Turning, then, to the role of the electorate in choosing a Prime Minister from the two or more candidates placed before them, the choice is made possible by the party system. The public are very far removed from politics, many electors having only the slightest knowledge of the issues, machinery or persons involved. The party system performs the dual function of so cutting down the options that electors can actually decide who will form the next government and of offering the electorate a shorthand or easy method of categorizing their preferences by bracketing certain attitudes and policies as Labour, Conservative or Liberal. As a result, one thing about which the voters are clear is that they are selecting the country's leadership for the coming four or five years, that they are arbitrating in the power struggle between the parties. It is therefore worth considering, as part of establishing how the leadership is selected, how the political system allows for two major and several minor parties and what effect this has on the process of choosing the Prime Minister.

It is often said in books on the electoral system that this method of electing one Member of Parliament for each constituency by a simple majority – 'winner takes all' – is seriously disadvantageous to third parties, such as the Liberals, and that this explains why Britain has usually had a two-party system. In fact, this is not true. The system gives a tremendous advantage to one candidate only, the candidate with a majority of one or more votes over his nearest challenger since that person is elected and none of the other candidates gets any benefit in the sense of being elected to Parliament. Only the winner is favoured in each constituency; the second, third and fourth parties fare equally badly in the sense that they are denied representation in the Commons.

Of course, if one takes the country as a whole, there is no necessary relationship between the extent of support obtained by a party and the strength of its position in Parliament. Viewed in party terms a British general election is a potentially unjust lottery. The prize of office can go to a political group less popular with the electors than another group which happens to have collected fewer seats in the Commons; this is what took place in 1951 and laid the foundations for thirteen years of Conservative rule. In terms of the nineteenth-century theory of representation, constituencies chose individuals to represent them – not party nominees. Parties were unknown to the constitution. If parties are ignored then unfairness between them, as in 1951, can be of no consequence. Nor was it possible to get excited about the peculiarities of election arithmetic before 1832 when the major cause of contention was the restricted and anomalous nature of the franchise. But since 1868 we have had a mass electorate and a Parliament dominated by a disciplined party system. Curiosities such as the 1951 outcome are accepted because, at least in the past, we have accepted the value of a two-party system as a means of securing stable government. Conservative and Labour leaders do not complain when luck runs against them in the hope of better fortune next time.

Arguments about the need to reform our electoral system will be reviewed in a later section of the book (p. 109). Here it must be stressed that present arrangements do not always place minorities at a disadvantage. If a political group has limited support, but support that is geographically uneven or 'lumpy', then it may defeat opponents in areas where it is strongest. At both the 1974 elections and again in 1979 the total of Plaid Cymru MPs was proportional to the extent of their support from the Welsh electors – entirely due to the concentration of sympathy for their cause in North-West Wales. Scottish nationalism is spread more evenly so the SNP has fared worse than Plaid Cymru.

One danger of the present electoral arrangements is that the most popular party could sweep the board. Except in 1931 this has not happened because parliamentary constituencies are highly mixed in their social composition, and it is the social or class composition which has the closest correlation with voting patterns in the UK. Though the class structure is very similar throughout the country, the proportions of the classes in each constituency vary. At one end of the scale there are Welsh valleys where the population is almost entirely working class and at the other, there are seaside resorts where the vast majority describe themselves as middle class with almost every variation of class content occurring in the intervening range of constituencies. Given that social class is an important factor in voting behaviour, this explains two things. First, it explains why an electoral system which favours only the winner, favours the Labour (and formerly the Liberal) Party in some seats and the Conservatives in others. Second, it explains why, however opinion swings from one party to another, it never wipes out either major party. The social composition of the 650 constituencies is sufficiently lumpy or uneven to ensure that the system still favours Labour in certain seats when the Conservatives are at their peak of popularity, while a Labour high tide still fails to engulf the seats where the uneven social scatter has heaped up a mass of middle-class people.

This is why the modern Liberal Party wins so few seats. From the 1880s, the Liberals drew their support largely from the lower-income groups and were saved from extinction in bad years by the factors that have been explained. Then this position was taken over by the Labour Party and since the 1930s Liberalism has become a series of attitudes drawing much the same level of support from each social class. Thus even when the Liberals have 19.3 per cent of the votes (as they did in February 1974), this tends to mean about that level of support in each constituency so that the other parties have little difficulty in defeating them. But if the six million votes (which represent 19.3 per cent of those cast) had been heaped up in any way, if Liberal support was 'lumpy' like that of the Conservative and Labour Parties, the Liberals would have won far more than the fourteen seats they gained in February 1974. Indeed most of these fourteen were due to the fact that there is a very slight tendency to concentration of Liberal support in the Celtic areas of the Scottish Highlands, North Wales and the South-West of England.

The reasons for changes in voting behaviour

Thus the party system in Britain is a product of three factors: the electoral system, the homogeneity of the country and the fact that class-based parties each have a body of seats where their position ranges from very secure to just winnable in a good year. But when voters turn to the alternatives before them at a general election, they respond to a wide variety of motives. As Butler and Stokes have pointed out in their superb study *Political Change in Britain*, working-class voters are much more prone to think in class terms and to consider that the task of the Labour Party is to protect their interests, while Conservative middle-class voters tend to place far less emphasis on this reason for political action and to explain their choice more in terms of what is good for the nation. In addition, as the electorate dies and is replaced, as social mobility has an effect, as real incomes have risen and living patterns have altered, as social tensions have declined, there have been cross-currents reducing the class aspect of voting behaviour. These movements have helped the Liberal cause. Religious affiliations in certain areas still have an observable effect on voters' choices. Also in those areas where one class and one political view is dominant, this tends to have a reinforcing effect so that a larger percentage of working men, for instance, vote Conservative in the South-East than in Wales.

In addition, the public has views on current issues, though whether this affects their voting depends on the depth of their feeling and the degree to which one party is regarded as being in favour of one solution and the other party as opposed. For instance, Labour has at various times been regarded as the party in favour of nationalization though it is significant that many Labour voters do not want any extension of nationalization. The identification of Labour with nationalization has fluctuated but the idea that Labour is close to the unions has grown, particularly since Mr Wilson reaped the advantage of the Conservatives' conflict with the miners in February 1974, and went on to fight the two elections of that year specifically on the grounds that only the Labour Party had a 'social contract' with the unions. Each party works to identify itself with popular and its opponents with unpopular attitudes on major issues. Thus the Conservatives have tried to identify themselves with lower taxation and efficient tough government and have attempted to label Labour as the party in favour of permissive social legislation, of soft responses to criminal behaviour, of nationalization and of economic failure. The Labour Party, in return, claims that Mrs Thatcher's brand of Conservatism produces even higher unemployment and the abandonment of much of the social welfare system introduced after the war. Labour alone can govern with the unions in a state of reasonable social harmony. Such propaganda only affects voting if the issue bites deep and the accusations ring true. Normally, voters who are attached to one particular party tend to accept the view of specific issues enunciated by that party's leaders rather than take a stand on current problems and then adjust their party loyalties. However, the massive fall in

Labour support in 1983 suggests that many former Labour loyalists were not prepared to follow the party's policy on unilateral disarmament, on Europe and perhaps on economic policy.

In all this, what part does the actual task of selecting an individual as the next Prime Minister of the country play? The answer is that the act of voting is complex in that the elector is choosing both a particular Prime Minister and government by a particular party. (It is interesting that the appeal of frontbench spokesmen other than the party leader plays virtually no part in electors' minds.) It is hard to separate the support for the party from the attraction of the potential Prime Minister and it is clear that in terms of political loyalty, most voters are thinking in the party shorthand they have acquired from childhood. However, the research of Butler and Stokes shows that the images of party leaders are highly personal, dwelling on such qualities as courage, integrity, ability and likeability rather than on political attitudes and that the force of these images – that is, whether the potential Prime Minister is attractive or not – does have a demonstrable effect on voting patterns. If the government is very unpopular, an unappealing Leader of the Opposition can be carried; similarly the hold of a popular Prime Minister can, in time, be eroded if his government is unsuccessful. As with so many aspects of the decision of how to vote, the appeal of the leadership is a definite factor but the key element remains the total impression the voter has formed of the party in question over a long period of time.

There is clearly no reason why the cumulation of class interests, family traditions, reactions to current issues and to the leaders, which together govern voting, should result in national support being divided fairly evenly between the major parties. Indeed in this century Conservative or Conservative-dominated governments have been in power for fifty out of the first eighty years. Before 1939 it was fashionable to talk of an 'electoral pendulum', a tendency for support to swing from one party to the other. Between 1868 and 1914 the Liberals and Conservatives each had a total of twenty-three years in power; similarly between 1945 and 1979 the Conservatives and Labour each had seventeen years in power. These equalities provide the basis for a theory that the longer a party is in office, the more voters it alienates. Since alienation is often a stronger feeling than satisfaction, the movement of opinion is likely to favour the Opposition.

However, since 1945 politicians and academic observers have

come to realize that the government has tremendous advantages over its opponents. In the first place, the government chooses the election date and may be able either to time this or to manage the economy so as to ensure that the country is enjoying an economic boom just before a general election. In addition, the government receives far greater publicity than the Opposition, and because it is actually governing and introducing policies, it can much more easily alter its image in a direction which fits in with the mood of the electorate, the Opposition being stuck with the impression it created in its last period of office. For these reasons, most politicians do not believe in any swing of the electoral pendulum. Indeed, many consider that an Opposition can do little to win power for itself. It has to create a good impression but the chief question is the record of the government. The way the question arises in the minds of doubtful electors is whether they wish to keep this government or not. But while the government has a built-in advantage as described, since the 1960s the Opposition has been aided by the fact that expectations have been encouraged to rise faster than the actual rate of increase in average wealth so that there has been a definite feeling of disappointment with the government of the day. This told against the Conservatives in 1962–3 and against Labour in 1967–9, in each case affecting the subsequent general election. But the old 'swing of the pendulum' theory also has some validity in the sense that a section of voters do believe that an alternation in power is desirable. There is an old maxim that power corrupts and absolute power corrupts absolutely. Thus when any party has held power for some time there is a mixed situation – special advantages and publicity accruing to the party in power as against the problem of satisfying the high expectations of the electorate and combating the conviction among a significant minority that a regular transfer of power is one of the beneficial features of British democracy.

The character of British political leadership

With this highly complex and shifting series of motives and with the choice of party leaders narrowed down by the pre-selection of the parties, what kind of leadership has the British public settled for in this century? There had been a total of eighteen Prime Ministers by 1983 and, not surprisingly, only two have been of working-class origin. The preponderant characteristic has been that twelve have come from families of reasonable wealth where the idea of taking

part in the government of the country is normal, while only six –
Lloyd George, Ramsay MacDonald, Harold Wilson, Edward
Heath, James Callaghan and Margaret Thatcher – have pushed
their way in from outside 'the establishment'. Yet it is notable that
the list does include the four most recent Prime Ministers, a fact
which suggests a greater element of flexibility has entered into the
pattern of recruitment to our highest political office since 1964.

The basic outlook of our Prime Ministers has been cautious, due,
no doubt, to an interaction of social background, personal
philosophy and age. Since 1964 it is arguable that Conservative
Prime Ministers have been more willing to encourage social change
than have their Labour counterparts. Another curiosity is that the
Conservatives, Edward Heath and Margaret Thatcher, have not
sought a similar direction for change.

The MPs who selected these people as party leaders knew them
well because the British system involves a long political
apprenticeship. On average, the premiers had served twenty-four
years in Parliament before being chosen as party leader and twenty-
six years before they became Prime Minister. Given this long
preparation for what was to be the climax of their careers, several
points emerge. The first is the relatively brief period they lasted, the
average being under five years. Also, despite the long
apprenticeship and exposure both to pressure and to the
observation of their fellow MPs, the nature of the premiership
imposed such strains that many fell ill and many exhibited qualities,
good and bad, which few even of their closer colleagues had
expected. Considering their health, in the period since 1945, Mr
Attlee developed eczema and attributed the resignations of Bevan
and Wilson to his absence in hospital; Mr Churchill stayed on after
many of the Cabinet thought his powers had declined to a level
which merited resignation; Sir Anthony Eden seemed to acquire a
nervous tension which interfered with his judgement even before he
was incapacitated by a bile duct obstruction, while Mr Macmillan
decided to give up the leadership because of his prostate operation.
At the same time, although the pressures of the office emphasized
attributes of character which were well known, other less expected
aspects also appeared. Few imagined that Mr Attlee would prove as
tough as he did, or that Sir Anthony Eden would be so tense and
reluctant to delegate. Few likewise anticipated that Mr Macmillan
would achieve such a personal ascendancy over the House, that Mr
Wilson would prove so cautious and conformist, that Mr Heath

would reveal such determination in carrying through both his policies and, when convinced, his reversals of policy, that Mr Callaghan would be so calm and dignified or that Mrs Thatcher would develop such dominance over her ministerial colleagues.

It is a further feature, not only of the loneliness, exposure and heavy responsibility of the post, but of the acute difficulties of British readjustment to the loss of worldwide power and possessions and to a new and much more competitive economic position, that few of these men have left office after their brief spells of power with their reputation enhanced. Mr Churchill paid in 1945 for the pre-war failures of his party at home and in foreign affairs. The Attlee Government did much and had its impressive personalities but again sank into gloom, purposelessness and a death wish by the end of five years. Conservative leaders in the 1950s had an easier time but Britain lost her chance to take a leading part in the construction of a united Europe, a failure which dogged British politics till the 1970s and there was the misconceived and abortive invasion of Suez which revealed a total misunderstanding of Britain's position in the world. Mr Macmillan's successes in office were eclipsed in his last year by the Profumo scandal and by the impression, created when he sacked seven of the twenty-one members of his Cabinet, that he was more interested in his personal survival than anything else. Mr Wilson started in a blaze of glory as an Opposition leader who could actually unite the Labour Party and then as Prime Minister who managed for seventeen months on a majority of six or less. But soon after his victory in 1966, his government was in the toils pushing a most unpopular policy of deflation and wage restraint. On top of this a sterling crisis forced Mr Wilson into a change of course in November 1967, when he had to accept devaluation of the pound and the withdrawal of British troops from east of Suez. Though the economy recovered as a result of these measures in 1969, the popularity of the government was slow to follow and he lost the election of 1970. Mr Heath had one great success and reward for courage in taking Britain into Europe. After reversing many of the policies on which he was elected, his restraint of incomes might have succeeded but he became involved in a conflict with the miners and just failed to win a seriously mismanaged election. Mr Wilson's second period of office, consolidated in October 1974 saw a series of economic crises, record inflation and unemployment. This legacy forced the Callaghan Government to borrow from the International

Monetary Fund and to adjust its policy to meet the views of the IMF. Adverse by-election results led to the loss of Labour's majority in the Commons. Finally Mr Callaghan discovered that the trade unions refused to accept his policy of wage restraint. In combination these events produced a feeling that ministers were no longer in charge of affairs and led to the Labour defeat at the 1979 election.

The record of national leadership has been feeble or uninspiring since 1918, except for the 1940s. Some people will argue that Mrs Thatcher has succeeded in recreating a sense of national purpose since 1979. The Falklands task force was victorious in 1982. Mrs Thatcher has negotiated firmly with other EEC countries to improve Britain's financial situation in relation to contributions to the EEC. She has used her powers of patronage more aggressively than any Prime Minister since Lloyd George. And she has stuck firmly to her economic policies in spite of rising unemployment and widespread concern over the consequences of unemployment especially among young people. The result is much stronger government than Britain had in the 1970s: whether it is also more successful government is a matter for argument.

6 Political leadership – the strength of the Prime Minister

Party loyalty, the whips and patronage

Once a party leader has either won a general election or has succeeded to the leadership of the party in power and thus becomes Prime Minister, he falls heir to a position of great authority. The degree of this authority varies but it is possible, by looking at the Prime Minister's security in office, the sources of his strength and the limitations which exist at a time of maximum weakness, to get some picture of the normal powers at the disposal of a premier.

The first and major factor which confirms the Prime Minister's position is the force of party loyalty. The majority party want their leader to be successful. If the leader's style, methods and policies are acclaimed, they also share in the benefits. They have assured the public that their party will govern well and meet the electorate's desires and the more this happens, the better they are pleased. But if a Prime Minister is encountering difficulties and if the government's policies are bringing unpopularity and press criticism, while some MPs may grumble, the normal reaction is to support their leader. After all, if these criticisms are not countered, the whole party will suffer and if disloyalty in the Commons did lead (which it has not since the 1880s) to the collapse of the government, then all the MPs would have to face a general election under the most disadvantageous circumstances. In general, a Prime Minister at his weakest and most exposed can be fairly sure that if the Cabinet decides to push on with a policy, party loyalty will see it through, though there may have to be some concessions or modifications.

Examples of such concessions can be found in the Conservative decision in 1982 to drop the idea of forcing local authorities to hold referenda if they wished to increase their rates beyond a certain level and the withdrawal in 1983 of powers in the Police Bill to enable police officers to seek evidence in confidential records. Labour Cabinets have been forced by backbench pressure to drop or modify major items of policy. Mr Wilson, in 1969, had to withdraw both the Parliament (No. 2) Bill – House of Lords reform – and the Industrial Relations Bill, the Dock Labour Regulation Bill was drastically amended in 1976, and the guillotine motion for the Devolution Bill was defeated in February 1977. Ultimately the devolution legislation was passed in 1978, but only after ministers had been forced to accept an amendment moved by one of their own backbenchers, George Cunningham, which required that if less than 40 per cent of the electorate were to vote 'Yes' in the referendum on devolution, then an order repealing the legislation was to be laid before Parliament. It was this provision which subsequently killed the legislation and hastened the general election which defeated the Labour Government.

Nevertheless, the examples of party loyalty are equally impressive. In 1969 Labour leaders never lost a clause of the Parliament Bill but the Chief Whip did not think he could carry a timetable motion. He then found that the bill was taking too long and dropped it because time was wanted for other measures. On the Industrial Relations Bill, despite the warnings of the Chief Whip, Mr Wilson was convinced that party loyalty would carry him through once the issue was put to the vote. He abandoned the bill only when the large majority of his Cabinet turned against him, though the objections on the backbenches certainly played a large part in producing this result. Mr Heath demonstrated what can be done by a determined Prime Minister when he drove through the bill to carry Britain into the European Community in 1972, despite sufficient Conservative opposition to put his majority at risk. He was aided by a few Liberal votes and Labour abstentions but it is impossible to say whether all the Conservative rebels would have persisted had they known that the result would have been the defeat of the government. In 1976, the Callaghan Government forced through five highly controversial bills, some of which deeply disturbed Callaghan's own party, when he had an overall majority of one.

In considering the nature of party loyalty, it is important to set aside the idea that it depends in any significant way on coercion or on rewards or that it is the product of the alleged spinelessness of MPs. Some writers and columnists have argued that there is nothing wrong with Parliament or the machinery of government; all that needs to be done is for backbench MPs to stand up and behave like men, to shake off undue subservience to the whips.

This attitude misunderstands the position, the party and the whipping system being part of the interlocking pattern of British politics. It shows a lack of comprehension to isolate certain sections of this pattern and attribute their form to the frailty of over 600 otherwise quite robust and unusually opinionated men. To understand party loyalty, it must be appreciated that most MPs have spent years in their party before election to the House. They have joined it, worked for it and probably stood as candidates once or twice before election. They identify themselves with the party's general approach and any serious failures of high policy are personal calamities for them. They may want to change aspects of policy, they may at times disagree with members of the Cabinet including the Prime Minister, but despite this they still wish the party to be successful. Because of this, they will defend the party in public, which means supporting the Prime Minister's actions in the lobbies and in the constituencies.

The idea that the whips continually exercise pressure on MPs has some truth but they do so largely in terms of party loyalty. The story of an aristocratic and autocratic Conservative Chief Whip, whose patience deserted him, seizing a doubting Conservative MP by the collar of his coat and seat of his pants and propelling him towards the door to the division lobby saying 'in five minutes you can do what you . . . . like with your conscience', is just possible, given that whip's well-known judgement in handling particular cases, but it is worth telling because of its unique character. The whips do have the sanction that they can put in motion machinery which could lead to the withdrawal of the whip. This would mean that the MP could not be readopted by his party at the next election. If the MP then contested the election as an independent, defeat is likely as only three MPs who have been opposed by their parties have held their seats at a general election since 1945. (All three were due to local disputes with the constituency parties.) On the other hand, no whip wishes to have to take such action, the press fastens on stories of rebels and splits which are damaging to the party and the effect of having to oppose a former member, even in a safe seat, is extremely unpleasant. The Conservatives very rarely use this weapon (they did it once in 1942) and though the Labour whips have done so a little more often, they also dislike the process. When it last happened in 1961 (six MPs were involved), the whip had to be restored in May 1963 in time for the 1964 general election.

For whips or leaders to threaten MPs is usually counterproductive. When Mr Wilson in February 1967 told Labour members at an 'upstairs' meeting of the party that 'every dog is allowed one bite, but a different view is taken of a dog that goes on biting all the time. . . . He may not get his licence renewed when it falls due', he did not create any alarm and was soon claiming that it was a joke that had been misunderstood. The forces at work were revealed in the 1968–9 session when, for a time, confidence in the Labour Party whips virtually broke down but though the government's majorities fell off on occasion and it sometimes could not go on as late at night as the whips had hoped, no division was lost and the government's position was never in danger. The force of party loyalty, reduced possibly in some cases to a mere desire for political survival, kept the rebels, the disillusioned and the disappointed attending and voting in the usual way.

It is sometimes said that another disciplinary weapon available is the threat of dissolution. But when a party has a secure majority, why incur all the risks and costs of an election just to teach some backbenchers a lesson? On the other hand, if a party is so divided that it faces defeat, it is not in a position to win an election and therefore will not call one. In May 1969 when Mr Mellish, the Labour Chief Whip, threatened dissolution if a motion to send the Industrial Relations Bill to a committee was defeated, the idea was greeted with scepticism. No one seriously imagined that if the government was defeated on a procedural issue, Mr Wilson would have asked the Queen for a dissolution. It was highly unlikely that a Prime Minister, who also had his feelings of party pride and party loyalty, would destroy his party by calling an election when it was divided, discredited and badly behind in the opinion polls. Most Labour MPs realized that in this case Mellish was trying, in a somewhat confused manner, to indicate the seriousness of the situation and to say that if the government lost its procedural motion, it would be so publicly and seriously humiliated that it would be hard for it to recover enough authority to go on governing.

The other often quoted method of ensuring support for the Prime Minister is through the distribution of rewards and patronage. (It is not without significance that the Chief Whip's official title is that of 'Patronage Secretary'.) Patronage can take several forms, the most important being the 100 or so posts in the gift of the Prime Minister, of which some eighty-five are in the House of Commons. With this number of offices, about one in four of the government side have a salaried post while a further group of about twenty-five unsalaried

Parliamentary Private Secretaries are appointed, making one in every three of the majority into guaranteed supporters of the leadership. For career reasons (discussed on pages 143–4), members are very eager to obtain ministerial positions so that the desire for office influences many outside the large number who actually hold posts. Conservative governments do distribute political honours, from peerages downwards, not simply to MPs but to prominent party workers. Since 1966 Labour Prime Ministers have abstained from this form of patronage. Finally, the whips have many minor gifts which they can use, ranging from places on committees of special interest to the MP in question, to membership of the Council of Europe or to inclusion in delegations on interesting visits abroad.

Yet though the force of these inducements is considerable, it cannot be compared with party loyalty nor can it be argued that loyalty guarantees certain rewards. It is true that titles under the Conservatives were almost always awarded in return for a long period of unvarying support in the lobbies. The ability to distribute titles provides a useful means of maintaining the loyalty and enthusiasm of MPs who no longer have hope of office and who contemplate retirement. As to posts in the government, the pathway to such promotion is somewhat obscure. It may be true that with certain Prime Ministers personal criticism will lead to exclusion but in some cases this has led to promotion. But there is evidence that both personal disagreements and rebelliousness on issues do not debar a backbencher from office. Indeed some backbenchers are appointed precisely in order to reduce the number of vocal opponents of government policy, others because a Left–Right or regional balance has to be maintained, while a Labour Prime Minister has usually wanted to keep a body of support on the party's National Executive Committee by appointing a number of the MPs on the Executive to his government. Thus no one can advise a new member as to just what degree or form of loyalty will lead to promotion. Mr Crossman once repeated to the author an aphorism of Mr Bevan: 'You can crawl up the ladder of preferment on your belly or you can go out, form a Left-wing group and kick your way into office, but do not try a mixture of the two.' It is not as simple as this, but the point is that none of these courses of action and no degree of personal success or failure materially affect the conduct of MPs in terms of party loyalty. Men who, whatever their talents, are clearly on the Prime

Minister's blacklist, men who have been dismissed, men whose ministerial careers are at an end and men who have long abandoned hope, all still support the leadership as regularly as the newest, most ambitious aspirant.

The fact is that the party system is the life-blood of the body politic in Britain. The mass electorate is primarily voting for one or other party and its leadership in the hope that those whom they prefer will form the government. MPs know that in the vast majority of cases they were not elected because of their own qualities or views but because they bore a party label and that their chief task in the eyes of the voters is to keep their leadership in power. Besides this little else matters. Men are drawn into a political life through the parties and while there is plenty of scope for individualists and a wide variety of views within the parties, the few who find themselves unhappy about the constraints of party loyalty soon find their discomfort spreading and they come to realize that there is no place for them in the House of Commons. Indeed some such system of internal regulation is essential. The MP would not know how to vote on the many complicated issues which he has no time to master, he would not be able to choose a leader or maintain a stable executive. The need for a party machine was illustrated in 1967–70 by the bewilderment of the single Scots and Welsh Nationalist MPs who had no party whip to let them know the next week's business and to guide them each time the division bell rang, and who had no overall political terms of reference from which to operate. Thus party loyalty is the main source of the Prime Minister's strength. It is not personal in that while one candidate or other in a battle over the leadership may have his special following, the whole party rallies once a particular man is chosen as leader and is an actual or potential Prime Minister.

Support of his colleagues, the Cabinet and the civil service

The second great source of strength of the Prime Minister is the whole supporting apparatus of government. This has several facets, the most important being that the premier is at the top of a chain of command which leads down through the senior ministers in the Cabinet, the ministers outside the Cabinet, ministers of state and parliamentary secretaries linking on to the senior civil servants and departments of state. But there is also the strength derived from the ubiquity of government and its great powers so that many elements in the nation both inside and outside politics look to the Prime

Minister or to the Whitehall machine. The sheer difficulty and involved nature of the decisions that have to be taken means that the initiative in proposing solutions lies almost entirely with the government. Besides the Prime Minister's position at the apex of both the ministerial and the official pyramids, he has the makings of a personal department in the Cabinet Office. It includes the Cabinet Secretariat and a Statistical Office. In addition, there is now a Special Policy Unit as well as the No. 10 Downing Street staff.

Not only has the Prime Minister these powers and opportunities but the Cabinet Office is responsible to the premier and now aids in remodelling the machinery, in altering the atmosphere and, if necessary, in rearranging the senior personnel in Whitehall. The Prime Minister arranges the ministerial hierarchy inside and outside the Cabinet and can indicate an heir apparent or allocate appointments, putting any challengers into thankless posts, so as to ensure that there is no crown prince. And if a reshuffle is not appropriate, departmental functions can be rearranged or Cabinet committees created to circumscribe particular individuals and thus, in time, alter the power structure both in Whitehall and in the party.

Most Prime Ministers have taken a special interest in foreign affairs and this tendency has strengthened their position within British government and has been itself emphasized by similar developments in other countries. It has, for instance, been the growing practice, especially since the First World War, for national leaders to deal only with other national leaders. Thus it has to be the Prime Minister who receives the American President or the German Chancellor and he or she can at any time decide to represent Britain at international negotiations. There is no absolute need for a premier to take charge of all important foreign problems. Mr Attlee left most issues and tasks in this field to Mr Ernest Bevin and, in his later years, Mr Churchill left more to Sir Anthony Eden than either Mr Macmillan or Mr Wilson did to their Foreign Secretaries. In contrast, Mr Wilson took over the exploratory stage of Common Market talks in 1966, the negotiations with Mr Ian Smith over the Rhodesian constitution and all the important East–West talks that included Britain. Mr Heath deliberately tried to avoid this kind of intervention but had to take charge of the crucial talks with President Pompidou in 1971 which paved the way for British entry to the European Community.

The same trend is evident in internal affairs, though in this area of activity it is much easier for the Prime Minister to insist on the responsibility of the appropriate departmental ministers. Thus Lloyd George tended to run the government himself through a series of *ad hoc* committees rather than through the Cabinet, but Bonar Law, reacting against him, insisted that deputations and difficulties should be sent to the appropriate minister. But, as governments have increasingly been held responsible for all events during their period of office, so the reputation of the Prime Minister has come to be at stake in all critical issues. For example, Macmillan, Wilson and Heath each tended to intervene in serious labour disputes, personally taking charge of the final rounds of talks with the unions and the employers.

Using the machinery of the Cabinet Secretariat, the Prime Minister can do much to frame the context within which decisions are taken. Most premiers have prior discussions with senior ministers and this has led to talk of 'inner Cabinets' or 'partial Cabinets'. Only Mr Wilson formally announced his arrangements at this level when he set up a 'Parliamentary Committee' in April 1968 to act as a steering committee on acute political issues which he replaced in April 1969 with a slightly smaller inner Cabinet with the same functions. But it appears that despite these bodies, Mr Wilson's conduct altered very little, most of his preliminary discussions being with the relevant ministers or with members of his own staff, though in 1969 he did dismiss Mr Callaghan from the Parliamentary Committee (leaving him in his office and in the Cabinet) for opposing a Cabinet decision on the National Executive of the party. In practice, no Prime Minister likes to go into the Cabinet without some idea of how his senior colleagues will react and he will usually consult some more than others. If this becomes frequent and convenient, talk of an inner Cabinet will arise.

In addition, the Prime Minister can decide when and what the Cabinet will consider and he can always propose that a matter should go to an *ad hoc* committee of ministers whom he can nominate. The best examples in recent times of the Prime Minister's control of the agenda, are that Mr Wilson's Cabinet barely considered the case for devaluation or for a military withdrawal from East of Suez from 1964 until November 1967, although an increasing number both of ministers and senior officials were thinking along these lines. It would have cut across the normal patterns of Cabinet conduct for ministers whose departments were not concerned, such as Mr Jenkins or Mr Crosland, to have sent a memo to the Secretary to the Cabinet asking for these issues to be put on the agenda for the next meeting. Such a proposal could only have come from an economics minister in the one case or the Chancellor of the Exchequer, the Foreign Secretary or the Minister of Defence in the other, or in either case from the premier. Mr Gordon-Walker in his book, *The Cabinet,* defends the failure to discuss the East of Suez question on the grounds that the Cabinet was subconsciously working round the problem and finally reached the central issue, to stay or withdraw, at the earliest possible moment when action was possible in late 1967.

The control of information can be illustrated by the fate of Mr Douglas Jay's paper, prepared by his department (the Board of Trade), on the industrial and commercial effects of entering the Common Market. Mr Wilson decided to handle the preparatory work on the British application in a Cabinet Committee chaired by himself. In this committee it was clear that there was a serious conflict between Mr Jay's paper and others which, coming from different ministers and departments, were much more favourable to entry. When the dispute could not be reconciled, the Prime Minister evoked the rule that the Cabinet will consider only opinions and not disagreements on matters of fact and Mr Jay's paper therefore was not circulated, though his continual efforts to reopen the issue finally led to his dismissal in August 1967.

In broader terms, the Prime Minister chairs the key Cabinet Committees on defence and overseas policy and long-term economic strategy, and can set up (and chair if necessary) *ad hoc* committees on critical matters, such as the Falklands campaign in 1982 (earlier examples in foreign affairs being the committees which ran the Suez operation in 1956, arranged Indian independence in 1947 or conducted the pre-Munich negotiations in 1938). The Prime Minister chooses the chairman and nominates the members of these committees. Mr Wilson introduced the practice that there was no automatic appeal on disputed issues from a committee to the full Cabinet; the chairman was given powers to refuse an appeal and to settle the matter himself. In addition, committees can be used to hold in check a difficult colleague, or bolster a weak one, Mr Butler having a committee imposed on him when he became Chancellor of the Exchequer in 1951, while Mr Tom Fraser was saddled with a committee, when he was Minister of Transport from 1964 to 1967, in order to push matters along. Mrs Castle, his successor, showed her fire and self-confidence by insisting that the committee be disbanded as soon as she took over the ministry.

Thus in both institutional and personal terms, the relations between Prime Minister and their senior colleagues are complex but normally emphasize and reflect the former's position of authority. As Sir Anthony Eden has put it:

> A Prime Minister is still nominally *primus inter pares*, but in fact his authority is stronger than that. The right to choose his colleagues, to ask for a dissolution of Parliament and, if he is a Conservative, to appoint the chairman of the party organization, add up to a formidable total of power. (*Full Circle*, p. 269)

Lord Butler's comment was that:

> I think that on the whole the Prime Minister has tended to stop being an equal among equals. There is a tendency not exactly to dictatorship . . . but to be the leader who does control everything, and things are getting more and more into his own hands. (*The Listener*, September 1965)

Sir Alec Douglas-Home's description of the situation was that:

> Every Cabinet Minister is in a sense the Prime Minister's agent – his assistant. There's no question about that. It is the Prime Minister's Cabinet, and he is the one person who is directly responsible to the Queen for what the Cabinet does. If the Cabinet discusses anything it is the Prime Minister who decides what the collective view of the Cabinet is. A Minister's job is to save the Prime Minister all the work he can. But no Minister could make a really important move without consulting the Prime Minister, and if the Prime Minister wanted to take a certain step the Cabinet Minister concerned would either have to agree, argue it out in Cabinet, or resign. (*The Observer*, 23 August 1961)

The chief reasons for the relationship illustrated by these comments are, as has been argued, party loyalty and patronage. The latter has more force with ministers than with backbenchers, because ministers have set their feet on the ladder of promotion and most would prefer to go further. Even if not bent on advancement, being ministers they all have something to lose. There is the additional point that those committed to certain policies wish to have the Prime Minister's confidence because this gives their proposals the best chance of success. Occasionally certain ministers achieve a position where they are virtually indispensable, while it is often the case that to dismiss one or more might not be worth the arguments that would take place over the issue which produced the break. But the old idea that a minister who resigns or is dismissed can be a serious threat because he may rally dissident feeling on the backbenches has little force nowadays; the backbenches simply do not have that degree of cohesion nor can such criticisms counter the normal effect of party loyalty. As a result, men who leave a government soon cease to attract attention; they revert to the status of backbencher and this explains why there has been a steady decline in the number of resignations on points of principle in the last twenty-five years.

The Prime Minister receives loyal and competent support from the civil service. However, the staff is fragmented into separate units. There is a small personal office which deals with political and constituency correspondence. There is a small staff attached to 10 Downing Street, keeping the diary, dealing with press and public relations, preparing for parliamentary business and dealing with patronage. The Cabinet Office staff serves the whole Cabinet and its committee system, but the Secretary to the Cabinet tends to act as personal adviser to the Prime Minister, and the Cabinet Office is used to give warning of issues and problems from government departments coming on to the Cabinet agenda. Clearly, the nature of personal relationships will vary greatly depending upon the individuals involved: Mr Heath is known to have had great respect for the advice of the late Sir William Armstrong, then Secretary to the Cabinet. Since 1974 the Prime Minister has also had a small group of non civil service policy advisers. Under Mrs Thatcher this group appears to have become stronger: Professor Alan Walters was appointed to review economic affairs, Sir Anthony Parsons advised on diplomatic questions and Mr Mount on family policy.

Should this support for the Prime Minister be formally integrated into a Prime Minister's Department analogous to other government departments, although much smaller in size? This question tends to conflate two separate issues. The first is whether existing civil service support for the Prime Minister should be strengthened and co-ordinated into a single hierarchy. In essence, the issue is whether the Prime Minister should be better briefed to deal with matters raised by Cabinet colleagues. How far should the Prime Minister be tempted to supervise a wide range of business or how far should Cabinet ministers be trusted to advise on matters within their departmental responsibility? Do we want an ever stronger presidential type of Prime Minister? Mrs Thatcher is known to prefer stronger personal briefing. Yet what happens if those with access to the personal ear of the Prime Minister have views that differ from the advice of the permanent staff in the responsible department? Will normal channels of advice be overborne by others based on less information and less experience of the problems involved? Here we come to the second issue raised by the creation of a Prime Minister's Department. Should it be staffed essentially by civil servants or should there be a strong input of party political opinion? Duplicate briefing by a second team of permanent officials seems wasteful. The alternative would be for the department to have a strong party flavour – to be a stimulus and challenge to the Whitehall establishment. Such a development would help the Prime Minister to counter orchestrated civil service pressure but it would add greatly to conflict and tension within the machinery of government. This is the major instance of the general issue of how far ministers should have political support when dealing with official business, a topic that is examined further in Chapter 11.

Right to choose the date of general elections

During the twentieth century the convention has become firmly established that the Prime Minister can choose the date of a general election. Thus the Prime Minister becomes the chief strategist for the party in office. There may be consultations with party officials, Cabinet colleagues and the Chief Whip, but the decision is the Prime Minister's. As the decision is personal, it follows that blame for misjudgement will be personal. Mr Heath never fully recovered his authority among Conservatives after losing the election in February 1974; Mr Wilson was weakened by losing the 1970 election; Mr Callaghan was blamed for not holding an election earlier – in the autumn of 1978.

But the right to fix the election date does give the Prime Minister a great advantage against his or her political opponents. It is always possible to seize a moment when the national mood seems to be favourable. There is little restraint on the Prime Minister. If the Opposition object to the timing of an election, then they can be accused of being unwilling to face the voters. Major legislation going through Parliament can simply be jettisoned, as was done in 1983. Important international engagements in the Prime Minister's diary can be broken or perhaps retimed, as again was done in 1983. Modern techniques of opinion polling which did not exist in the earlier part of this century help to show the Prime Minister when the moment is suitable. It follows that there is a substantial bias in the British system of government which favours the party in office. In the 1970s this bias was not noticeable because of the degree of dissatisfaction which the electorate felt for successive governments. Nevertheless, the advantage for the ministerial party is still there even if it does not produce victory on election day.

It would be possible, as is done in many other countries, for parliaments to be elected for a fixed period of four or five years. The election date would be known automatically in advance. There are two main objections to this arrangement. If as the result of a major political crisis or erosion of support at by-elections the government lost control of the Commons, then the case for an immediate election would seem very strong. This situation could be met by having a provision that Parliament should be elected for a fixed term unless the government had earlier been defeated in a vote of confidence in the House of Commons. Such an arrangement would both retain essential flexibility while limiting the power of the Prime Minister. The second objection is that if the date of the election is fixed then, as in the USA, election campaigns last a very long time. For months ahead of polling day all developments of public policy would be viewed in terms of party advantage. Parliamentary business would tend to become a permament election campaign as Parliament's life visibly ebbed away. The public might well get tired of even more polemical activity between politicians. However, a democracy should not shy away from constitutional reform because it could provoke more political discussion. Even so, it must be recognized that a system of fixed-term parliaments would not wholly eliminate the potential bias in favour of the party in power; ministers can always manipulate the levers of economic policy to try to produce a more hopeful atmosphere on election day to convince waverers that things are moving in the right direction.

7 Political leadership – the limitations on the Prime Minister's power

Limitations of party loyalty and Cabinet control

None of the powers that have been described are without limit, though in some cases the surprising fact is how remote the limits are. For instance, party loyalty is greatest for a successful Prime Minister who looks like winning any foreseeable election, but if there are mistakes and ground is lost in the opinion polls, then party loyalty still holds, because no MP on his side wants an election under these conditions. Matters have to be pretty desperate to reach the position when either other loyalties begin to loom larger than party loyalty or MPs begin to wonder whether party loyalty would be better served by disloyalty to this particular premier. In the case of the Conservatives, this has happened only once in recent history, when many felt that Neville Chamberlain was so directly responsible for leading the country close to disaster in the Second World War that he had to go (though even then he retained his majority, for only 33 out of 417 Conservatives voted with the Opposition and 66 abstained). This has to be balanced against such examples as the way the Conservative leadership was able, despite many warnings, to lead that patriotic and pro-military party into appeasement in the 1930s, to lead it into and out of the Suez expedition in 1956, and into and out of support for the settler-dominated Central African Federation in the same decade. On the Labour side, a prior loyalty can be revealed if the Prime Minister comes too deeply into conflict with the unions or with the fundamentals of socialist faith. Yet Ramsay MacDonald was able to retain the party loyalty of the vast majority of his backbenchers through all the difficulties of the 1929–31 Government with mounting unpopularity and increasing unemployment, until he decided to walk out on his party. Had he stayed as a Labour Prime Minister and fought it out with his critics, he might well have won a majority at a party meeting. Similarly, despite severe by-election setbacks and mounting economic problems, Mr Wilson was able to carry his party into a wage restraint policy and then, in 1969, on the issue of trade union reform into a head-on conflict with the Trades Union Congress, in defiance of Labour Party conference decisions, against the wishes of many MPs and after a period of acute government unpopularity, before the bonds of party loyalty showed any signs of snapping. At the last stages of the Industrial Relations Bill a minority of members did feel that their loyalty to the unions or their principles might drive them to vote against their party leader, but Mr Wilson always reckoned that had this been put to the test, party loyalty would have triumphed. Mr Heath also drove his party hard over entry to the European Community and over reversals of policy on industry, increases in public expenditure and a statutory incomes policy, all without serious challenge to his leadership. Mr Callaghan survived even greater tensions.

A more normal and regular limitation on a Prime Minister than the very remote possibility of a breakdown of party loyalty lies in the relationship with ministerial colleagues inside and outside the Cabinet. The limitations arise in several situations. When a Prime Minister is chosen or wins an election, greater power is conferred upon him, but the immediate objective is to end any old party feuds and to draw everyone round the new leadership. So most new Prime Ministers are inclined to include in their Cabinets or other ministerial posts those men whom they have just beaten in the contest for leadership or their chief lieutenants when in opposition. Thus it would be unwise to omit certain individuals and better if places could be found for a whole series of groups whom the Prime Minister, on purely personal grounds, might have preferred to exclude. For example, it would scarcely have been possible for Attlee to have left out such men as Ernest Bevin, Stafford Cripps or Herbert Morrison just as Mr Heath would not have contemplated the omission of Sir Alec Douglas-Home, Mr Maudling or Mr Quintin Hogg when he was forming his Cabinet. Whether this should be described as a constraint or not is dubious because Prime Ministers want the best government they can assemble and in both the cases mentioned, Mr Attlee and Mr Heath would have certainly felt great regret if men of such ability and experience had refused to serve.

But none of this must be taken as evidence that a politician can force himself upon a hostile Prime Minister. Both Baldwin and Neville Chamberlain were able to exclude Mr Churchill in the 1930s. Mr Heath would not have Mr Enoch Powell in his Cabinet.

Mrs Thatcher kept him out of her Shadow Cabinet, and Mr Callaghan was able to refuse Mr Jenkins the Foreign Office in 1976, which encouraged him to go to Brussels, and Mrs Thatcher kept Mr Heath out of her Cabinet in 1979. While most party leaders wish all strands of party opinion to pull together when a new government is formed, the longer a ministry lasts, the more it reflects 'the manpower policy' of the Prime Minister. Given success, the premier's strength grows and it becomes easier to sack senior ministers or to let them go if there is a dispute. Thus Mr Macmillan was able to lose three Treasury ministers in 1958, Mr Thorneycroft, Mr Powell and Mr Birch, saying that it was only 'a little local difficulty', while Mr Wilson felt able to accept one of Mr George Brown's regular resignation gestures in 1968. Of course the Prime Minister can always arrange Cabinet shuffles designed to ensure that the Cabinet reflects more closely the views of 10 Downing Street. Even a senior Cabinet figure like Mr Prior can be partially isolated by sending him away to deal with the intractable problems of Northern Ireland. Mr Walker could be kept away from the centre of events by confining him to peripheral issues such as agriculture and energy. Other Cabinet colleagues were sacked by Mrs Thatcher – Sir Ian Gilmore, Mr St John Stevas, Mr Carlisle and, most notable of all, Mr Pym. New recruits to the Cabinet and to posts of central responsibility represented the 'dry' stream in Conservative philosophy – witness the rapid promotion of Mr Brittan, Mr Lawson and Mr Tebbit.

On the other hand, while a Prime Minister whose policies are unpopular can purge the government in order to give it a fresh image or to indicate a new approach in certain fields, there is a limit to what can be done. For instance, Mr Macmillan was able to sack seven of his Cabinet of twenty-one in July 1962 but he could not have repeated the exercise in that Parliament. Similarly, when Mr Wilson's policies ran into difficulties after July 1966 and there was a forced devaluation in November 1967, he took Mr Jenkins as Chancellor of the Exchequer and probably could not then have dismissed him without a catastrophic collapse in confidence. If the political situation deteriorates seriously and there is discontent in the party and a potential challenge to the Prime Minister, the position may well depend on relations with the senior five or six members of the Cabinet. The backbenchers and junior ministers may complain and cabal but they can achieve nothing (discussed in more detail on pages 80–2) if there is no alternative leader and some co-operation from among the senior ministers in the government. Thus the criticisms of Clement Attlee in 1947 which led some ministers to suggest that he stood down in favour of Ernest Bevin never amounted to a serious challenge because Ernest Bevin refused to countenance any such move. Similarly, the talk of removing Mr Wilson in March and April of 1969 foundered on the fact that while there was an alternative readily available, Mr Callaghan, none of the influential members of the Cabinet were prepared to move. Had two or three of the top seven been prepared to support Callaghan, the whole picture would have changed.

Thus the Prime Minister has to take the state of the party, the government's standing and the position of leading colleagues into account. At all times, but particularly if serious unpopularity is encountered, these factors may affect the Prime Minister's decisions. But if there is a record of success, scope increases and there is almost total freedom to select and promote any colleagues.

Within this framework, the more normal limitations arise from the day-to-day operation of the Cabinet system. Here the Prime Minister has the advantages already listed of choosing the men, passing the agenda, chairing the main committees and preparing the ground with preliminary talks; he or she can decide if and when to intervene during the discussions, whether to allow the argument to continue by postponing a decision or when to halt and sum up the sense of the meeting. Yet, in almost every government, the Prime Minister has been overruled on certain issues, though most ministers agree that when this hapens, it is a little surprising and a sign of misjudgement in one form or another. Mr Gordon-Walker in this book, *The Cabinet*, gets the emphasis exactly right when he announces in somewhat surprised tones that 'Mr Harold Wilson and his Foreign Secretary were once overruled by the Cabinet on a matter of great importance'. If this happens frequently, confidence in the Prime Minister will wane.

In practice, two or three ministers give overall direction and tone to a government. Their views are known and are rarely and reluctantly challenged by the less influential members. For instance, Mr Wilson, Mr Callaghan and Mr Brown set the general lines for the Labour Government for some time after the 1964 general election. In the early years of the Thatcher Government the Foreign Secretary, Lord Carrington, the Home Secretary, Mr Whitelaw and the Chancellor of the Exchequer, Sir Geoffrey Howe each carried considerable weight. Different Prime Ministers have set about running their Cabinets in different ways, but with much the same result. Mr Attlee was brisk. He would call on the minister concerned and one or two others and then sum up the sense of the meeting. Mr Churchill tended to indulge in long reminiscences and anecdotes but commanded tremendous respect. Mr Wilson, on controversial issues where he was himself undecided, tended to go round the table collecting voices. (This is a better description than 'taking votes'. The Lord President beside him would keep the tally and this led to newspaper leaks giving lists of 'fors' and 'againsts'.) Mr Callaghan faced special tensions and allowed thirty hours of discussion on the terms of the IMF loan to Britain in late 1976 before he stated his position and concluded.

In meetings of this kind where important business is being rapidly transacted by politicians with an overriding common purpose, it is clearly wrong to talk in simple terms of Prime Ministerial dominance. On the other hand, several experienced ministers have pointed out to the author that a premier who cannot get what he wants out of the Cabinet does not deserve to hold such an eminent post. At the same time, no leader wishes to give the impression of brow-beating or overruling his colleagues. The purpose of Cabinet meetings is to keep members informed of major policy developments (the Foreign Secretary regularly reports on what he has been doing), to settle inter-departmental conflicts and to test opinion on the larger policy issues that are facing the government. Often, on these questions, the Prime Minister may not have a clear view. He may be waiting to see how a situation is developing and how opinion is forming among the public, in his party and among his colleagues. But once the Prime Minister has formed a view and wants to ensure its acceptance, the odds are heavily in his favour. For instance, if the division of opinion is serious and opposed to him, the premier can see those who may be likely to disagree with him one by one, as Mr Wilson did in the sterling crisis of July 1966, when he tackled each devaluer in turn until the opposition crumbled, leaving only George Brown to threaten and then to withdraw his resignation.

The seats around the Cabinet table are arranged in order of importance, the most influential posts carrying places opposite to or close beside the Prime Minister. He will invite the senior ministers, especially those with such important or wide-ranging responsibilities as the Treasury, foreign affairs or the leadership of the House, to contribute and it is a brave junior Cabinet minister (already overburdened by a heavy departmental load) who will challenge these more experienced, senior men. Also the circulation of information is selective, only a few of the Cabinet receiving the bulk of Foreign Office telegrams. Moreover the burden of their own work usually prevents the departmental ministers from reading even those telegrams of major importance which are circulated to the whole Cabinet. Richard Crossman, when Minister of Housing, once told the author that he had never said a word on Vietnam, but he had become so worried that (in 1967), he decided for once 'to be a Cabinet Minister'. This meant that he deliberately neglected his own work and waded through the mass of paper on Vietnam so that he was in a position to put his own views. Thus, though there is an element of discussion and decision-making in the Cabinet, the Prime Minister and those he has chosen to be his principal lieutenants are in a strong position. To insist on putting a view and to be clearly in a minority damages a Cabinet member and there is always the restraint caused by the knowledge that soon there will be another ministerial reshuffle and some members will move inwards along the table closer to the Prime Minister while others will move out altogether. It was noted above how Mrs Thatcher altered the balance of opinion in her Cabinet after 1980 by redistributing jobs. Even if the Prime Minister loses an argument in Cabinet, some of the 'victors' may subsequently be punished for disloyalty. Thus after Mr Wilson and Mrs Castle lost the support of almost all the rest of the Cabinet over the Industrial Relations Bill 1969, some of those who took the lead in opposing them were subsequently punished. Mr Marsh was sacked. Mrs Hart was moved out of the Cabinet. Mr Shore found that his ministry, the Department of Economic Affairs, was abolished. Mr Crosland was taken away from his chief interest – economic policy.

The history of the proposed Industrial Relations Bill of 1969 has been referred to many times in this book because it was a period of such strain for Mr Wilson and the Labour Party that it brought out many of the underlying relationships in politics and revealed the points at which the Prime Minister's sources of strength reached their limits. In the early months of 1969 first Mrs Castle, the Secretary of State for Employment and Productivity, and then the Prime Minister both came to believe that the economy required strong action against unofficial strikes and that to check these strikes would be electorally popular. But to take such action was to confront one of the founding sections of the Labour Party and to unite against the leadership the Left, the trade union members and many others who doubted the wisdom of such legislation. Various groups mobilized on the backbenches to try and defeat the bill, or, if there was no other alternative, to remove the Prime Minister. They found that there was no proper machinery for the latter purpose and the Prime Minister remained convinced that sufficient MPs never would vote with the Conservatives if it meant the defeat of the government. He was probably correct, but the fate, only a month before, of the Parliament (No. 2) Bill seemed to provide an alternative method of blocking the measure. The procedural motions to send the bill to a committee or to endorse a guillotine could be defeated (on the assumption that no government would resign on such procedural issues) and then the bill could be talked out on the floor of the House. Mr Mellish, the Chief Whip, inveighed against this possibility, threatened dire consequences and even an election but, at the end, told the final Cabinet that he could not guarantee the passage of these motions.

Until this point, Mr Wilson had been secure against the backbench muttering because there was no concerted opposition to him in the Cabinet. The Home Secretary, Mr Callaghan, had indicated his opposition to the bill but was joined by none of the other senior members nor was there any agreement among the backbenchers as to which of these ministers they would prefer as an alternative to Mr Wilson. Then Mr Mellish made his announcement. The Cabinet, with the exception of Mrs Castle, one by one turned against the bill and urged Mr Wilson to settle with the TUC. Yet he was not prepared to be instructed in this way. He left the last Cabinet to meet the TUC and refused to make any concessions. At this stage the senior ministers who had remained loyal to him until the last meeting began to fear that the Prime Minister would come back to the Cabinet, announce deadlock with the TUC, and then insist either that the Cabinet would agree to legislation or he would have to tender his resignation. To forestall this, Mr Crossman contacted the Prime Minister and pointed out that senior ministers would even prefer a government led by Mr Callaghan to a collapse and a Conservative victory. Mr Jenkins may also have pressed the Prime Minister to settle. When such powerful voices were raised, Mr Wilson probably realized that at last he was in real danger, but, whatever the precise form of the pressures mounted at this stage, he then returned for a second meeting with the TUC, found an acceptable formula which would allow him to jettison the Industrial Relations Bill and reached a settlement on this basis.

The moment this was done a sigh of relief swept the Labour Party and all the normal forces of party loyalty rallied again behind Mr Wilson. Moreover, by the summer of 1969 it was getting too close to a general election for arguments about the leadership and there was a dramatic (though short-lived) improvement in the government's standing in the opinion polls. As a result, Mr Wilson was back on a pinnacle of authority, able to force through measures (such as the amalgamation of the Prices and Incomes Board with the Monopolies Commission) which many of the Cabinet opposed. He was able to make a major reconstruction of the machinery of government in October 1969 without telling even the so-called inner Cabinet and he was able, as has been said, to punish most of those who had recently resisted him.

The party outside Parliament as a constraint

This episode also reveals the extent to which the annual conference of the party can be regarded as a constraint on a Labour Prime Minister. In theory, the Labour Party annual conference has an important role in the life of the party. It elects the National Executive, which is the governing body of the party, and the resolutions passed at the conference are the policy of the party; those which are carried by a two-thirds majority have to be included in the election manifesto. Opposition from the National Executive can become a serious embarrassment since internal disputes are always damaging and so Labour Prime Ministers have tried to preserve a favourable majority by deals with the union members and by making MPs on the Executive ministers in the government. Often opponents of official policy are elected to the National Executive. Until the leadership of Mr Gaitskell, the conference had not rejected the stand taken by the party leader on a major issue and many in the party assumed that if this happened, there would be the most serious repercussions and that such a division could not persist for long. Mr Gaitskell took this view in that he was deeply shaken when the conference in 1960 rejected the defence resolution which he had supported in favour of one embodying the policy of the Campaign for Nuclear Disarmament. He said he would 'fight, fight and fight again' to bring the party he loved back on to what he regarded as the correct course and, in 1961, the decision was reversed.

In power, Mr Wilson, and subsequently Mr Callaghan, was able to treat the conference less seriously and simply ignored or failed to become excited about defeats. Thus a special conference in 1975 voted by a majority of nearly two to one in favour of leaving the European Community. The majority of the Labour Cabinet took no notice. In 1976 the conference opposed the holding of direct elections to the European Parliament; the Labour Cabinet later introduced the necessary legislation into Parliament to authorize these elections. Two years later the conference rejected the Prime Minister's anti-inflation policy of limiting wage and salary increases to 5 per cent by a majority in excess of two to one. On this occasion the conference vote was influential because the policy was not based on statute but depended for success on popular consent. So party opinion can hamper Labour ministers. In opposition, the conference is even more formidable because the leader of the party is not Prime Minister and members of the National Executive are not eclipsed by other powerful ministers.

Mr Callaghan as Prime Minister was in constant conflict with the National Executive Committee of his party which became increasingly dominated by Left-wing opinion after 1974. The conflicts were sometimes over matters of party organization and more often over policy. In particular, there was serious trouble over the party manifestos for the 1979 general election and for the election to the European Parliament. The Prime Minister was regularly out-voted. He was reported to feel bruised and humiliated by the treatment he received at his own party headquarters. The NEC had little effect on the policy of the Labour Government because Labour had no effective majority in the House of Commons. Its activities were also resented by Labour MPs of the Right and Centre of the party.

The relations between a Labour Prime Minister and the party conference are not quite the same as those of his Conservative counterpart, both when the Conservatives are in opposition and when they are in office. The Conservative conference has none of the constitutional powers and assertive independence of the Labour conference. There is a greater trust of the leadership but Conservative leaders can be seriously embarrassed. Mr Heath found his position continually under fire at these gatherings and every speech he made to his party conference was a test of his capacity as a Conservative leader. While his strength and the respect for him enormously increased after he won the general election of 1970, a defeat at a conference on a matter where, for example, Mr Powell's views were opposed to the government's was still regarded as an exceptionally serious blow which should be avoided if at all possible. In this sense, the thesis of the late Professor R.T. McKenzie in his *British Political Parties* is correct, that the power structure within the parties and the relations between the leader and the rest of his party are very similar in both the Conservative and Labour Parties because in each case the relationship is governed by the power the political system confers on the Prime Minister, though the Labour conference has more influence, especially when that party is in opposition.

Professor McKenzie's argument is less satisfactory if it is extended to suggest that the motives people have for joining the parties, the atmosphere within them and the techniques each leader must apply in order to hold his party together are also similar. Professor Samuel Beer is right to emphasize in his *Modern British Politics* that the approach of the two parties to those problems, their outlook and spirit are radically different, though the facts of a nation's position in the world and the long-term nature of social and economic development does mean that the margin open for political change is small. In the sense that these limitations operate equally on both parties, there is little difference. However, each party finds that the pressure groups react to it in a different way and each party's approach to problems has a different flavour though, at the same time, no political leader wishes to be at loggerheads with the rank and file. In this sense, for the leaders of both parties, open challenges and defeats at the party conference are an ominous sign.

Governing through the House of Commons

It is argued or even simply asserted in many books that the chief limitation on the Prime Minister is Parliament and that this is the main task of the House of Commons. This is quite wrong and contrary both to the belief of contemporary politicians and to their practice. For the majority of MPs, as has been argued, the task in the Commons is to support their leaders. They regard the conflict inside the House as an extension of the struggle for power in the constituencies, their duty being to rally to the party. For the government, the Commons may be a nuisance in that its procedures dominate the timetable of departments and periodic attendance is required from busy ministers. But the Commons is also one of the agencies through which the government operates, enabling it to explain its policies and defend its record. Nothing pleases a Prime Minister more than to hear his cohorts behind him cheering as he scores points off the Opposition. For the Opposition, the objective is not to alter what the government is doing – that is its responsibility – the task is to explain to the public the Opposition's case for becoming the government after the next election.

Of course, the position was entirely changed in two years before the 1979 election. The Labour Government had no secure party majority of its own in the Commons. For eighteen months it relied on a pact with the Liberals. Thereafter, the government depended on the wish of the Scottish Nationalists to keep Labour in office until the referendum on devolution had been held. So in this exceptional situation the Commons was in control of the government and not vice versa. The Cabinet suffered a number of defeats, sometimes caused by their own backbenchers. Then the 1979 election produced a secure Conservative majority; the government whips were again in command and normality was restored.

In so far as the House of Commons does constitute a constraint on the Prime Minister, the pressure comes from the government's own backbenchers. The resistance of the Opposition is expected and, in this sense, taken for granted. Among government backbenchers, the normal attitude is one of loyal support, but the leadership knows that if it moves in certain specific directions, it will encounter objections, for example from the Left in the Labour Party or, in the case of the Conservatives, from those in favour of firm law and order policies and strict control of immigration. The leadership of a party, aided by the whips, has an excellent sense of what will, and what will not, arouse objections. At the same time, the leadership knows that in most circumstances it can survive such objections as the Conservatives did over British entry into the European Community or, more recently, over its policy towards the payment of social benefits. Similarly, Mr Wilson and Mr Callaghan survived even stronger opposition to their attitude towards Europe and to their economic policies. But no government wants a conflict if it can be avoided and this desire for harmony does have a marginal effect on a Prime Minister and on his senior colleagues which it is very hard to assess with precision. The reason is that the effect is a matter of influence, not of direct, clear-cut power to accept or reject. Thus it is possible, when searching for examples of such influence, to find cases when one minister concerned will say there was a modification in order to meet backbench pressure, and another minister equally involved with the same measure will deny that this was the reason, attributing the modification to his insistence or to an outside pressure group. When the author put a list of possible cases of backbench influence to Mr Wilson in mid 1967, he went through each carefully to demonstrate that on no occasion was he consciously deflected from his original purpose, even over mode of presentation or timing, by any estimate of what dissident groups on his backbenches might say. On the other hand, when he encountered greater political obstacles in late 1967 and in 1968–9, it would seem clear that backbench pressure had at least a marginal effect. Likewise, it seems probable that Mr Heath's changes of policy in 1971 and 1972 were due to external factors such as the level of unemployment and the rate of world inflation rather than to backbench pressure, but this must have had some influence, for example when the government was surprisingly defeated over immigration regulations in 1972 and 1982.

The way in which backbench pressure operates will be analysed in greater detail in Chapter 10 but in considering the position of the Prime Minister, the first and hardest task is that of formulating policies and of securing the support of ministerial colleagues for them. Then putting the policies through Parliament is a process which, if the government is reasonably successful, will be relatively simple. Debates make promulgation and execution of the policies easier. Yet all political leaders have a developed sense of the reactions of those around them. The Prime Minister wants both party and public approval and, other things being equal, will always prefer the method of solution which will improve morale on the backbenches; the leader can rely on party loyalty to carry government measures under almost all circumstances but he would rather cement than strain this loyalty.

Governing through the civil service

Just as Parliament is one of the agencies through which the government operates politically, it operates administratively through the civil service and here again there is a reciprocal influence on the Prime Minister which is hard to locate and estimate with accuracy. Crude suggestions either that politicians who know their own minds ought to be able to do exactly what they like with the governmental machine or that senior civil servants seek to win over or mislead ministers must be discounted. But it is also clear that senior civil servants, really able people who have spent their whole lives in government, whose duty is to advise ministers as to the best course of action, are bound to have an influence. Some of this derives simply from the complexity of modern society and the need for long-term policies. Thus public expenditure is planned over a five-year period and each summer 'hard' decisions are taken for three years ahead. So any government will inherit commitments in public expenditure, foreign policy commitments in the shape of external alliances, trade and defence agreements and commitments in the form of fixed expectations on the part of the electorate. It is part of the function of the civil service to point out these limitations to new ministers.

But a Prime Minister and the Cabinet may feel that the limitations are greater than those arising from the continuous nature of administration. This may occur when ministers find that they have inherited departments with elaborate and positive opinions as to how policy should be operated or when departments argue that to adopt certain policies would create too many administrative difficulties. While senior civil servants will always try to meet a minister's wishes, if they do consider that a policy is mistaken, they are bound to say so and a minister who wants to overrule such advice faces a very hard task in devising alternatives and in carrying them out. On the other hand, it is equally exhausting for a minister if the department has no policy to recommend, as this means that the politician has to collect the evidence and to think through a problem, when time is short and the necessary experience and expertise lacking.

It has been widely reported that Mrs Thatcher has been deeply dissatisfied with the performance of some of the most senior civil servants. The complaint arises from a feeling that there is a reluctance to adapt to the policies of the government particularly in regard to reducing public expenditure and cutting back on the range of state activity. Such reluctance is not wholly surprising. The top civil servants in each department were, in the early 1980s, men who had spent their whole careers in an atmosphere in which the public service had become used to undertaking more tasks. Since 1945 both Conservative and Labour Governments had followed policies which involved ever wider responsibilities for the state. So civil servants were being asked to assist in a change of direction which ran contrary to the experience of a lifetime. And, in a sense, the change was uniquely painful. An expanding system means more opportunities for those who work in it; a contracting organization is faced with loss of jobs and poorer promotion prospects.

Tension between ministers and civil servants is concealed, so it is difficult to know just how serious it is. But it is notable that Mrs Thatcher appointed influential personal advisers to assist her. Sir John Hoskyns was her first adviser; after Sir John resigned he argued publicly that senior civil servants should be politically more in tune with ministers. He was succeeded by Mr Ferdinand Mount who had previously published a book stressing the importance of the family and urging that it should be regarded as a more important, self-reliant social unit. Mr Mount was reported to be responsible for stimulating ministers to propose policies that would fit into this conception and probably reduce public expenditure on welfare. Professor Walters, known as a supporter of monetarist economic theories, was chosen to advise the Prime Minister on economic questions. After the Falklands crisis in 1982, Sir Anthony Hopkins, formerly Ambassador to the United Nations, was asked to advise on foreign affairs. Thus a small but highly influential team was assembled in Downing Street to assist the Prime Minister, a team chosen not simply on the basis of their ability but also because of their opinions. Mrs Thatcher did not invent the idea of political advisers; they had been used to some extent by every government since 1964. However, their impact on Downing Street from 1982 onwards appeared to be greater than ever before. Fears (and hopes) were expressed that an embryonic Prime Minister's Department was emerging.

Mrs Thatcher was also reported to take a close personal interest in appointments to senior civil service posts as they fell vacant. On occasion, officials known to her personally were chosen when, by the normal canons of seniority, they might have expected to wait a little longer for major promotion. The implication is that those who enjoyed preferment had opinions that were pleasing to the Prime Minister.

These developments raise two major issues about the civil service. Should the Prime Minister have a separate department able to provide advice and support on major policy questions? Should the non-political basis of civil service appointments be regarded as sacrosanct or should ministers work with officials who, broadly speaking, share their opinions? The second of these questions, which is fundamental to the whole character of the public service, is postponed until Chapter 11.

What is the case for providing the Prime Minister with independent sources of advice? The Prime Minister is expected to be concerned with all major aspects of policy. In a complex world she or he will require briefing on any issue that needs discussion with ministerial colleagues. But if other ministers are briefed by their departments and the Prime Minister is less well served then the leader of the government is at a disadvantage. It is difficult to win an argument if one is less acquainted with relevant facts. So it is perhaps natural that a Prime Minister should look for more help of the highest quality. The objection, however, must be that a Prime Minister's department, if it were developed, must constitute duplication of effort. What is the purpose of having an extensive and expensive system of policy advice in the Treasury and the Foreign Office if its efforts can be offset by the work of another, and presumably, much smaller group of officials in 10 Downing Street? Civil servants in the traditional departments cannot be expected to welcome competitive advice from Downing Street, especially advice which, arguably, is less well informed. A Prime Minister's department would be less welcome to civil service mandarins than the Central Policy Review Staff. Nor can Cabinet ministers be expected to enthuse at the idea. But without more personal support a Prime Minister may well feel unduly constrained by the effect of advice from civil servants, often unknown and unseen, and who she cannot control.

Relations with the pressure groups

Probably the greatest limitation on a Prime Minister and his government comes from the various power blocks in the community, their power being largely negative; to refuse to co-operate, to strike, to fail to participate or to follow new rules. In some cases, this non-cooperation may come from the public at large rather than from specific pressure groups. For example, over the years it has been established that no amount of exhortation will end absenteeism at work or, in times of balance-of-payments problems, persuade Britons to holiday at home. The relations with industrial, professional, regional or religious pressure groups can vary from one party to another and from one Prime Minister to another. Pre-war Conservative administrations viewed the trade union movement with some suspicion but Mr Attlee, on the other hand, expected to retain, above all, the confidence of the leaders of the larger trade unions. When the Conservatives came to power in 1951, they went to great lengths to convince the TUC that the latter's close association with government built up between 1945 and 1951 was not at an end. There was steady consultation and co-operation throughout the 1950s while the Labour Government, elected in 1964, tried to maintain similar relations with the Confederation of British Industries and with its members. When the Conservatives returned to office in 1970, there was a short period when this pattern was broken but then extensive consultations took place on incomes policy coming to an end, somewhat surprisingly, with a direct confrontation between the government and the miners. The Labour Government which took over in 1974 based its appeals to the electorate and its continuance in office very much on its capacity to make and maintain 'a social contract' with the unions. This was carried to such lengths that by 1977 54 per cent in one poll said that Mr Jack Jones, the leader of the Transport and General Workers Union, had more power than the Prime Minister.

In this field the lessons of recent years are complex. It is clear that pressure groups that act in a manner contrary to the interests of their members or to the public interest can be challenged and defeated by the government. For example in 1911 and 1948 the British Medical Association refused to accept major health proposals made by the government and found in the end that it was abandoned by the doctors. In 1982 Mrs Thatcher's administration overcame industrial action by health service workers. But other experience shows that governments are much less certain to win when dealing with pressure groups than they are to get legislation through the House of Commons. Admittedly, some bills are discussed with interested parties before being presented to Parliament. Outside bodies have a life and will of their own. This remains true even where, as with the BBC and British Rail, they operate subject to a degree of state control. In conflicts with them as well as with totally independent bodies the government has to be careful to choose its ground and to have public opinion on its side. The government cannot simply say 'We make laws and they must always be obeyed'. Law must be acceptable as fair and reasonable if it is to be successful: the fate of the Conservative's Industrial Relations Act 1972, is a salutary warning. There is a special problem for the Labour Party if it is in conflict with the unions, since they are built into the power structure of the party and can challenge a Labour government not merely by external confrontations, but internally through the party conference and by enlisting the support of trade union-sponsored MPs.

Thus the Labour Government of 1964–70 faced great problems in putting its wage policies into effect and was left in 1969 with an effective choice between continuing a statutory prices and incomes policy and introducing a new Industrial Relations Bill. It chose the latter but, in the end, lost both. The Conservatives after 1970 found, to their dismay, that they did not have the easy and automatic backing of the community for all aspects of their policy in this field. When public opinion, at least in part, accepted that the National Union of Mineworkers had a case during its strike in 1972, this helped the miners inflict a humiliating defeat on the government. When the same government got into a further conflict with the miners and failed to rally support, it lost a general election called specifically to strengthen the Prime Minister's hand. On this occasion the public preferred peace to a request to show 'who governs Britain'. There were even those who said that the election was irrelevant to the struggle with the miners.

The conclusion is that this is the key area of political action in internal affairs. The Prime Minister receives his mandate from the people; they expect him to govern but there are sub-leaders and representatives for subsections of the community whom he has to convince, appease, cajole or, if necessary, isolate and defeat. It is in this area that much of the real opposition to a government comes between elections, though the penalty of failure is not to hand power to these groups of sub-leaders. They cannot govern. The result, if the public accept the criticisms of its current political leadership, is to hand power over to the Leader of the Opposition at the next general election, who then becomes Prime Minister to try and handle these relationships in a manner which will produce better results and be more acceptable to the country.

As a result, there is a constant temptation for political leaders to encourage conflict or at least to back outside groups which might make life difficult for the government. Mr Wilson often attacked external forces on the Right in high finance for example, or on the extreme Left pointing to 'closely-knit groups of politically motivated men' who, he alleged, were behind certain critical strikes.

At least since 1945 there has been a general tendency for the government to consult with important pressure groups about important issues that concern them. Employers' organizations, trade unions, local authority associations, religious and welfare bodies join in a trek to Whitehall to put their point of view. Those who are consulted regularly expect to achieve some degree of influence. Consultation became traditional. Sometimes bargains were struck with interested parties which were then presented to Parliament for ratification in the form of legislation. This form of multiple participation is known as political pluralism. To an extent it modifies the influence of the party in power and reduces the status of Parliament.

Mrs Thatcher's administration paid less heed to outside bodies. In particular, a tendency developed to avoid trade unionists. They were less often asked to serve on advisory committees and boards. The National Economic Development Council and other bodies still operated but they seemed to have no impact on government thinking. The theory and practice of pluralism were in disfavour. Some trade union leaders were deeply affronted. The moderate leaders were the more offended: Mr Reg Basnett was more upset than Mr Arthur Scargill. Right-wing leaders wanted to participate in framing consensus policies; Left-wing leaders wished to have nothing to do with what they regarded as a deeply reactionary government.

The crucial issue is whether consultation, compromise and pluralism are desirable. Mrs Thatcher's view is that they are a recipe for weakness. On this analysis pluralism has led to inflation, inefficiency and Britain's industrial decline. When he first became Prime Minister, Mr Wilson often spoke about 'the smack of firm government': with Mrs Thatcher Britain actually felt it. The acceptance or rejection of pluralism is not a straightforward issue between the parties. Many on the more extreme Left share Mrs Thatcher's distrust of too much consultation. But the trouble is that if ministers talk only to party supporters and do not listen to critical advice, then they may well be surprised at the adverse consequences of their own policies. Ministers must govern but they should not be deaf. If they get too far out of touch, the electorate has a chance to impose a corrective at the next election.

The mass media

The acid test of the reality of democracy is the extent to which the means of mass communication are free from state control. In Britain, the level of this freedom is high. The press is controlled by its owners and editors. The main constraint placed upon it is the law of libel which protects the reputation of private individuals rather than the government. Editors may be asked not to publish information that would be harmful to national security but this arrangement does not spare ministers from criticism.

The British Broadcasting Corporation and the Independent Broadcasting Authority enjoy a large measure of independence. There is a constant stream of political controversy on both radio and television. Programmes are expected to provide political balance. Broadcasting authorities keep a careful tally of appearances by MPs and ensure that equal opportunity is given to Labour and Conservative spokesmen. How much access should be given to minor parties is a delicate problem. The allocation of time for party political broadcasts and election broadcasts is settled through negotiations between the political parties and the BBC and IBA: the government, as such, has no role in these discussions.

Ever since its inception the BBC has been highly conscious and jealous of its independence. This tradition dates from the freedom enjoyed by the BBC at the time of the General Strike of 1926, was confirmed in relation to domestic services at the time of the Second World War and continued with the Suez crisis in 1956. Politicians often resent the influence of broadcasters and envy their ability to control communications. Thus during the Falklands war in 1982 many Conservative MPs were irritated by a 'Panorama' programme which emphasized doubts in this country about the wisdom of government policy. The new Channel 4 also upset Conservatives because of an alleged Left-wing bias; Channel 4 was required to produce programmes to cater for minority interests, e.g. teenagers and ethnic groups, and these programmes tended to deal with topics that previously had received little attention on television.

A common complaint is that those who control the mass media also determine the agenda for political discussion. It is true that the editor of a popular current affairs programme will have more impact on everyday political conversation than the average MP or even the average minister. Because the editors of newspapers, or radio and television output are not elected, they are open to the charge that the influence they wield is non-democratic. Yet it would be a sad day if ever the pattern of political argument were decided by politicians alone. Topics on which the parties agreed would be ignored; topics which were embarrassing would be evaded. The main ground for criticism now should be that access to the media is restricted because the means of communication are limited. The number of newspapers is declining and the press now has a strong Right-wing flavour. On the other hand, the number of radio and television stations has increased and the broadcasting of political argument has grown immensely. Today it seems extraordinary that before 1939 the BBC itself imposed a ban on political controversy. After the war this rule was relaxed but a new restriction emerged which prohibited the discussion of issues due to be debated in Parliament. This gag disintegrated under the pressure of the Suez crisis and the restriction was formally dropped in 1957. Making fun of ministers became acceptable in the early 1960s with the television satire programme 'That was the week that was'. Those in high office were treated with less respect. Interviewers like (Sir) Robin Day became famous for giving ministers a hard time. Senior Labour politicians were incensed by the treatment accorded to them in 1970 in 'Yesterday's Men', a programme which discussed how former Cabinet ministers were now using their time. In days past, MPs ambitious to succeed had to perform well in Parliament; now they have also to do well under the television lights before a vastly greater audience. Although the press is in decline, the vigour of publicized political debate is stronger than ever before.

Of course, ministers will attempt to use the mass media for their own purposes. The Prime Minister is in a position to control, through the press aides at Downing Street, the public relations of the government. As Crossman put it, the press are 'fed with the Prime Minister's interpretation of government policy and . . . present him as the champion and spokesman of the whole Cabinet' (*Inside View*, p. 67). The press accept this relationship because of the value of No. 10 as a source of news, so many newspaper men wish to remain in good favour with the Prime Minister and the supporting public relations staff. The foreign trips of the Prime Minister usually draw considerable press and television coverage as do the receptions for statesmen visiting Britain. Mrs Thatcher's unannounced trip to the Falkland Islands in January 1983 was extensively covered by a BBC television team which happened to be there when she arrived: Downing Street then subjected the BBC to strong and successful pressure to make film available to Independent Television News so that ITV viewers would not be deprived of the sight of the Prime Minister's activities. Such manipulation of publicity helped to make Mrs Thatcher seem increasingly important, while others among her ministers declined relatively in reputation. Mr Wilson was also very conscious of the techniques of the mass media; Conservatives came to suspect him of regularly contriving some exciting release on the opening day of their annual conference in order to blot them out of the headlines. In normal circumstances, the Prime Minister holds the political initiative and can, to a large extent, choose when and how to act. This situation confers a constant advantage over the Leader of the Opposition who usually has to react to events.

   Yet, on balance, the public impact of political argument on radio and television is probably not favourable to ministers. As fresh policies are announced, ministers are expected to explain and defend them. Studio interviewers will subject them to stiffer questioning than they will suffer in Parliament. Opposition spokesmen add their criticisms. The same process will operate in reverse if the Opposition produce new policies, but this happens less frequently. And the Opposition proposals are not restrained by the cares of office. Of course, if the Opposition has internal quarrels, then the media will be merciless in exploiting them. Here the Labour Party suffers because it tends to bicker much more often and more publicly than do Conservatives.

   The impact of newspapers is less great than in the past. In the early years of this century, Prime Ministers were keen to be on good terms with the powerful men in Fleet Street. Those who owned papers were often elevated to the Lords. 'Press Baron' was a term in daily use. Party leaders were wise to treat newspaper magnates with care. Part of the Conservative press made life very difficult for Stanley Baldwin in 1930, while attacks on Sir Anthony Eden in the pro-Conservative *Daily Telegraph* in early 1956 were such that the Prime Minister felt it necessary to issue a statement saying he did not intend to resign. In 1965 Mr William Rees-Mogg (later the editor of *The Times*) wrote a feature in *The Sunday Times*, 'Why Home Must Go', which appears to have been a major factor in making Sir Alec Douglas-Home decide to resign. Labour leaders are less subject to this kind of pressure as there are no quality papers that are influential in the Labour movement. Attacks on a Labour leader from Conservative sources will not be taken seriously.

Today, greater public attention is concentrated on the news and current affairs programmes on radio and television. Newspaper owners and editors count for less. Broadcasting is less opinionated and a better medium for conveying information than the press. The BBC and IBA have no editorial opinion on items of party controversy; their job is to ensure balance in presentation. Television has greatly reduced the effect of politically biased journalism. The constant exposure of politicians to viewers who support another party or no party does show the public that these people are not unreasonable, that they have a case that can be stated and such evidence does make denunciations of political opponents as total blackguards much less plausible.

A further consequence of this greater intimacy of political debate is that ministers, even Prime Ministers, find it less easy to command respect because they hold positions of authority. Respect has to be secured by success. When things go well, the government finds it easy to hold its own in controversy. When things go ill, the spotlight of publicity adds to the difficulties. And ministers can never know what the investigations of journalists may uncover. If the best safeguard of liberty is unceasing vigilance, the existence of free mass media and a multiplicity of media add strength to the safeguard. The stimulation of public discussion is a major check on the arbitrary exercise of power by government.

8 Political leadership – can the Prime Minister be sacked?

The broader limitations on the Prime Minister that come from public opinion will be considered in the next chapter. The other crucial test of the strength of political leadership in Britain is whether a Prime Minister can be dismissed other than by the electorate at a general election. How much control do party supporters have over a Prime Minister or a Leader of the Opposition? A party leader needs initially to find favour with party selectors. How easy or difficult is it for the party selectors to effect change? The position is different between the Labour Party and the Conservatives; the position of a Prime Minister is also distinct from that of a Leader of the Opposition.

A Prime Minister has far stronger defences than a Leader of the Opposition. Normally the Prime Minister will have led the victorious party at the previous general election and thus enjoys some element of personal mandate from the voters. An Opposition leader can make no such claim; if he led the party at the previous election, then he suffered personal rejection by the electorate. A Prime Minister wields the weapon of patronage. If pressure to force resignation is unsuccessful, then patronage can be used to promote the faithful and demote the faithless. No politician in Opposition can have such power. A Prime Minister may also be able to distribute responsibilities in such a way that there is no obvious successor to his office. Those who collude against a Prime Minister are open to the charge of plotting to achieve higher political office; those who act against a Leader of the Opposition can claim to be trying to improve the chances of their party gaining power to the benefit of the whole country. To move against a Prime Minister is to admit that your party has been giving the nation poor leadership. A party that has just lost an election can afford the indulgence of a party row while the leader is being changed. The instinct of a party in power is much more to stick together. Thus a variety of factors, institutional and behavioural, ensure that the occupant of 10

Downing Street is far more difficult to replace than her (or his) principal adversary.

Strength of a Labour leader

The Labour Party has never dismissed a leader since 1922 although George Lansbury decided to resign after attacks made on him at the party conference in 1935. Ramsey MacDonald was not challenged as leader of the party; he left the position of his own volition. Attempts were made to remove Clement Attlee in 1947 and Harold Wilson in 1969 while they were in office. In 1960 Hugh Gaitskell was faced by a formal challenge from Harold Wilson; at a vote among Labour MPs Gaitskell won by 166 to 81. In the early months of 1983 there were rumblings against Mr Foot's leadership.

There are two methods of trying to change leadership, by private negotiation or by public campaign. The smoothest, least unpleasant technique is to bring pressure on the leader to resign. This method requires considerable unanimity among senior members of the Cabinet or Shadow Cabinet that the leader should go and, second, on who should take his place. The first condition is not easy to satisfy and the second condition can be even more difficult. So the pressures on Attlee, Wilson and Foot all failed. Indeed, a vigorous, determined political leader is unlikely to give way because of discussions behind closed doors.

If private pressure fails, the alternative is a public campaign. Such an exercise must be greatly damaging to the unity of a party and to its public image. For the Labour Party, contests for the leadership can be especially hurtful as the issues tend to be about policies rather than personalities. It is not whether A would be a better leader than B because of his personal abilities; the quarrel is about whether the policies advocated by A shall be adopted by the party or, alternatively, whether what B wants to do shall be accepted as the party's objective. Thus the leadership contest can become a fight between gladiators representing Left-wing and Right-wing or perhaps Centrist tendencies within the party. Intra-party argument is stimulated. Disarray within the party is made even more obvious. Labour's political opponents can only benefit.

The creation of an electoral college in 1981 (described in Chapter 5) to choose the Labour leader and deputy leader may well have strengthened their position. The choice is no longer a matter solely for MPs. Trade unions have a voice and so do constituency Labour

Parties. Thus a challenge to existing leaders must stimulate widespread argument covering a span of many weeks. No longer can the contest be conducted through discreet lobbying in the corridors of the Palace of Westminster. It is not simply that the electorate has widened out of all recognition; there is also a prospect that a Labour MP will be under pressure from his local party to use his vote in a particular way. Each year there is an opportunity for the leader and the deputy leader to be challenged. So each year there is an opportunity for widespread dispute which could do great harm to the image of the party. Such damage can only be avoided by not having a contested election. In the past a difficulty about attempting to replace the leader was often that there was no clear successor. Now this problem is aggravated by the fact that a new leader may be imposed on the Parliamentary Labour Party that it does not want, through the voting power of trade unions and local Labour Parties. Indeed, the disparate character of the electorate makes the outcome of an election harder to predict with certainty. In these circumstances a majority of Labour MPs may generally be keen to avoid change. And the influence of the Parliamentary Labour Party in deciding whether leadership elections shall be contested is still substantial, for Labour MPs meet together regularly in a way that cannot be matched by representatives from trade unions or constituency Labour Parties. The MPs can establish an atmosphere which either favours or inhibits contests for leadership.

As the election rules were altered quite drastically in 1981, events before then are a poor guide to what may happen in the future. The full implications of the new system are not wholly clear. Before 1981 a leader could in theory be dismissed by a vote of no confidence at a meeting of the Parliamentary Labour Party. Now the PLP does not have the power to choose a leader, so it cannot dismiss him. Of course an adverse vote in the PLP would be a sign of a major crisis of confidence in the leader, who might well feel the necessity of resignation; alternatively, the leader could stay until or unless he was ousted by the electoral college.

In February 1983, Labour suffered a disastrous defeat at the by-election in Bermondsey. The morale of the party was shattered by the loss of a safe seat to the Liberals; the position of Mr Foot as leader seemed to be under threat. A month later the mood changed when Labour won a by-election at Darlington with an increased majority and Mr Foot's position became secure again. But if Mr

Foot had resigned, what would have been the consequence? In the short term, Mr Healey, as deputy leader, would have taken over. But for how long? Would he have acted as leader until the next party conference in the autumn or just for a few weeks until the electoral college was summoned? What time interval must elapse before the electoral college can meet in a crisis? Some trade union leaders feel that they should not vote in a leadership election until they have consulted their members and such consultation takes time. Inevitably, a rushed election must be less democratic. In 1983 there was an additional problem – the imminence of a general election. If the leadership contest had been postponed, then Labour would probably have gone to the polls with an acting leader. This arrangement might have damaged the credibility of the party, as the Conservatives would certainly have claimed that the acting leader was likely to be replaced by someone with more extreme opinions.

There is little doubt that Labour's electoral college system has come to stay and that it will make the leader more responsive to a wider range of opinion. Yet it does not follow that the leader's position has been weakened, for the difficulties and potential political costs of replacing a leader have been made greater.

Strength of a Conservative leader

In the case of the Conservative Party, the position of the leader is almost identical, although a Conservative Prime Minister is in an even stronger position than his Labour counterpart, while a Conservative Leader of the Opposition is slightly weaker. The reason for the difference is that the Conservatives are accustomed to being in power and regard it as only natural and proper. They therefore tend to be more severe on leaders who have lost power or who do not look like winning back power than the rank and file of Labour MPs, many of whom have no basic objection to being in opposition. Thus the Conservatives sacked A. J. Balfour in 1911, Austen Chamberlain in 1922, Baldwin was nearly removed in 1930, Sir Alec Douglas-Home was part persuaded, part urged to leave in 1965 and Mr Heath was rejected in 1975. All these occurred when the Conservatives were in opposition. A further factor is that most Conservative leaders have had both a high sense of loyalty to the party and other sources of activity and satisfaction on which they can fall back. As a result, they have been less tenacious of power once their leadership was widely questioned. Mr Baldwin did fight successfully to hold his position (the Labour Government was declining and an election was possible), while Mr Heath was the victim of the new procedure for're-election activated by those who disliked his style.

In office, Conservative Prime Ministers show the full degree of power and security that has been described in the case of Labour Prime Ministers. There were no attempts to remove Baldwin or Neville Chamberlain before the last crisis. Mr Churchill was criticized for staying on when his health and strength seemed to be declining in early 1955 but very few of his colleagues were prepared even to mention the matter to him. Sir Anthony Eden, on the other hand, was widely and openly criticized soon after he became premier, particularly in the columns of the *Daily Telegraph*. Before this challenge became serious, there were the disastrous events of the invasion and withdrawal from Suez. Eden was widely criticized for his general nervousness and interference in departments, for his serious misjudgements and lack of candour, and for both going into Suez and for calling a cease-fire. He returned from sick leave in December 1956 and resigned in January 1957. However, there is no evidence that his colleagues or his party wanted him to leave at that moment. The Conservative Party had suffered a terrible blow to its morale and wanted to hang together. Any immediate repudiation either of the Prime Minister or of the Foreign Secretary, Mr Selwyn Lloyd, would have seemed like a confession of error. Sir Anthony actually resigned because his doctors told him he could not carry on.

The other case in which it has been suggested that a Conservative Prime Minister was edged out was that of Mr Macmillan in 1963. The facts are that the government's and the Prime Minister's credit had both declined seriously in 1962 and in early 1963 Mr Macmillan had to repudiate suggestions that he was going to retire. Some Conservatives felt he had handled the Profumo scandal badly, others that he was too old and that he was by then associated with an old-fashioned approach and a certain lack of success. In October 1963, hit by a prostatic obstruction which required an operation, he resigned. What drove Mr Macmillan to announce his resignation was the view, later proved wrong, that his prostate trouble was malignant and that he would be weakened and incapacitated either for a very long time or permanently.

Thus the only Conservative Prime Minister to be rejected by his party while in office in this century has been Neville Chamberlain in May 1940. This was at a time of national disaster, in a war, with defeat staring the country in the face when Neville Chamberlain's cautious, doctrinaire and almost half-hearted leadership seemed to epitomize the nation's inadequate response to the German challenge. Yet even then, the government's majority was still eighty-one (thirty-three Conservatives voting against and some sixty abstaining) and both Mr Chamberlain and Mr Churchill thought at first that Chamberlain could carry on but as the leader of a national or coalition government. It was the Labour Party's refusal to serve under Chamberlain which killed this idea and, once it was realized that there would have to be a new Prime Minister, Churchill soon emerged as the only possible candidate. (Chamberlain for a moment toyed with the notion of Halifax as Prime Minister but he was not the man for the occasion, he was in the House of Lords and himself refused to contemplate the idea.) The Conservative Party elected Churchill as their leader but only after he had been appointed as Prime Minister.

So it can be seen that the Prime Minister has a very strong position and while this can become even stronger when he is successful and looks like remaining in office for a long time, much of his power and invulnerability remains even during periods of political adversity. The forces of party loyalty, control of patronage and the support of the governmental machine remain intact except in the most unusual situations and even then, a Prime Minister has great resources with which to alter, evade or surmount these unusual dangers. It is true that the office is a lonely one, that few speak to the premier with complete candour and that holders of the office have tended to worry, to overwork and to tire themselves out. Under these circumstances, and particularly with certain types of personality, premiers may suspect plots and fear cabals but the objective powers of the office remain. By the time a politician reaches the premiership, he is usually well aware of how to use them.

9 The leadership and its relations with the electorate; the state and the citizen

Politicians and the public

The assumptions which underlay the Westminster model were that the politicians had beliefs and known methods of handling problems, perhaps even a list of policies and that the electorate had its views, the voters picking those leaders whom they regarded as being most appropriate for the time. The rejected party might change its mind or the situation might alter, the government might fail or the voters might decide on another approach by the time of the next general election. But the democratic process was an interaction between the leadership and the led in which Parliament played the vital roles of explaining the issues to the people and of reflecting the electorate's views on government policies with the constant possibility that Parliament could go on to intervene and alter these policies or remove the government.

Now Parliament plays a much diminished part (discussed in Chapter 10) and since the government knows it will remain in office till the Prime Minister chooses to call the next election, the relationship is a much more direct, if rather muddled one, between the leadership and the voters. Also the old view of two relatively independent sets of opinions reacting on each other is over-simplified. Now the politicians in part tackle the problems on their merits and in part try to pick up the prevailing mood of the electorate. At the same time, the advocacy of the party leaders helps create the climate of opinion and the standards by which the politicians are themselves judged. Thus, at the general election of June 1970, the electorate was disappointed that the expectations raised by the Labour Party had not been fulfilled. In part, this led to scepticism about the possibility of sustained and rapid growth and in part it encouraged concentration on rather different issues. There was irritation about the rate of inflation, about high taxation, alleged spongers on the social services and worries about the increased level of crimes of violence. The Conservatives reacted to this mood, which suited them, by framing and stressing policies on these issues while the Labour Party and, in particular, Mr Wilson responded by fighting a totally negative campaign. In the two elections of 1974, there was disappointment over the Conservative record and distrust of the Labour Opposition but the latter crept ahead because it seemed better able to avoid the stresses of head-on conflict with the unions. In 1979 the Conservative victory was entirely predictable in the light of preceding events. For two years the Labour Government had been without a secure Commons majority and appeared to cling to office through the support first of the Liberals and then of the Scottish Nationalists. The government's attempt to restrict wage and salary increases to 5 per cent had broken down in the midst of a wave of strikes which had produced great social dislocation in the severe winter just before the election. In addition, Labour supporters had been irritated by the restrictions on public expenditure imposed by the government since 1976.

It is dangerous for a political system if the parties in turn fail to achieve the targets they set themselves. Yet some targets are hard to achieve, especially in a single five-year term, yet it might be thought that if a party promises to cut taxation, it should be able to redeem this promise. But it is quite possible for politicians to encourage attitudes and expectations which are mutually incompatible. Thus the public have come to expect a certain standard of comfort in hospitals or a certain level of support if they are unemployed and parents expect that children who achieve a certain scholastic standard will be able to enter a university. Yet these standards require public expenditure and party propaganda may create a situation in which the voters expect both improved services and tax reductions. The unfortunate aspect is that if one side of the equation has to be sacrificed, the disappointment is far greater or of more political significance than the pleasure felt at the achievement of the other side. A further unrealistic attitude which both political leaders and the public encourage with equal enthusiasm is an exaggerated notion of what any government can achieve. Thus, if anything unfortunate happens, the public will blame the government and the politicians are usually ready to assume responsibility or at least to allow the Opposition to blame the government. This is bad for public confidence in the system since there are, in fact, many things about which a government can do nothing. One reason for the confidence felt in the late Victorian system was that voters had been carefully indoctrinated with the view that large parts of the nation's life were outside the competence of the government. It was accepted that booms and slumps, public mores, prices and so on were settled by forces outside the political arena. Thus when politicians said they would òr would not give Ireland Home Rule, provide free elementary education or end church rates, they could do as they had promised. It is possible, with the present relations between government and the governed, not merely that the former tries to do too much and that the latter expect too much but that because of these exaggerated expectations, faith in the system is being undermined. This may explain why, at a time when the tasks of government are set so wide, the public's enthusiasm for democracy is less positive.

Parties and electors

Party leaders have their greatest contact with party supporters and the electorate on the occasion of a general election. An election is a major catalyst for the political system. Rulers become dependent on the wishes of the ruled. Politicians out of office have a chance to improve their fortunes. Hope and uncertainty are everywhere. Opinion polls will prophesy but they are sometimes wrong, they may disagree and the election campaign itself may affect the balance of opinion.

At the start of a campaign each party produces a manifesto that sets out the party's policies which, in the event of success at the polls, becomes a programme for action by the new government. Very few people read these documents carefully, especially as in recent years they have tended to become longer and more complex. It follows that not many voters are swayed by a conscientious study of the whole of these documents. But it would be quite wrong to write off the manifestos as unimportant. Their influence has grown steadily, perhaps to an unhealthy extent.

In days past political leaders preferred their manifestos to be little more than a general rallying cry containing a general statement of party philosophy. This view was satirized by Disraeli: ' "I am all for a religious cry," said Taper. "It means nothing, and if successful, does not interfere with business when we are in." ' Certainly, it is convenient for leaders to be free from commitments, but the modern electorate may want to know what politicians will do if elected to office. In 1945 the Conservatives used as their manifesto

'Mr Churchill's Declaration of Policy to the Electors', which was a fairly short statement containing some splendid rhetoric but few specific proposals. Subsequently, there was some feeling in Conservative circles that the form of their manifesto had contributed to their defeat. The pattern today is for a manifesto to include a statement on each main sector of public policy and to give a series of undertakings intended to form the basis for subsequent legislation.

There are a number of aspects to the importance of manifestos. They are a symbol of a moral contract between political leaders and the ordinary voter. Rival parties set out their stalls. The electors have the right to expect that the winners will do what they said they would do. In this sense the manifesto gives a much broader significance to an election than the fairly simple process of choosing someone to represent you in the House of Commons. And while the manifesto sets the course that a Prime Minister is expected to follow, it also strengthens the position of those in office against anyone who tries to obstruct those actions designed to implement their promises. The doctrine of the mandate argues that ministers must be allowed to carry out election pledges. Thus, the Conservative-dominated House of Lords feels impotent in the face of legislation based on the election manifesto of a Left-wing government. Perhaps even more important is the use of the manifesto to overcome objections by civil service advisers to what ministers seek to do. Mr Crossman argued that the manifesto was 'the battering ram of change'. In 1974 when Mr Benn was appointed as Secretary of State for Industry he is reported to have instructed his senior civil servants to read the sections of the Labour manifesto relevant to their department. Then there is a third and quite different aspect to the importance of these documents. They can be used not simply to protect ministers against critics but also to drive ministers on. If ministers develop second thoughts or cold feet about the wisdom of past promises, they can be told by party zealots that they are morally obliged to do what they said they would do. Thus the doctrine of the mandate has evolved from legitimation of action to a requirement for action. Particularly in the Labour Party the manifesto is seen as a means of ensuring that a Labour Cabinet will carry out party policy. However, the same idea is spreading among Conservatives; in 1982 when Mr Whitelaw the Home Secretary introduced a minor liberalization of immigration rules he was faced with a considerable Right-wing revolt supported by a claim that he was acting contrary to the party's statement of policy at the 1979 election. Prime Ministers, both Conservative and Labour, speak of the extent to which they have carried out election promises.

As manifestos are important, the question of how they are drafted is also important. For the Conservatives, there is no problem. It is accepted that the leader is in charge, so if the party is in power then the Prime Minister has the last word on the contents of the programme. For Labour the problem is more awkward. The party is built on a belief in intra-party democracy: in theory, the annual conference is the final arbiter of the party's constitution, conduct and policy. Under Clause 5 of the Labour Party Constitution the contents of the election manifesto shall be decided jointly by the National Executive Committee, elected by the annual conference, and the Parliamentary Labour Party's Committee. The party leader leads the PLP side. There may be considerable friction between the parliamentary leadership and majority opinion on the NEC over what the programme should contain. Both Mr Wilson and Mr Callaghan delayed calling the meeting to draft the manifesto until the last possible moment, after the date of the election had been announced. At this stage the Prime Minister or leader has a virtual veto on the contents: any evidence of a major row over the manifesto would be seized upon by Labour's opponents as a sign that the party was hopelessly split and therefore could not be trusted to govern.

It can well be argued that the growing emphasis on the weight attached to manifestos is unhealthy and damaging to the quality of representative parliamentary government. Stated in its crudest form, the doctrine of the mandate is a fraud. The claim that a majority of voters have sanctioned all the proposals advocated by the government party at the previous election cannot be sustained. In the first place no party now secures a majority of votes at a general election. Second, all voters are not fully aware of all the policies put forward by the party they support. Third, even if an individual does know a great deal about party policies, it does not follow that he approves of everything that any one party wants to do. Indeed, survey evidence has shown consistently that there is substantial objection by voters to many of the ideas of the party they support.

There are further objections to being tied to the details of a manifesto. Conditions change, especially economic factors. What may seem possible when a policy is drafted may look a great deal more difficult when the time comes to put planning into practice. Particularly for opposition parties, denied the official information available to ministers, there may be a failure to appreciate the cost and other implications of what it is proposed to do. Changing circumstances and better information change opinions. Is it right to demand that ministers must continue with policies they no longer believe in? For their part, ministers like to claim steady consistency; to renege on a policy, to make a U-turn is seen as a sign of weakness. In reality, bitter experience may make it highly desirable to alter the approach to a problem.

While there can be pressure to honour specific pledges, ministers still have much room for manoeuvre. Some questions may be ignored by the manifestos; there was no mention of applying to join the EEC by the Conservatives in 1959 or by Labour in 1966. Issues can also be fudged: the Labour promise in 1974 to renegotiate the terms of entry to the EEC is a notable example. Both Conservative and Labour Governments have adopted various methods to limit wage and salary rises; these tend to have no counterpart in election programmes beyond general statements on the need to control inflation.

An election campaign is not normally conducted on the basis of competition between manifestos. The populace give a verdict on the basis of the past record of the government. If there is satisfaction with the way ministers have conducted the affairs of state, then ministers will remain in office; if there is sufficient dissatisfaction, ministers will be replaced. However, the 1983 election did not quite fit this model. No doubt the Conservatives obtained some advantage from the successful Falklands campaign, but public discussion during the campaign concentrated on the major proposals in the Labour Party's manifesto *The New Hope for Britain*. Unilateral nuclear disarmament, quitting the EEC and a vast programme of public expenditure to stimulate economic recovery became the crucial issues. The Conservative manifesto was ignored. The content of the Labour programme and the well-publicized rows in the party over policy questions reduced Labour support. In these untypical circumstances a manifesto did have a major impact upon opinion.

The conclusion must be that when people vote they are, in essence, choosing a government but not setting down a pattern of how the state shall behave for the next four or five years. Without question, manifestos have value in that they explain to the public what each party wants to do; they also help political accountability by providing a yardstick against which the Prime Minister and the Cabinet can be judged. The various arguments about the need for or the consequences of the moral authority of a mandate all exaggerate the role of a manifesto. And the argument chosen is always suited to meet the immediate convenience of the politician who uses it.

A similar position arises in relation to discussions about the electoral system. The present system gives an advantage to the major parties alternately, so it is retained. Conservative and Labour politicians accept that the 'first past the post' principle deals harshly with smaller groups whose support is thinly spread, although a minor party with concentrated sympathy does not fare too badly. Thus, in the 1979 election for the European Parliament none of the eighty-one seats allocated to the United Kingdom were won by the Liberals although the Scottish Nationalists obtained one: the Liberals collected 1,690,638 votes while the SNP total was only 247,836. At the 1983 general election Labour won 209 seats and the Liberal/SDP Alliance won twenty-three. Yet the total Alliance vote was over 90 per cent of the size of the Labour vote. The standard defence of our present arrangements claims that such discrepancies are but a minor blemish when weighed in the balance with the benefits we enjoy. 'First past the post', it is claimed, gives the party that gets more votes a clear lead in seats over its major rival and so provides a secure majority in the Commons; thus is provided the base for stable government and the prospect of continuity of policy for four or five years following the election. In this fashion the democratic voice of the electors can be transformed into strong, determined and effective administration.

Critics argue that this rosy picture does not relate to the facts. In 1951 the Labour Party obtained more votes than the Conservatives and their highest-ever percentage of the total poll, yet the Conservatives found themselves with a majority in the Commons. In 1950, 1964 and twice in 1974 the general election failed to produce a majority or a sufficient majority to provide a clear prospect of single party government for the full term of a parliament. It follows that in four of the twelve elections held since the last war, the electoral system has not produced the type of result that is said to be its great merit. Of course, if the minor parties get stronger there is an increasing possibility that an election will fail to produce a single party majority. The increase in the number of Ulster seats in 1983 from twelve to seventeen further adds to the prospect that these members could have substantial influence in a closely balanced House of Commons.

The traditional doctrine is open to another fundamental challenge. Single party government is said to be good because it avoids the need for coalition and compromise that is associated with more complex electoral systems. However, the history of France and West Germany since 1945 shows that other fairer electoral systems do not necessarily lead to coalition governments. And the fact that our rate of economic progress has been manifestly slower than in other democratic countries of Western Europe undermines the claim that our electoral system gives us successful government.

The inequalities in the electoral system do not apply simply as between parties. They exist also as between geographical areas and, therefore, between people living in different places. Scotland and Wales are both over-represented at Westminster: Scotland has seventy-two seats and Wales thirty-eight; if all constituencies had an equal number of voters their allocation of seats would be, respectively, fifty-eight and thirty-two. It may be asserted that rural areas more distant from London are more difficult to represent and therefore some element of advantage should be given to such places. The logical consequence of this principle would be that urban areas adjacent to London should have below-average representation, i.e. more voters per constituency. In practice, this does not happen. After the 1983 redistribution of seats the lowest number of voters to be found in an English constituency was at Kingston-on-Thames with 45,000; at the other extreme the Isle of Wight had 88,000 voters. The voice of each individual was roughly twice as powerful at Kingston as on the Island. The reason for this discrepancy is that constituency boundaries are made to fit in with local government. The Boundary Commission, which reviews constituency boundaries at up to fifteen-year intervals, has taken the view that parliamentary seats should be divided out between shire counties and metropolitan districts depending upon their population: Kingston just qualified for two seats but the Isle of Wight did not. So the principle that justifies more seats for Scotland and Wales is completely ignored in England.

It is certain that the first past the post system affects the behaviour of voters but exactly how much can never be precisely known. People are well aware of the electoral history of their own area; they know who is likely to win, who may possibly win and who has no chance. During an election campaign the regular publication of opinion polls shows the same thing at national level. So if it is believed that a constituency will be won by A or B and that other candidates are certain to lose, then to vote for anyone other than A or B is to 'waste' a vote, or so many people may feel. Alternatively, if you feel greater sympathy for Party C but the national opinion polls are reporting constantly that the election will be won either by Party A or Party B, then again you may well feel that the real contest is between Parties A and B and that you should join in making the crucial choice between them. Thus the election system dissuades people from voting for minor parties especially if they are not particularly strong in the local area. Over the years it is the Liberals who have lost most from this 'wasted vote' argument. Yet there are areas in which the Liberals regularly come first, or second by a convincing margin, where the wasted vote theme damages Labour or, more rarely, the Conservatives.

Our electoral institutions do not have the merit of consistency. The system of single member constituencies does have the advantage of improving the contacts between an MP and those he represents both by reducing the number of people each MP speaks for in the Commons and also by ensuring that this responsibility of representation is undivided. In local government, however, these merits are ignored, and multi-member wards are the norm. Even the steadfast rejection of proportional representation has admitted an exception. For Northern Ireland this system was adopted in 1979 for European elections in order to ensure that one of the three members sent to the European Parliament should represent the Roman Catholic minority. Presumably it was felt that the choice of three Protestants would further unsettle the province and possibly cause adverse comment in the EEC.

Britain has an electoral system virtually unchanged from Victorian times except in relation to the breadth of the franchise. It is unfair between parties, unfair between areas, unfair between individuals. Further, there is encouragement for people to vote for candidates and causes other than those they genuinely prefer. Various calculations have been made about how the outcome of a particular general election would have been different had the electoral law been different and based on some form of proportional representation. Such calculations are ingenious but, surely, wide of the mark. They assume that voting behaviour would be unaltered even if the election rules were altered. For that assumption there is no basis whatever. If the rules of the game are changed it becomes a different game and people will play differently. A change in election law could make a substantial alteration to the party composition of the House of Commons.

There are big obstacles to such a change taking place. As the Conservative and Labour Parties tend to profit at least alternately from the present pattern they do not want to change it. Conservative and Labour MPs may fear that reform in election procedures may cost them their seats at the subsequent general election. For Labour there is the virtual certainty that any type of proportional representation would eliminate the possibility of a Labour majority in the Commons that could introduce fundamental socialist measures. Thus the advocates of change face a massive opposition from established interests. Their only hope must be that the existing system will produce parliaments lacking a clear-cut party majority. At the stage at which electoral reform becomes a real possibility, a new issue will arise. Exactly what should the new electoral law be? Democratic countries have a variety of systems. A wide choice is available for the reformers. Each system has merits and disadvantages. Should the Commons ever get round to accepting the principle of electoral reform, there will be a second and intense round of argument about the details of the reform.

Contacts through officials and pressure groups

When a party is in power, its own machine diminishes rapidly in importance as the Prime Minister at once acquires a much larger and expert body of advisers in the form of the civil service. By far the best-documented stream of information reaching ministers about public reactions comes from their field force, the officials handling the application of policies to actual situations. For example, it is the large and highly skilled group of officials engaged in research, advisory and administrative services which tells the Minister of Agriculture just how the farmers are faring, while similar groups warn the Minister of Education of changes in the school population and of the response to new projects in further education, and alert the Minister of Trade and Industry about impending mergers, closures or developments in industry. This method of contact has tended to be overlooked by commentators because it is compartmentalized and specialized by function but it is the main way in which a government finds out whether its policies are working and decides what needs to be done next.

One difficulty is that the civil service, understandably, like to be certain about public reactions to the policies they are applying or intend to introduce and for this they turn to the representatives chosen by the various interests. The most extreme case is in agriculture where the 1947 Act obliges the government to consult each year with the leaders of the producers' organizations, that is, the farmers' unions. It is easy to appreciate that if such bodies exist (and they cover most producer but few consumer interests), it is much simpler for civil servants to deal with them than to attempt to find out how the bulk of doctors, farmers, companies making paper or local authorities will react. It is understandable that neither the civil service nor the pressure group leaders are ready enough to admit that sometimes the latter do not accurately represent their members' views. If these leaders have to be re-elected at intervals, they may also have a political game to play within their organizations and they may have to appear more moderate or extremist than the average of the people they represent. Pressure group leaders may not be able to assess their members' wants or they may wish to use their position to press their own views. Extreme examples are the way the larger trade unions move from the Right to the Left of the Labour Party, or vice versa, depending not on swings of opinion among their members but on the views of the general secretary of the day. At times there are clear indications that a gap exists, as when the farmers took to demonstrations in 1970 in part because they considered the leadership of the National Farmers' Union was too moderate or too much in cahoots with the government. The author recalls a minister defending a policy on the grounds that all the members of the major pressure group concerned wanted it and when, meeting the secretary of the pressure group on a later occasion this was mentioned, the official said, 'My members want it! I have never asked them and I would have an awful job putting this policy across if I did', but it was true that he felt that the government was on the right lines and had said so.

Such divisions inside pressure groups cannot be carried too far. Ministries are successful inasmuch as their policies yield the desired results and if the pressure groups are wrong in their estimates of reactions and if the result is that policies misfire, the pressure groups or their leaders will soon be discredited. There has to be a certain relationship between the minister, his department, what it wishes to achieve, the outside bodies that have to be dealt with and the general public, because if any one of them gets too far out of line, the actual operation of the policy or the service begins to falter and this soon becomes evident. But the effect of relying on this institutionalized method of gauging public reactions is that it places too much emphasis on those groups or sectors of opinion that can readily be organized. The author once obtained permission to study the preparation and passage of a piece of minor legislation, a bill dealing with the fishing industry. In order to find out the reactions of those involved and to estimate the financial assistance and the form of the new legislation that was needed, the officials had consulted all the interests involved. It had taken a period of nearly two years to meet the owners of the trawlers (through their federation), to talk to the fishermen's representatives, the port authorities, the marketing and transport concerns, the retailers and some large firms involved in canning and processing the fish. As a subsidy was called for, the Treasury were involved and when they insisted on a lower rate than the ministry had indicated, there had to be a second round of consultations. The officials were a little taken aback when it was pointed out that two key groups had not been consulted – the public in the form of consumers and in the form of the subsidy-providers or taxpayers. Yet the civil servants could scarcely be blamed, for there is no fish-eaters' union or anti-fish subsidy league to talk to. In traditional political theory, this is the task of Parliament, but the House of Commons was, as with most legislation, presented with the final negotiated product so that these general interests were never specifically considered. Normally this is not necessary, as it can be assumed that the public want plenty of cheap fish, but as the government expands its activities and plays a larger part in people's lives, the sense that they are not being considered has spread among the public. Moreover, this can lead to administrative errors which at best cause irritation and at worst explosions of anger. An example of the kind of reaction which an elected representative of the public might detect or foresee which would possibly escape a civil servant occurred in the last war. Then, at the worst stage of the submarine war, the most critical shortage was of shipping space. A division of the Board of Trade calculated that the total consumption of toilet paper required two shiploads of wood pulp per year, that more than one newspaper per family was sold and that if the government announced that for the duration of the war no more toilet paper was to be made but people could use old newspapers, two ships would be released to take supplies to the army in the Western Desert. Such a proposal reached the Cabinet and was torn up by Mr Churchill who said the shipping space saved would not be worth the blow to morale that would be caused.

Opinion polls

These generalized and unorganized responses of the public which ought to be channelled through Parliament, now reach the leadership in a variety of ways, the chief ones being public opinion polls, by-election results, the mass media and politicians' hunches formed as a result of their own experiences and contacts, while the atmosphere in the House of Commons plays a relatively small part. (It is curious how the House tends to make MPs Westminster-orientated and cuts them off, to some extent, from the moods and reactions of the mass of the non-political public.) Probably the most influential of these sources of opinion is the regular polls provided by such organizations as Gallup and National Opinion Polls, though there was some scepticism after most of the polls failed to predict the results of both the 1970 and February 1974 elections. Nevertheless, politicians have become fairly sophisticated over polls and look chiefly at the overall party ratings and at the responses to individual proposals. It is appreciated that the standing of a party is not necessarily affected by its attitudes on single issues and that some issues have much more effect in forming or altering party support than others. A party can be associated with an unpopular policy much more easily if the other party is in agreement or if the issue does not link up with existing patterns of political belief. However, it is possible to observe political leaders following public opinion on specific issues. For instance, in the lead up to the 1970 general election, both parties were committed to seek entry to the Common Market but found that this was an unpopular policy, so that each tried to suggest that it would take a tougher line in seeking 'adequate safeguards' for Britain. Similarly, when law and order became an issue, though several leading Conservatives, including Mr Heath, voted for the abolition of capital punishment, every effort was made to try and identify Labour as the abolitionist party.

Broadly politicians have sensed that, as Butler and Stokes have demonstrated (*Political Change in Britain*), certain reactions among the public are central to changes in party allegiance, the chief one being the overall impression as to whether the government is or is not competent in running the economy. This is revealed by the reactions to the question, 'Are you better off than you were this time last year?' The politicians also appreciate the 'salience' (to use Butler and Stokes's word) of certain issues; the deep dislike of trade union methods, hostility to layabouts, dislike of high taxation, worries about coloured immigration and so on. The effect is not to produce a subservience to gusts of public feeling but to force ministers to pay continuous attention to public reaction to their economic policy.

Perhaps the most influential opinion surveys are the private polls commissioned by the major parties on how different categories of voters are reacting to major policy questions. According to Professor Kavanagh the Conservatives decided to emphasize council house sales because of advice from polls that such a policy would be popular. Also during the 1979 election campaign attempts were made to ease the fears of pensioners that Conservatives would increase indirect taxation: the private polls had warned that this fear could be politically damaging. In the Labour Party the National Executive has been divided over whether to engage the services of pollsters. Some members believe that the party should advocate policies in which it believes as opposed to policies that are reported to be popular. However, Labour has used polls to some extent. It has been said that private survey material was a main reason why Mr Callaghan did not, as many people expected, hold an election in the autumn of 1978.

By-elections

By-election results similarly require discriminating interpretation. They are a poor guide to the outcome of subsequent general elections because conditions at a by-election differ from those at a national appeal to the people. Fewer people vote. And voting has a different significance. At a general election, a government is chosen. A by-election, with rare exceptions, does not determine the fate of a government. The occasion can be used to give ministers a warning by those who are not sure that they want to turn them out.

Minor parties also do well at by-elections because the issue is not which of the major parties shall form a Cabinet. Further, they can concentrate restricted resources into a small area. The Liberals have got great encouragement from by-election successes, starting with Torrington in 1958 and Orpington in 1963. The publicity attracted through a by-election victory will consolidate the position of the MP in his constituency and help him to retain it at subsequent elections: David Steel, Alan Beith and Clement Freud have been assisted in this way. The successes of Welsh and Scottish Nationalists at by-elections in 1966 and 1967 brought their cause into prominence and paved the way for further advances at the 1970 and 1974 elections. These by-elections also forced the major parties to take action. The Wilson Government established the Commission on the Constitution while the Conservatives established their own inquiry under Sir Alec Douglas-Home to examine the case for a Scottish Assembly. More recently, the credibility of the new Social Democratic Party and the concept of the SDP/Liberal Alliance was greatly enhanced through their gains at Crosby (Mrs Shirley Williams) in 1981 and Glasgow, Hillhead in 1982 (Roy Jenkins).

Although by-elections are dubious barometers of political opinion, they can still be of major importance. If a government does unexpectedly well at one or more by-elections then there may be a temptation for the Prime Minister to call an immediate general election: just such a success in Hull North in January 1966 encouraged Mr Wilson to have a general election in March. Equally, the adverse publicity associated with by-election losses will encourage ministers to avoid embarrassing contests. In fact the rate at which vacancies occur in the Commons has fallen; in the 1955–9 Parliament there were fifty-one by-elections, between 1979 and 1983 only nineteen. Backbenchers are less frequently promoted to the Lords or given appointments that require resignation: those contemplating retirement will be urged to stay. It is also notable that the decline of the Labour Party is well illustrated by their record at by-elections. Between May 1971 and October 1982 the party did not gain a single seat from their opponents at a by-election in spite of the fact that for over half this period the Conservatives were in office: during this period the by-election gains of other parties were Liberal eight, Conservative seven, SDP two and SNP one. It was the loss of Labour seats be-tween 1974 and 1977 that destroyed the slim Labour majority gained at the October 1974 election and led directly to the Lib-Lab pact that sustained the Callaghan Government for eighteen months.

Referenda

A new form of communication between our national leaders and the electorate was used twice in the 1970s. A referendum was held in 1975 on whether Britain should stay in the European Economic Community. Four years later voters in Scotland and Wales were asked for an opinion on the devolution legislation that had been passed by Parliament. Both referenda were merely advisory and final decisions rested with Parliament. However, in the devolution case the government had to bring before Parliament an order to abort the legislation if fewer than 40 per cent of the electorate indicated support for it.

Referenda are widely used in other countries. It is not uncommon for a constitutional amendment to be referred to the voters in this way. In Britain, polls on specific issues have been held only on local matters. A decision by an urban local authority to seek wider powers through a private bill could be challenged in a town poll. There could also be a local vote on whether cinemas could open on Sunday. Both these opportunities for consulting opinion have now been withdrawn. Welsh districts can still vote every seven years on whether pubs should open on Sundays; since 1982 only two districts, Ceregidion and Dwyfor, remain 'dry'. Clearly, these exercises in consulting opinion on trivial issues formed a weak precedent for holding referenda on such major questions as the European Community and devolution. Indeed, the town polls on proposals for wider urban powers were terminated by the Local Government Act 1972, because of low participation. The only important exception has been in relation to Northern Ireland. In 1973, a referendum was held about remaining in the United Kingdom.

How, then, did the referendum fashion start? In both cases, the European Community and devolution, the appeal to the people was needed to paper over difficulties within the Labour Party and, in particular, between Labour MPs. When the Heath Government succeeded in taking Britain into Europe in 1973, the Labour Party was deeply divided on the issue. A compromise policy was worked out: a Labour Government would renegotiate the terms of Britain's membership and the results of the renegotiation would be submitted to a popular referendum. After Labour's electoral successes in 1974, this programme was put into practice. Then devolution caused dispute in the Labour movement. The concept could cause difficulties for the centralization of power needed to create a socialist state. If it led towards a break-up of the United Kingdom, the Labour Party in England would probably become a permanent minority party. If devolution for Scotland produced greater state aid for industry in that area, the prospect was that other areas, especially the North of England, would suffer a competitive disadvantage. So to make devolution acceptable to its own backbenchers, the Labour Government had to accept demands that a referendum be held on the issue.

It may be argued that it is a good idea to ask for people's opinions more often, that formal participation in the processes of democracy should not be restricted to election day. Nevertheless, government by referendum is incompatible with the theory and practice of representative government. Not everyone can join in the making of decisions, even major decisions. It is not practicable. So communities choose spokesmen to represent them. They are chosen largely because of their views but also because of their personal suitability. The elected representatives can then devote their time to the study of public policy and their accumulated knowledge and experience should help them to carry out their duties wisely. One expects the average MP to be better informed than the average voter. The House of Commons is not a microcosm of society. It ought to be better at making judgements than a random sample of 650 adults. In so far as this theory breaks down, it does so largely because the Commons fails to reflect contemporary opinion, because opinion has changed since election day.

The referendum concept seeks to bypass the elected representatives. On some matters, perhaps the most important matters, they are to be ignored. Leaders will communicate directly with the people. But when will this occur? And on what terms?

Where a state has a written constitution, the constitution can define when referenda are required. Britain has no such constitution. So referenda will be held, if at all, on an *ad hoc* political basis. The government will decide what questions shall be put to a popular vote, when they shall be put and how they shall be put. Referenda are used in totalitarian countries to provide support for the policy of the dominant élite. In France, General de Gaulle used referenda to maintain his personal supremacy. As noted above, the two referenda held in this country were organized to suit the convenience of one political party. To allow governments to put questions to a popular vote is to strengthen the hand of government. And the result of a referendum can be influenced by the way a question is worded and perhaps by the date of the poll.

If government policy is not upheld at a referendum, a very awkward situation could arise. What would have happened if the vote on Europe had gone the other way? Presumably the Wilson Government would have promoted legislation to extract Britain from Europe – a policy to which most of the Cabinet were strongly and publicly opposed. It would have been no solution for the Opposition to have taken office for the Conservatives were more strongly in favour of Europe than the Labour Party. Of course, as referenda in this country are merely advisory, the Cabinet could ignore the result. But to do so would provoke a storm. The alternative is to accept the popular verdict; in this case a government is forced to follow a policy of which it does not approve. Such an outcome destroys all sense of government responsibility, for ministers cannot be held responsible for policies imposed on them. So far this type of difficulty has been evaded. In 1975 the majority of the Cabinet won the day. In 1979 the Cabinet lost but within weeks a general election led to a change of government. However, there is no guarantee that an adverse referendum result will force the government into an election.

Some issues are more suitable for submission to *vox populi* than others. When the question is straightforward, well understood and clear-cut, the case for a referendum is strongest; when the question is intricate with many aspects and involves assessing a balance of advantage, the electorate is least qualified to judge. This analysis provides justification for local polls on the powers of urban authorities or on what people may do on a Sunday. It also suggests that continued membership of the European Community was the worst possible topic for a referendum. Few electors in 1975 understood the complexities of the European connection. Probably some politicians were also inadequately informed. There were fears that the complicated nature of the problem would deter electors from voting. In fact, the turnout was 65 per cent, only slightly lower than the turnout for a general election. But on what basis had people voted? It is likely that personal decisions were often made on the basis of which leader or leaders were trusted. Wilson, Jenkins, Heath and Thorpe were felt to be better guides to the situation than Benn and Powell. It was easier to judge the men than the issue.

There are powerful arguments against adopting the referendum as an accepted part of the process of British politics. Nevertheless, the idea has a strong appeal. The British brand of parliamentary democracy is no longer regarded as a very successful form of government. 'Let us consult the people' is a cry which is difficult to oppose. Élites are a natural target for popular criticism. If people express a view which Parliament then follows, that is a restraint on the power of the élite at Westminster. It is democracy in the most pure, Athenian sense. Some Left-wing opinion, especially in the Liberal Party, is attracted by this prospect. But while referenda will diminish Parliament, it is far less certain they will diminish the authority of the government. If the Cabinet can decide when and how to hold a referendum, the device will be used only when ministers think it will be to their advantage. This analysis is not disproved by the Labour Government's failure at the devolution referendum; this case was exceptional because the Cabinet was not firmly in charge of events due to the lack of a parliamentary majority.

There is another school of thought that favours referenda, a view not based on political principle but founded on a shrewd calculation of the probable consequences of making direct appeals to public opinion. Evidence drawn from many countries shows that referenda tend to favour the *status quo* and seek to evade change. The British votes on Europe and devolution both support this theory. Had the referendum on Europe been held in 1972 on whether we should enter Europe, the result probably would have been different because the *status quo* would have been different. So those with Conservative inclinations may come to favour the referendum device because they think, probably correctly, that it will act as a brake on change. The Italian referendum on divorce in 1974 is sometimes used as an argument against this conclusion. It is true that the voters favoured civil divorce against the wishes of the Roman Catholic Church. However, divorce had been allowed by legislation passed in 1970; the question was whether the law should be changed. In conformity with the thesis above, the voters supported the *status quo* which, in these particular circumstances, meant that the conservative view was defeated.

The Conservative Party is now tempted by the idea of direct democracy. It favours greater use of ballots in industrial disputes. There is much interest in schemes of constitutional reform which incorporate referenda. They are seen as a check upon a future Labour Cabinet, dominated by the Left-wing, which might introduce fundamental political, economic and social reforms.

There is also some Left-wing sympathy for the idea of wider popular consultation; the obstacle is that the outcome tends to be unsympathetic to radical causes. In August 1981 the Labour-controlled Coventry Council arranged a local referendum which offered a choice between better standards of public service or lower rates. The result was a handsome victory for lower rates. Mr Heseltine, then Secretary of State for the Environment, thereupon included a provision in a Local Government Bill to limit the power of local authorities to impose higher rates without the consent of local electors in a referendum. This proposal was uniformly condemned by local government, irrespective of party loyalties, as being an attempt by the Conservative Government to undermine what was left of the independence of local authorities. The plan was dropped.

Personal contacts

The final line of communication between the Prime Minister, his colleagues on the frontbench and the public is personal contacts and impressions. By the time most political leaders have been in public life for twenty years, they believe they have some idea of what is acceptable to the electorate. This may be a hunch, or simply a reliance on the views of specific persons. Some political leaders sniff the atmosphere at meetings or in their constituencies. They form some impression of how a policy is being received and such perceptions do play a part in their attitudes to proposals. And there is usually a fairly rapid check on the accuracy of their perceptions in the form of by-elections and opinion polls, all of which serve to remind politicians that a general election is never more than four and a half years off.

Put together, all these contacts give a picture of how political leaders and the public react to each other. It is a remote kind of contact because the leaders are obsessed with politics and power while the public are only remotely interested. Most citizens would rather not have to concern themselves with any political issues and if they have to react in any very positive way, this is usually a sign of failure on the part of the politicians.

The public's reactions to politics

The reasons for changes in the public's attitudes are complex and hard to analyse but it is evident that after a period of time, the public's mood alters. Only rarely in Britain do the public demand radical reforms. At the time of the 1959 general election, there was a mood of gratitude, of relief that living standards were rising. Coinciding with the 1964 and 1966 elections, the atmosphere was one of moderate restiveness, of disappointment that living standards had not risen faster and a feeling that Britain had missed several boats and needed to be brought up to date. By 1970 the prevailing sentiments had moved to the Right, against the concept of widespread provision of welfare, against high taxatien for the good of others and in favour of a tougher application of the law in all forms. The party leaders in part form and in part react to these moods. By their previous campaigns, they create expectations. By their successes and failures they fulfil or disappoint these hopes and by their propaganda they try to convince the public that the other party is responsible for whatever is unsatisfactory in the current situation. As the public's mood shifts, so both parties adjust and move in the same direction, though usually the traditional view of a particular party makes it easier or less easy for it to fall in with certain changes of mood. Thus in 1963–6, the Conservatives became regional planners and talked about growth and modernization of industry but these arguments came more naturally to the Labour Party and it benefited most from this trend in thinking. In the late 1960s, the Labour Party was pushed into emphasizing the restrictions it had imposed on coloured immigration, its efforts to clamp down on 'scrounging', and its interest in reducing direct taxation, but all these arguments seemed more appropriate in the mouths of Conservatives and they gained most support from the emphasis on these issues.

As Henry Fairlie has put it in his book, *The Life of Politics*, the parties are like buses which move along and if they miss the public at one stop, if everyone has boarded the other bus, they drive on with new paint and advertisements hoping in time to arrive at a stop where the public are still waiting and find the rival bus a less attractive conveyance.

In this interaction, it may appear as if the public are largely passive, acted upon by the political leaders. While there is some truth in this, the electorate can retaliate and alter the context in which decisions are taken and the reaction of the rank and file, either spontaneously or through their organizations, can have a great effect on the success or failure of government policies. In some cases the possible reactions are obvious – voting for the other party, registering a protest by voting for third-party candidates or not voting at all. But it is also possible collectively to refuse to accept a government policy. For instance, the experience of the various attempts to control incomes since 1966 has shown that these will ultimately collapse unless there is a complete statutory prohibition on all increases. Then public reaction may change. There can be support for proposals to cut public expenditure but great dissatisfaction when the consequences of cuts become apparent. The Heath Government panicked in 1972 when unemployment reached one million and it threw its policies on public expenditure and aid to industry into reverse. The Thatcher Government, faced with even greater pressures, has so far avoided such spectacular U-turns. Unemployment is not always such a sensitive issue as it used to be: the Callaghan Government was not seriously troubled by a jobless total of a million and a half. The general public may become bored and deadened by bad economic news but it still recognizes failure. In 1979 the breakdown of the government's incomes policy, the dislocation caused by strikes and dislike of high taxation combined to produce the Conservative victory at the general election.

One of the dilemmas facing governments is that the public may have been encouraged to want incompatible things. Thus there is a desire for rising standards of living but also a reluctance to accept short-run policies such as incomes restraint which may be necessary to produce investment and greater growth. It is in this sense that it is sometimes said that Britain could become ungovernable.

Direct action

Strikes, even with political motives, are an accepted feature of industrial society, but with the growth of interlocking industries, elaborate transport systems and an intensely competitive situation in foreign trade, strikes can rapidly draw in the government and can be used to break its wages and industrial policies or simply to step outside the normal bargaining procedures. New groups entering upon these procedures, such as nurses and teachers, have served to indicate declining confidence in the normal machinery for adjusting disputes. Interruptions to the electricity supply cause grave social dislocation. The miners' strike of 1974 put industry on a three-day week. In the winter of 1978–9 a strike by some gravediggers caused much offence. Strikes by hospital staff or by firemen necessarily provoke an outcry. In 1982 a long and bitter dispute over pay in the National Health Service led to a limited amount of sympathetic industrial action by other workers in spite of the fact that such action had been made illegal by the Employment Act 1982. There is no doubt that public opinion dislikes strikes. Attitudes towards trade unions are also influenced because the unions are linked in the public mind with industrial action.

Direct action has spread from industrial disputes into attempts to alter public policy. Since 1968 university students have occupied buildings from time to time as a protest either against some university decision or sometimes against some aspects of government policy on education. In 1970 farmers disrupted traffic to try and get a better price review. In 1975 inshore fishermen blocked inland seaports. Easily the most important and successful example of direct action was the 1975 general strike by Protestant workers in Ulster which effectively stopped the attempts at 'power-sharing' with the Catholic minority. In 1980 the TUC organized a 'day of action' to protest at the policies of the Conservative Government.

Protesters may claim to be above ordinary law because of the injustices they suffer. Of course, the existence or severity of injustice is a matter of opinion. In extreme cases, protesters resort to force rather than reason. Nevertheless, they gained some support in that they sometimes seemed to gain results which endless discussion through the 'normal channels' failed to produce. Demonstrations also provide good visual material and so achieve greater publicity on television and in the press than do orderly representations. Thus the case of the protesters becomes known to a far wider audience. Often the protest may gain considerable sympathy, for example, parents blocking a road to demand a pedestrian crossing where children have to cross a busy road to go to school. Yet the underlying philosophy of direct action must be that might is right. The consequence is that the strong and the determined gain; the weak and the scrupulous lose.

Why do people obey the government?

These activities have given some point to a question that in the past has seemed somewhat unrealistic or abstract in Britain, namely why do people obey the government? In the jargon of political science this is put in the form of, 'What gives a political system its legitimacy?'

Clearly if all citizens actively or passively resisted or refused to obey a government, its authority would collapse. Since earliest times, systems of authority have put forward reasons why their subjects should respect and obey them. Perhaps the government was that of the father of the tribe or the clan to be obeyed because of filial duty, perhaps power lay with a king to be supported because he was God's appointed vicar on earth or perhaps the system rested simply on long-established custom and awe. When he wrote in the 1860s, Walter Bagehot (in *The English Constitution*) argued that the reason why people accepted the decisions of the government was that they thought it was all the work of Queen Victoria. The monarchy had tremendous traditional respect and reverence from the aristocracy, the middle classes and the illiterate masses. It was a symbolic or dignified government everyone could understand. Behind this dignified monarchical front, the real (or 'efficient' in Bagehot's terms) government was free to operate through the Cabinet and the House of Commons.

The implications of Bagehot's thesis was not necessarily that if the people ever did realize how and by whom they were ruled, they would at once treat their political leaders and the institutions of government with scorn. He might have retorted that once education was as widespread among the masses as it was in the ruling 'ten thousand' in 1865, all would be well. The unique virtues of a system of government by open discussion with a delicate balance between executive and legislature would then be appreciated by everyone. But several aspects have changed in the ensuing century. In the first place, the monarchy clearly cannot lend legitimacy to the rest of the machinery of government. It has respect and affection but this is needed to maintain the monarch's own position as a ceremonial head of state. Nowadays certain standards, stricter than those the community expects of its own members, are imposed on the monarchy and, while the Crown is generally cheered, when Edward VIII wished to marry a divorcee he had to abdicate, and when the Duke of Edinburgh expresses the mildest of opinions on current affairs the press descends upon him. The monarchy is no longer an institution whose acceptance can cloak or cover all the controversial actions of the government. Indeed, the slightest sign of a controversial action on the part of any member of the royal family causes immediate trouble and is hastily disavowed.

Nowadays, any legitimacy that British government is going to get has to come from its own powers and virtues. The general public today is probably as well educated as the political classes were in Bagehot's period but they lack the same feeling that the government is 'theirs', that it is run by them for a homeland and an empire which they are privileged to guide and lead. The identification of a small élite with a system which confers great prestige and power upon them as individuals is necessarily different from the attachment of 40 million adults even if they, a hundred years later, are relatively well educated and informed on political matters. This mass electorate has taken the place of the illiterate and awestruck citizenry of Bagehot's day and while the mystique of monarchy has gone, there is the same feeling of being on the receiving end of government, the same feeling that 'they' do things to 'us'. If anything, this is intensified since modern governments tax, regulate, aid and supervise the average citizen so much more than the governments of a hundred years ago. At the same time, the special virtues remarked on by Bagehot have gone. Government by discussion, where a good case wins the day, where strong feelings penetrate Parliament, alter the balance of forces and produce a different result, is no longer in operation. When the electorate now pause and survey the government, they see a massive complex of authorities with no clear sign of public control, with no clear channels by which pressure can be exercised and results achieved. To put one party in power and then, four or five years later, to replace it with another seems to make little difference. Much that affects the individual can be traced to no specific persons or institutions; decisions seem simply to emerge from the machine and local or individual complaints apparently have little effect.

In this situation, the public tend to judge the system by the material results of government. In this they are encouraged by several aspects of modern culture. On the one hand, the entire weight of advertising emphasizes that the good life depends on the volume of new consumer goods the individual or the family can purchase. On the other, the politicians encourage people in the belief that they, the governors of the country, are responsible for everything that happens and therefore ought to be able to solve all problems. Very, very seldom does one hear a minister in Parliament in answer to the question, 'What have you done about X?' say, 'X is none of my business', or 'X is quite outside the area of governmental activity'. If, after this, the results are not as people want, there is no special legitimacy on which the government can fall back. It is obeyed because it is there, because it is backed by the police and the courts and there is little evidence of a special reverence for our democratic system. It is not easy for observant members of the public to point to any facts that demonstrate that the British system is markedly better than those of other more or less democratic countries in other parts of the world, though there is still in certain circles a pride in the degree of freedom and tolerance. But there is no special reverence for Parliament and politicians are viewed with a mixture of feelings, a mixture of hope that they can live up to the omnicompetence they claim, of hope that they will provide the leadership any country needs and of contempt if they fall below the targets they have set themselves. If, then, the question is repeated – 'What gives the British system its legitimacy?' – the answer is a mixture of satisfaction, tradition and inertia. It is accepted because nothing better offers, because of the residual national pride which fails to see any advantage in foreign methods, because there is no positive motive for change and because the system till 1974 provided a steady rise in living standards. The theory that the voters did choose the government and therefore ought to obey it until they have time to choose another has some force, and respect for the institutions does go beyond a willingness to support or put up with the government of the day. There cannot be any denying the truth that if people are not satisfied with what they have got, they can at least participate in throwing the government out at the following election. For those who do not wish the party in question to be out of power, it is comforting to reflect that the amount of past practice which is open to change by a new administration is relatively small. At one time, before the populace were enfranchised, democracy was seen as a method of making sweeping, indeed revolutionary changes in the structure of society. While this was likely, those with property and power resisted an extension of the right to vote. But as Victorian Britain became a little more prosperous and working men had something to lose, they came to accept and, in Bagehot's time, almost to revere the system of government. Then they could be safely admitted 'within the pale of the Constitution'. The parties accepted that commitments by past governments had, by and large, to be honoured and a Cabinet did not try to undo all the work of the last. By the 1970s it is even more true than before that the decisions that can be taken in any five-year period alter only the margins of public policy, though the cumulative effect on the political atmosphere can be considerable. But the result is that the frustration felt by the supporters of a defeated party is quite tolerable. But it is precisely this position that causes much of the apathy. While few wish to see sweeping changes which would carry the country back into a *laissez-faire* era of the pre 1930s or would impose rigid Marxist patterns of the kind being applied in Eastern Europe, much of the criticism of British politics and politicians springs from disillusionment about the system's capacity to push through changes, to achieve anything at all. In recent years, each party in turn has promised rapid growth in the economy, each party has sought to end terrorism in Northern Ireland, each party has tried to control wages in order to restore the balance of payments and reduce unemployment; yet by and large each party has failed in these objectives. These failures were serious not only in themselves, but they undermined confidence in the capacity of British democracy to produce satisfactory results, and now it is precisely by its capacity to produce results that the system is judged.

Personal freedom

This may be a little unfair and many Britons who have travelled abroad have a vague perception that in Britain, personal freedoms are more secure and individual liberty is more respected than in many comparable countries. In the United States, a Bill of Rights was embodied as a group of amendments in the constitution, and citizens who feel these rights have been violated can seek a remedy in the courts, even if the threat comes from the United States government itself. This method has been followed in many countries, some of which have incorporated a list of freedoms based on the United Nations Charter of Human Rights in their constitutions. In Britain, the opposite method has always been applied. Apart from principles built upon ancient charters and the restrictions on the power of the Crown imposed in the years just after 1688, there are no formal guarantees of liberty, the assumption being that citizens are free until they encounter limitations placed on them by the need to avoid damaging the freedoms of other citizens. For instance, freedom of speech means that an individual can say what he likes, provided he does not defame others. Freedom to enjoy one's property again is only bounded by the condition that it cannot be used in a manner that will injure one's neighbour, though public authorities can acquire an individual's property compulsorily if this can be shown to be in the public interest. No one can be arrested or detained except upon a criminal charge and after conviction or for debt or contempt of court or, in certain special circumstances, if the person is a lunatic, mental defective or infant.

At the same time, this area of freedom depends on the support of an active public opinion and of a Parliament which is eager to protect it. The growth of terrorism in recent years has meant that there has been greater interest in trying to protect the ordinary citizen from violence than in protecting the legal rights of individuals. The Prevention of Terrorism (Temporary Provisions) Act 1976 is each year extended by Parliament for a further twelve months. The act allows the police to detain suspected terrorists for two days without charge; the period can be extended to a week with the consent of the Home Secretary. Residents in Ulster can also be sent back there from the mainland of the United Kingdom. Such exclusion orders can be made in the reverse direction, i.e., people can be sent back from Ulster, but so far this has not been done. These powers are controversial not simply because they limit personal freedom but also because there is no clear evidence that they are effective. The vast majority of those detained under the 1976 Act are subsequently released without any charges being brought against them. And it is difficult to see how the level of violence in Ulster will be reduced by stopping suspected terrorists from leaving the province. Equally, it is understandable that England, Scotland and Wales do not want uncivilized behaviour to be brought in from across the Irish Sea.

The place of the courts

Other countries with written constitutions accept the principle of judicial review. A court is able to rule that a law is of no effect because it is contrary to the supreme constitution. In Britain all laws are of equal validity. There are no dominant rules against which laws can be judged. The concept of judicial review is limited to testing whether public bodies have exceeded their legal powers in a particular instance, and offers an opportunity for an individual to obtain redress against an improper exercise of power. In the 1970s the courts seemed to become more willing to give rulings against government departments. Thus in 1976 the Secretary of State for Education was told that Tameside must be allowed to make its own decisions about policy for secondary education; the Secretary of State for Industry was told he could not prohibit Mr Laker from running Skytrain services to North America; the Home Secretary was told he could not stop people buying television licences early to avoid a price increase. Then in 1982 it was ruled that the subsidy policy of the Greater London Council for public transport fares was unlawful. The GLC case is remarkable because the judges did not challenge the legality of the principle of subsidy: the illegality was caused by the amount. Indeed, a further test case in 1983 showed that a lower level of subsidy was legally acceptable. It is also notable that the London Labour Party had contested and won the 1981 GLC election largely on their policy for transport subsidies. Certainly, an election result cannot itself alter the law. However, in this instance the courts were coming dangerously close to a clash with the electorate.

When there is dispute over the interpretation of the meaning of a law, judges can and do disagree. The Court of Appeal can overrule the decision of a lower court. The House of Lords can reject the findings of the Court of Appeal. A Lords' decision is commonly made by five judges, so it is possible for an ultimate decision on a highly contentious matter to be made by a vote of three to two. It is clear that the interpretation of statutes is not a precise science, leading to an undoubted result. Sometimes the outcome seems to rest on the character of judicial opinions. Lord Denning, who presided over the Court of Appeal until he retired in 1982 at the age of 83, was in favour of flexible interpretation of laws so that justice could be done. The difficulty is that different people can have different views about the nature of what is just. It is arguable that if law is widely felt to be unjust then Parliament, not the judges, should make the necessary reforms.

These issues are relevant to the larger question – whether the courts should play a wider role in protecting individual liberty against the state. Many influential people, particularly lawyers, have argued that we need a Bill of Rights to help secure our freedom against the actions of public bodies. Such a development would make it easier for the courts to rule in favour of individuals. At first sight the idea is attractive, but there are serious obstacles. What precisely would a Bill of Rights contain? Would it be a set of principles the exact effect of which would emerge in subsequent lawsuits? If so, the personal influence of judges would become important. And there could well be dispute about which principles to include. Right-wing politicians want to defend property rights; Left-wingers care about civil liberties.

What would be the status of the Bill of Rights in relation to other laws? If British tradition were followed so that it had no special status, then the whole or part of the bill could be repealed by a government with only a narrow but secure Commons majority. Such an arrangement offers little protection against the ambitions of ministers. Yet if a Bill of Rights were made in the form of a supreme law, particularly difficult to amend, then the concept of parliamentary sovereignty would disappear. In consequence, we would start to be governed by the past. People who pass a fundamental law are attempting to impose their views on succeeding generations. Citizens of the United States in 1789 have had an effect on events in that land ever since. But circumstances and values change with time. Why should the attitudes of the past determine the affairs of the future?

It is unlikely that a Bill of Rights will become a serious political issue. The idea is favoured mainly by those with Right-wing opinions, especially when the Conservatives are out of office. Inevitably the proposal would stimulate a major public debate covering profound issues – the proper functions of the state, individual rights, the nature of law, the influence of judges and the powers of Parliament. Any government might be wary of opening up arguments on this scale.

Public inquiries and administrative tribunals

One area where the courts might have become more involved in critical problems of the relations of the state and the individual is the vast group of cases arising from the development of economic and land-use planning, where land has to be acquired and planning permission granted (or withheld). If a dispute arises in such cases, the aggrieved citizen appeals to the minister, but instead of turning to the courts, the latter sets up a public inquiry. The reason for this procedure is that English (and Scots) law has tended to regard the task of the court as determining matters of fact, leaving the judge then to apply the law. But in arguments over what would be the best line for a motorway, where a factory would best be sited and so on, there is not the same clear division between fact and law. The motorway could be built on one of several routes, and there is no law or legal principle which could guide a judge in saying that X route was fairer, would make a better motorway or do less damage to private interests than route Y. For these reasons, it was decided to use the form of a public inquiry but the decision whether to accept the outcome of the inquiry lies with the minister whose department was often a party to the original dispute. The extent of the problem can be measured by the fact that the annual number of planning appeals is about 7000.

There have been objections to this form of proceeding which reached a peak after the Crichel Down case in 1954 when it was revealed not only that officials of the Ministry of Agriculture had behaved inefficiently and unfairly in handling a dispute over the compulsory purchase of a piece of land and its subsequent resale, but that there was a legal way of reviewing such cases. As a result a Committee on Administrative Tribunals and Inquiries was appointed under Sir Oliver Franks and its Report (Cmnd 218) in 1957 set the pattern for the future development of these bodies. It accepted the system but urged more uniformity, careful application of the principles of 'openness, fairness and impartiality', with the right to legal representation, reasoned decisions, a system of appeals and, in the case of inquiries, the publication of the inspector's reports to the minister. The total effect was to make the civil service 'Franks-minded' and these principles were, broadly speaking, applied in subsequent years. There have been occasional problems since, such as the 'Chalk pit' case, but in 1962, the government accepted that if new evidence appeared, the minister must give the parties concerned an opportunity to comment on this before he accepts or rejects his inspector's report.

There are many different kinds of administrative decisions in which the public has an interest but where other considerations of cost to taxpayers or side implications on other parts of the community have to be taken into account. It is hard to devise procedures suitable for all the different types of case. One example is the procedure set up by the government for the closure of a railway line under the 1962 Transport Act. This procedure has often caused great heart-burning. It required British Rail to announce an intention to close a line and then evidence could be fed to a Transport Users Consultative Committee on the question of hardship and on the planning aspects to the regional planning council. The exasperation was caused by the fact that British Rail was not obliged to explain the economic and financial problems it was facing in running the line, it was not required to try economies or improvements before announcing an intention to close and the minister could still decide to close, even if it was agreed that there would be both planning problems and hardship caused.

Simpler considerations of equity apply when the state has either conferred a right or imposed obligations on citizens (for example, by granting social security payments or levying a tax), as in these cases it is only fair that the legislature's intention is carried out and that the rules are applied equally and impartially. But here again, these issues have not been left to the courts but have usually been entrusted to special administrative tribunals, boards or hearings. The impact of these bodies on the public is considerable; Rent Tribunals have dealt with as many as 15,000 cases a year and Industrial Injuries and National Insurance Tribunals with 50,000 to 60,000 a year.

But though the intention is to produce a mixture of informality and the rules of fairness that normally apply in a court, most citizens feel overawed, puzzled or outsmarted when they are called before such bodies and encounter a well-briefed property company lawyer, an employers' counsel or a tax inspector.

So considering the entire system of determining disputes between the individual and the state, it cannot be said that the situation is satisfactory. In part this is because there are great gaps where no body exists to listen to complaints about harsh or unfair decisions (the Crichel Down case could not have been taken up in this way). In part it is because of the complexity which means that citizens, even if they are of considerable professional status, have little idea of how to proceed in cases of dispute. As a result, a confused suspicion spreads that everything is managed by a vast complex of bureaucratic organizations far away from the individual concerned (for many Scots and Welsh, they suspect literally far away in London, for Londoners far away in a psychological sense), a suspicion that remote, not very well-informed officials apply rules without much thought about the particular case and the persons affected.

There have been suggestions as to how this problem could be remedied. A number of experts on constitutional matters have argued the case for a general administrative appeal tribunal which would be the final authority on all such issues. This exists in France in the form of the Conseil d'État but the Franks Committee (though not empowered to examine situations where no tribunal existed) reported against such a council to hear appeals from tribunals and appeals against a minister's decisions after an inquiry. The government accepted the committee's arguments that the existing variety of tribunals were all supposed to be expert in the particular field of administration in which they were working, that these proposals would mean an appeal from an expert to an inexpert body, and that the effect of a Conseil d'État or administrative court being the final court of appeal would be the creation of a body of administrative law. British lawyers had, since the Middle Ages, tried to establish the principle that the state had no special privileges before the law, and that to create a body of administrative law might be interpreted as a move away from that principle. Under the Franks Committee's recommendations, appeals on points of law lay with the ordinary courts so that the old common law principles would still, as far as possible, be applied in these administrative cases. Second, and probably more important in the government's eyes, was the very British conviction that a minister's decisions were political, they should be final and the only resort against them should be political criticism. It is entirely against the British tradition of an almost unfettered executive to create situations where a court could veto decisions or pass on the justice or administrative good sense of a minister's actions.

The ombudsman

Another method of attempting to bridge the gap between the citizen and the state, or at least of removing the frustrations and sense of impotence felt by some citizens, was to appoint an ombudsman. This was proposed in 1961 by a committee under Sir John Whyatt (set up by the British Section of the International Commission of Jurists) which also made other recommendations about a general tribunal to hear appeals on discretionary matters not covered by other tribunals. The ombudsman was to consider cases of maladministration or unusually harsh or unreasonable decisions. Public interest was aroused by the proposal, but the Macmillan Government turned it down in 1962 on the grounds that it was incompatible with the final authority of the minister in question, and that a citizen with a grievance could get at the minister through his Member of Parliament. The Labour Party included the proposal for an ombudsman in its 1964 election manifesto and, after coming to power, produced a White Paper in 1965 and passed the necessary legislation in 1967.

The act provided that complaints to the ombudsman, or parliamentary commissioner as he is called in the act, can only be presented through a Member of Parliament and the subjects which he can investigate do not include local authority matters, the nationalized industries, personnel questions in the armed forces or civil service, the police, government contracts or the health service. Also the ombudsman cannot examine the wisdom of ministerial decisions, he can only consider cases of maladministration given the existing policies determined by the government. In so doing, all departmental files have to be made available, though a minister may forbid the publication of information in the ombudsman's report. Where the parliamentary commissioner finds that injustice has occurred he can suggest that action be taken to right the wrong, but he cannot insist. It is for the responsible minister to decide whether to make redress, for instance by the payment of compensation. The convention is that the advice of the commissioner is accepted.

However, it must be stressed that this is a system to review the quality of administration; it is not a method of appealing against the decisions of civil servants. For a complaint to be upheld the parliamentary commissioner must find an element of 'maladministration': a decision must have been influenced by 'bias, neglect, inattention, delay, incompetence, ineptitude, perversity, turpitude or arbitrariness'. The concept of maladministration is a little imprecise, but it does not cover a case where a government department has exercised its discretion within the limits of the law and after having reviewed the situation in a proper manner. The departments that are the subject of most complaints are the Inland Revenue and the DHSS.

The parliamentary commissioner reports to a select committee of backbench MPs. The committee tends to provide support and encouragement for the commissioner. It has sometimes urged him to take a broader view of his role and the rule that this system can be approached only through an MP has been largely circumvented. Now, if the commissioner receives a complaint directly and it appears worthy of further inquiry, the letter will be sent to the complainant's MP with a note from the commissioner to inquire whether the MP would like the matter to be investigated.

One major defeat for the commissioner was the Court Line affair. In 1974 Court Line collapsed; it was a large travel firm with other interests. About 50,000 holidaymakers were stranded abroad and a further 65,000 lost deposits on holidays already booked. Rumours about the financial instability of Court Line had been circulating for some time, and six weeks before the crash Mr Benn, then Secretary of State for Industry, had given the Commons a firm assurance that holidays booked with Court Line were safe. The commissioner found this statement blameworthy and suggested that compensation to the holidaymakers was appropriate. The government rallied behind Mr Benn and refused to pay compensation from public funds. It is arguable that the commissioner was not established, nor is he suitable, to deal with this kind of incident. If ministers themselves make errors that adversely affect many people the sanction is a row in the Commons which damages their political credit. The commissioner can handle only mistakes within the closed domain of the bureaucracy. That position rests not on law but on political reality.

Many of the cases sent in by MPs were outside the commissioner's terms of reference. As a result there had been steady pressure to expand the system and in April 1974 a local government ombudsman was established for England and Wales and in May 1975, a further local government ombudsman for Scotland was appointed. Again, these ombudsmen could only be approached through councillors elected to the relevant local authorities. Northern Ireland was ahead in that the commissioner for complaints was established in 1969 as part of the reform programme brought in at that time to try and alleviate the grievances of the minority community. This commissioner can be approached by the public directly and can hear complaints against both local government and certain public bodies and organize a reconciliation. In September 1973, health service commissioners for England, Scotland and Wales were introduced, patients getting access only after a preliminary complaint to the responsible health services authorities had been made with an unsatisfactory result.

Enforcing the law: the army and the police

When laws have been enacted and have to be applied in particular cases, they are, in the last resort, enforced by the courts (though the courts have been tending to watch the claims of the executive with some care) and then by the police. The military have been used in Northern Ireland in the 1920s and again since 1969. Either in time of emergency or in time of war, special powers can be taken by the government. These methods of enforcement play little part in the normal political life of the country. The forces themselves are governed by military law set out in the Army Act and there is no such thing as martial law. The powers and duties of soldiers in a situation such as the 1969 riots in Londonderry and Belfast are different in degree and not in kind from those of the ordinary citizen. All alike are under an obligation to try and stop riots, though soldiers clearly have a greater responsibility in that they are equipped and brought there for that purpose. Officers and men must exercise their own judgement whether to use force and, if so, how much. The normal courts continue to operate (unless there is an actual invasion or loss of control of a wide area including the place where the local court sits) and all alleged offences committed during the riots, including any accusation of excessive use of force by the military, can be tried in these courts.

Of much more consequence to most citizens is the position of the police, as they are the coercive aspect of the state with which people are regularly in contact. Here also, the vast expansion in the activities of the state and in the complexity of society have led to many more people being involved in such contacts. The police have not merely the old, central task of the detection and prevention of crime but, because they are an available force, they have been used for many aspects of social welfare work, investigating cases and keeping contact with those under some kind of supervision. Also the growth of private car ownership and of traffic has involved them with many who, in former days, would never have had any dealings with the police. The public's attitude to the police is somewhat ambivalent, as there is a strong desire for firm enforcement of law, a strong desire to support the police in their efforts to cope with lawbreakers and yet inevitably a percentage of those who have had dealings with the police have also had complaints or have resented the way they have been treated. Thus in this aspect, as so many other of the state's relations with the citizens, the awe has gone, there is no automatic respect and the police are judged very much by results, results which are complex in that they involve the ability to crack down on certain categories of offenders while dealing fairly and impartially with the public as a whole.

Worries about the relations between the police and the public led to the appointment of a royal commission under Sir Henry Willink in 1959. It considered two major issues, the most suitable size of force – local, regional or national – and the question of public accountability. The problem was that until then chief constables in charge of a police force had been responsible for their administrative efficiency to the local Watch Committee (or Police Committee in Scotland) from which they drew half of their funds. Also the actions of the police had to be justified in that the propriety of their proceedings had to be accepted by the courts. But in the enforcement of the law fairly, impartially and efficiently, the chief constables were not under any external control, though the Home Secretary has, in some sense, a responsibility for law and order throughout the country. (In the Metropolitan area, he is the police authority.) The report of the commission was followed by the Police Act 1964. It provided that the local police authority would still be the source of pay and equipment and could discuss the efficiency with which these were utilized by the police force. The Home Secretary (and Secretary of State for Scotland) was given general powers of supervision and inquiry, for which he was responsible to the House of Commons, but still fought shy of claiming responsibility for the efficient operation of individual forces in particular situations. This was still the exclusive task of the chief constable. At the same time efforts were made to increase the efficiency of the police by cutting down the number of separate forces, which by 1976 were reduced from 125 in England and Wales and thirty-three in Scotland to forty-three and eight respectively.

Yet the chief sources of complaint, the conduct of individual officers in particular situations and the overall handling of certain episodes such as student protests, strike pickets or demonstrations, have continued. Besides alleged brutality and the death of various persons in police custody, there was also a suspicion of widespread corruption in the Metropolitan Police. The slow progress made in investigating such matters also stimulated criticism. While there is considerable public support for the police and for the enforcement of law and order, the respect for the police has been undermined by a number of factors. There is a temptation by the police to take short cuts or fabricate evidence when they know who is the villain; there are special problems of policing in relation to ethnic minorities; there is the general tendency among the younger generation to question authority; there is the increasing involvement of normally law-abiding members of the public through traffic offences with the police and there are the doubts created by episodes such as those described above.

Since 1964 proposals have been made that an independent

element should be introduced into the procedure governing complaints against the police. A sustained campaign in the Commons led to the establishment of a new Police Complaints Board in 1977. Chief constables remain in charge of decisions about punishment of police officers, so their ultimate responsibility for discipline is unchanged and undivided. Nevertheless, questions of guilt and questions as to whether a complaint from the public is justified can, in serious cases, be heard by a tribunal at which the independent members will be in a majority. So it should be more difficult for erring members of the police force to be unduly protected by disciplinary procedures that are no longer wholly internal.

Relations between police and public again became a centre of attention after riots took place in a number of inner-city areas in April 1981. The main incidents were in South London at Brixton, but trouble arose also in a number of provincial cities. Many police and protesters were injured and there was considerable damage to property. The Conservative Government was sufficiently alarmed by these incidents to ask a senior judge, Lord Scarman, to undertake an immediate investigation into the cause of the trouble. His report confirmed the widely-held view that there were three basic reasons for discontent: social deprivation, unemployment and racial tension. Social deprivation and the lack of leisure facilities for young people in inner-city areas led to frustration. Unemployment produced idleness, economic hardship and an incentive to crime. High crime rates led to strong police activity against the chief suspects – black youths: the black community then came to feel that the police were biased against them. Lord Scarman's report argued that the police in Brixton had responded well to a difficult situation but he also made criticisms of police behaviour, which had been sometimes insensitive and occasionally showed signs of racial discrimination. He favoured more community policing and better liaison between the police and leaders of ethnic minorities. One important recommendation, that racial discrimination should be made a specific offence in the police disciplinary code, was subsequently rejected by the Home Secretary on the grounds that such a change was unnecessary.

The police have a truly unenviable role. They represent society's front line of defence against disturbance and disorder. Equally, we want them to pay equal respect to the rights of all individuals. Criminals and political extremists have an interest in stirring up discontent against the forces of law and order. There are no easy solutions to this situation. Yet it would help if the quality of leadership in the police could be improved.

10 Governing through Parliament

The role of Parliament

The old nineteenth-century role of Parliament as a body which chose the government, maintained it and could reject it, which operated as an intermediary between the electorate and the executive, has gone. In a political system dominated by the direct relations between the leadership of the country and the voters, the major function of Parliament has altered. Now Parliament is one of the agencies through which the government operates and it is the place where the struggle for power continues in a restricted form between elections. Those who were brought up on the older theories of the Westminster model in which, despite party loyalties, there was a balance between the executive and the legislature as a whole, expect that the House of Commons will still regard its main functions as being to consider and amend legislative proposals from the government (and from private members), to scrutinize public expenditure and to expose government policies to continual questioning and debate. In practice, there are shadows of the first two functions remaining and the third has been incorporated into the power struggle aspect of the Commons. But for ministers, shadow ministers and most MPs on both sides of the House, the division that comes to mind is not between the executive and the House but between the government and the Opposition. The main function of MPs is to support their leaders, to attack the other side and to score the maximum points with the electorate in preparation for the next general election. In 1964 and 1966 a number of Labour backbenchers who believed in the older, more historical functions of the House were elected. They wanted to restore, to some small extent, the House's powers to scrutinize and, on occasion, to resist the executive over items of legislation, finance and general policy but their attitude was greeted with genuine surprise by many older members and by others in their own 'intake'. For these more orthodox members, the machinery of the House had to be used to protect Labour ministers and to project their achievements. They thought that it might be excusable to exploit situations to promote the individual MP's career within his own party or to look after constituency interests, but it was quite inexcusable to open up opportunities for the Opposition to criticize the government.

For the Prime Minister and his colleagues, the House can be useful in providing a forum in which they can explain their policies and it is, in any case, necessary to legalize government actions and to vote money. But many ministers regard the House as a drag. Question time has become increasingly taken up with party claims and counter claims or with constituency points, while debates often strike ministers as largely a waste of time. The ministers who like the House either do so because, in their opposition days, they enjoyed its fellowship and had few other contacts in London, or they feel so confident of their capacity to score off the Opposition that they like revealing their talents. They are conscious that their strength with the Prime Minister and chances of promotion bear some relation to their performance in the House and to their popularity in the parliamentary party. But the House may well seem a curious, wayward, ill-informed, trying body to ministers with busy departments to run and managing the House may constitute a distraction from their chief and more interesting task of governing the country.

Turning from ministers to backbenchers, for the younger, more ambitious members the task is to defend their party and to make a reputation for themselves so that they will, in due course, be promoted to a junior office or, on the other side, to a shadow post. The object in this case is not money or prestige. A junior minister in one of the less important departments has no very glamorous task. He cannot speak in or out of the House on subjects outside his department. He cannot write for the papers or take part in television programmes and his sole opportunities in public are sharing the replies at question time and answering for the government in adjournment and sometimes in wider debates which concern his ministry. The motives for seeking office are partly that the life of a backbench MP soon becomes unsatisfactory and offers so little scope for achievement, for registering even the smallest impact on a restricted area of public life, that the average MP looks with envy on any minister who has a positive job to perform, however limited the field. One quality of backbench life which is distracting for those with a professional or commercial training is that it lacks coherence, and there is an aimlessness which is debilitating. Constituency work takes some time and leads to a multiplicity of minor preoccupations but it by no means occupies the entire day. Then the questions arise; should the MP speak in a debate? – he may not be called. Should he sit on a select committee or will the work go unnoticed? Should he try to write a newspaper column? An article is more likely to be accepted if it says something new but this might annoy some of his party leaders. All the time he is encouraged to dabble in this or that to no lasting effect and the relief that such an MP feels when given an actual job, a place to go from 9 a.m. onwards with a definite task to perform, something to do which stretches his capacity more than drinking tea, gossiping and writing letters, is enormous.

For the man who enters the House at a later age who does not expect to get and perhaps does not want office, there is no point in continual exertions to catch the limelight and this is the kind of member who is particularly prone to regard his function as supporting his leaders. On the Labour side, there is a solid body of such members who inhabit the Tearoom. On the Conservative side this element is based in the Smoking Room, and is composed of the men with estates or directorships who do not see the House as their primary source of prestige or income. They, likewise, would find it most unusual and uncongenial if they were expected to devote themselves to constraining and criticizing a Conservative Government.

There are groups who take a different view, but they are a minority. The Left in the Labour Party use the House to register their protests against Right-wing men and measures, whichever party is in power, though many of them consider that once this is done on the floor of the House and the outside public has been informed of their dissent, they will support their leaders in committee and in the division lobbies. Only a few, largely of the younger members, consider that at least for the first few years after an election, the House as a whole should keep a wary eye on the government and seek to support or influence its policy irrespective of the line taken by the official Opposition. These members are interested in the issues, in extracting information from the government, in finding out precisely what is being planned, how policies are to be applied and whether the machinery of government is working well but, as has been said, this is the approach of a minority and, if well done, simply suggests to the more orthodox

MPs that the person concerned ought not to be a backbencher but is either seeking office in a rather unusual way or ought to be in some other occupation.

This analysis of the House of Commons is put forward and supported in rather different ways by two very able contemporary commentators, Mr Henry Fairlie in his book *The Life of Politics* and Mr Ronald Butt in *The Power of Parliament*. Fairlie argues, in the same fashion as that employed above, that Britain has an executive-dominated legislature, that the House of Commons can do little to stop a government and that its traditional functions are largely meaningless. But he adds the value judgement that this is desirable because it exists and cannot be undone. Fairlie emphasizes that the House has no corporate feeling, it cannot stand apart from the government, and the parliamentary reformers' idea that the House can recover some of its former powers is both impracticable and, in his judgement, undesirable. It will not happen because the House cannot reform itself; it can only act with the permission of the executive. In other words, the executive has to propose to the House that reforms should be instituted and why should any executive wish to make rods for its own back? Does it make sense, Fairlie asks, to expect the government to set up committees to scrutinize its work and to expose it to criticism when the government itself would have to table the motion setting up the committees, fix their terms of reference, select the members and appoint the chairmen? For Fairlie, the task of the House is as it is, to keep the party battle going. The accountability of the government arises simply from the ministers' desire to win the next election and, as individuals, to have the minimum of embarrassment and the maximum of political credit. These motives can be exploited to good effect by skilful MPs who understand the system and work with it rather than try to change it.

Ronald Butt arrives at much the same conclusions and he adds certain extra points. His political position is conservative and though some of the ultra Left share his views, they are typical of the older Conservative members. Such members are often landowners or men of wealth who have little ambition for office and no concept of the House as a countervailing power to watch over the executive. In their eyes, to seek to strengthen the critical functions of the House is pointless, since they tend to trust the (normally Conservative) government. In strong personal positions and moved by loyalty, they back their Prime Minister. But if these men do rouse themselves to tell the premier that something is going wrong, he takes notice. The Labour Party equivalent is a serious rebellion by the trade union loyalists. Such actions are quite exceptional on both sides, taking place only a handful of times during each political generation, but then with definite effects. Conservative members dismissed Chamberlain (in their eyes), vetoed Mr R. A. Butler for the leadership and nearly stopped the Retail Price Maintenance Bill. Labour members smothered an incomes policy and helped kill legislation on industrial relations in 1969, and the 1976 Devolution Bill. With this evidence of House of Commons influence and reading the journalistic and academic comment about the ineffectiveness of Parliament, Mr Butt felt he had to argue that these comments showed a misunderstanding of the situation. He cited the various occasions when premiers had been influenced to prove his point. Moreover, all this influence was exercised without any reforms, select committees or other institutional changes proposed by the more theoretically minded parliamentary reformers. (The author interviewed an archetypal example of the older kind of Conservative. This was Mr J. G. Stuart, later Viscount Stuart of Findhorn, who was asked if, after all his years in the House, there were any reforms he would like to see carried out, any changes at all? 'Yes,' replied Mr Stuart, 'there is one thing I have always thought ought to go. We ought to abolish the special allowances paid to the Leader of the Opposition. It is quite ridiculous to pay taxpayers' money to encourage someone to oppose the Queen's Government.')

Yet, part of the argument that the Commons' powers, whatever their value now, have declined as compared with a century ago, is an historical one about the relationships between the executive and the legislature in Victorian Britain. Butt also attacked the accepted view in this case, quoting statements by politicians who thought that in the 1850s and 1860s Parliament was so strong it was becoming hard to maintain an effective executive. These views could be quoted to suggest that though Parliament was more powerful in these years, some Victorian politicians regarded this as an undesirable departure from the British tradition of a strong executive capable of controlling and commanding Parliament except on a few special occasions. Even on its own terms, this is a selective view, as only the 1846–60 period was one of unusual instability (Peel's 1841–6 Government was strong enough as was the Palmerston Government after 1860) and the estimate of executive–

legislative relations inherent in the Westminster model is based on a broader period from 1832 to the 1890s, when most commentators accepted that a reasonable balance had been achieved.

How the executive gained control of Parliament

Before joining battle on the value judgements in the theses of Fairlie and Butt, both of which agree basically with the assessment given here of the powers and role of the House of Commons today, it is worth establishing the facts, both historical and contemporary. In the period from 1832 to the 1880s, the number of party issues (nine-tenths of one party voting together) fell to 25 per cent of all divisions under a Liberal Government in 1860 and 31 per cent under the Conservatives, this low level of party cohesion being much the same from the 1830s to the early 1880s. The House could and did sack governments (such as Russell's first Cabinet in 1852, Aberdeen's ministry in 1855, Lord Palmerston in 1858, Russell again in 1866 and Gladstone in 1885) without having to face a general election. It could and did reject, revise and remake legislation on the floor of the House (such as the 1858 India Act or the 1867 Reform Act). Individual ministers were censured and driven from office by the House, examples being Russell in 1855 and Ellenborough in 1858. The House controlled a large part of its own timetable, it had a corporate spirit and it could force information out of the government, the best example being the stream of diplomatic Blue Books in which the Foreign Office had to reveal the course of its negotiations with foreign powers almost as soon as the events had occurred. Select committees were set up by the House with full powers of investigation. Sometimes they did more than just report, and drafted legislation which could be adopted and introduced either by the government or by a private member. There can be no doubt, then, that the loose nature of party discipline, the small electorates, the relative security of the private MP against the executive, all gave the House not merely much greater power than it enjoys nowadays but powers which altered its entire role and position in the system of government. Under these circumstances the House had an independence and authority which would be utterly alien and unfamiliar to MPs accustomed to contemporary conditions.

During the Victorian period, in order to exercise these functions of controlling, scrutinizing, appointing and removing the executive, the procedure of the House was adapted to suit these tasks. It is generally accepted that in order to watch over an executive, the system of supervision has to be constructed in parallel so that information about the salient issues is extracted at the right time and the process of scrutiny is based on this information and takes place when the decision is still open. In the nineteenth century, the first step in legislation was a motion asking leave to introduce a bill. At this stage the bill was not printed but the sponsors explained why they felt legislation was necessary and the lines on which they were planning to draft the measure. This gave warning to the outside interests and to members and gave them time to gather their thoughts and explain their views before the first reading, which was purely formal but provided for the printing of the bill.

The second reading debate then dealt with the principle of the measure and could go on as long as members wished to speak, the government soon sensing whether it could proceed or whether modifications were needed. Once past this hurdle, there came the committee stage taken on the floor of the House, when detailed amendments could be moved clause by clause, and again all amendments had to be taken and this stage went on until each had been dealt with. Finally, there was the third reading debate when the House had to look at what it had done to the draft bill during the committee stage and decided whether to pass the measure.

A similar stage-by-stage supervision obtained in financial matters. Since the 1790s, administrative reforms had gathered together the raising and spending of money into an annual exercise in the hands of the Treasury, the process being completed by the Exchequer and Audit Departments Act in 1866. To permit proper supervision, Gladstone devised a 'circle of control' which followed the same annual cycle. In the spring of each year, the House considered the civil and military estimates and could and did move and carry reductions in individual items in Committee of the whole House called the Committee of Supply. Then in early April, at the end of the financial year, the new taxation was set out in the Budget and listed in the Finance Bill which was discussed in Committee of the whole House, the Committee of Ways and Means. The money for expenditure, as set out in the estimates and finally authorized for expenditure in the Appropriation Act, was passed to the Treasury which in turn handed it out in a carefully controlled flow to the spending departments. At the end of the year, the accounts from all these departments went to the Comptroller and Auditor General, an official of the House of Commons, who put the audited accounts before the Public Accounts Committee of the House to ensure that every penny was spent in the way set out in the Appropriation Act. So the House watched over estimates, money raising, money allocation, its actual expenditure and the legality of what had been done.

So long as the House was not bound by strict party ties and so long as it had control of the major part of its own timetable, the general task of commenting on and questioning government policy was relatively simple. There was no need for a question time, since a member could intervene in business by moving a motion on a number of pretexts and raise any subject in an immediate debate. If the House was worried, the government could not refuse a full explanation nor could it return to its other business till members were satisfied. The House might decide to act on its own by appointing a committee to inquire into the matter or a private member might move resolutions or introduce his own measure.

This pattern of parliamentary activity was rapidly altered (though much of the descriptive language remained the same) in the twenty-five years before the First World War. The electorate increased, party battles became much more intense and for the government, over 90 per cent, indeed up to 97 per cent, of divisions in the House became party divisions in that over nine-tenths of the party voted as the whips indicated. With these changes went a different attitude to legislation. For radicals such as Randolph Churchill (Conservative) and Joseph Chamberlain (Liberal), the task of the House was not to talk over and often talk out measures. If a party had been elected on a given programme, this was an indication that the public wanted these measures passed. This was an early sign of the leadership reaching over the heads of the House to the electorate. The voters had pronounced and the newer, more radical leaders considered that the House should then give up its extensive powers; the measures endorsed by a majority at the polls should be passed with reasonable rapidity. This view, the increasing tempo of legislation and the use of the procedures of the House to obstruct measures (by Conservative backbenchers, called 'the Fourth Party', by 'the colonels' opposed to the abolition of purchase of commissions and then by the Irish) led to the first restrictions on private members' capacity to interrupt or hold up business whenever they liked – or whenever they could get the House to listen to them, for there was always considerable self-discipline.

The new Standing Orders adopted in 1882, after Speaker Brand had intervened in 1881 to stop a forty-one hour sitting, allowed the closure of debate by a simple majority. Further changes were made between 1887 and 1891, the process being largely completed by A. J. Balfour between 1895 and 1902. In 1902 Balfour brought in his 'reforms', called 'Balfour's railway timetable', because under them, the government took control of virtually all the time of the House. It decided what was to be debated, for how long and when the final vote was to be taken, so that the government could plan its legislative programme and could forecast accurately when each legislative train would reach the various stages on the journey to enactment.

These parliamentary procedures rest upon the government's command of a majority. If this does not exist then both the government and its control of the timetable collapse but while the one lasts, the other is intact. The government now announces each Thursday the next week's business. Private MPs rise and ask for time for this or that motion or debate which they particularly want, but normally the only concessions the Leader of the House will make is through 'the usual channels', that is in private discussions with the opposition Chief Whip. This is because both frontbenches accept that it is the function of the House to permit the two sides to state their cases, and each party in power has respected the right of the Opposition to determine the subjects of debate for about one-third of the total time of the House.

The methods used for controlling debate are the power to apply the closure by a simple majority, though normally the majority must consist of a hundred members; the power to send bills upstairs for their committee stage to a standing committee and the power, when bills are taken on the floor of the House or in committee, to impose a guillotine. This is a preliminary timetable resolution which requires the vote to be put on certain clauses at a certain time, irrespective of whether all the amendments to the clause or to previous clauses have been discussed. Whether a guillotine has been imposed or not, the Speaker has the power to select and group amendments in order to cut down the number and to confine debate to the salient points, but even with this power of Speaker's selection, a guillotine may mean that blocks of amendments are never reached.

This control by the government of the life and work of the House is pervasive and for most purposes has ended any corporate sense of 'the House' as a body which could oppose the government of the day. It is safely assumed that a government can obtain the passage of virtually all the bills it introduces. This is true also of amendments. Professor Griffiths, in a study of the committee stages of bills covering the period 1967–71 found that 907 amendments were moved by ministers, of which 906 were carried. Backbenchers moved 3510 amendments, only 171 being carried and most of these were not opposed by the government.

Besides this control of measures, the government also controls the processes and personnel of the House. Acting through the Leader of the House and the Chief Whip (aided by the Opposition Chief Whip), the government appoints the members of select committees, nominates the chairmen, and can guide the committees by suggesting suitable subjects. The whips agree to give a certain amount of time for private members' bills and private members' motions, but they then encourage all their own backbenchers to ballot for these opportunities. They also circulate among their backbenchers suitable motions and advise about appropriate and acceptable bills for those who come out high up on the list of names which emerge from the ballot. Of course, members can disregard this advice. Once on a committee, a backbencher is relatively safe and select committees have been known to reject government suggestions as to suitable subjects and go their own way. Indeed, there is now a tendency for select committees to show some greater independence of spirit, particularly since 1979 when they were first appointed on a systematic rather than an *ad hoc* basis. Nevertheless, their recommendations can still be ignored.

The way this government control has come to be accepted as normal and proper can be seen by the irritated reactions of ministers and whips on the odd occasions when something goes wrong. For instance, after the day's business is over, which is normally at 10 p.m., the government can put through unopposed items (such as the nomination of committees) but if an MP shouts 'object' the matter is postponed. If this is repeated on several occasions, the government can either give up the proposal or take government time, have a short debate and then push the matter through. But though the only effect of this kind of obstruction is a minor rearrangement of government business and a slight delay, the reaction of the whips and the Leader of the House can be intense. The culprit is sent for and denounced, for this is regarded as a very serious crime. The most spectacular case where the government lost control of the timetable was in the spring of 1969 over the Parliament (No. 2) – House of Lords Reform – Bill. The situation was abnormal in that the substance of the bill had been agreed between the two frontbenches, but when the inter-party talks broke down (over a Rhodesian order), the Shadow Cabinet gave their members a free vote and a group of them resisted the measure. The normal forces of party loyalty did not help the government precisely because there was no official opposition. So the ministers in charge of the measure felt they could not bring in a guillotine or send the bill to a committee upstairs because most of the Conservatives would have voted against and, not being an issue of confidence between the parties, sufficient Labour dissidents might also have voted against the government to leave it in a minority. So the bill had to be taken on the floor of the House and all selected amendments had to be debated and voted on. As a result, though the government won every division, after nine days only five out of twenty clauses had been passed. This would have been counted as a great success and a reasonable rate of progress in the 1850s or 1860s but was so unprecedented and so humiliating, given the contemporary assumptions about government control, that the bill was dropped.

The effects of the timetable and work of the House passing under the control of the government have been widespread. One sign of the degree of power and independence of a legislature is its capacity to extract information from the government. In the nineteenth century, the House of Commons forced successive ministries to publish collections of dispatches dealing with Britain's relations with foreign powers shortly after the events had taken place, simply so that the House could judge whether the policies had been appropriate. As party discipline tightened and governments could rely on regular majorities, motions 'that papers be laid' on given subjects were increasingly resisted. Thus the flow of this information began to decline in the 1890s reaching a trickle, mainly on peripheral issues, by 1914 and ceasing totally after 1918. The contrast can be seen by comparing the information available when the Commons in 1856 forced the publication of all dispatches dealing with the origins of the Crimean War before hostilities were over, and the capacity of successive governments to keep the House and the public in total and persistent ignorance of what led up to the invasion of Suez in 1956. In the latter case, no information, other than private memoirs, has been published and though Labour leaders talked about revealing all the secrets when they won power, once in office in 1964, they also refused publication. The other great method of investigation and discovery of information was by the appointment of select committees, governments often feeling that they could not oppose motions seeking to elicit the facts on any situation. Again, party loyalty stopped this process. All major inquiries are now initiated by ministers who prefer to rely on royal commissions or departmental committees, which may sometimes contain a couple of MPs. Of course, one of the new breed of select committees can review any matter that falls within its ambit, but their reports tend to lack the prestige of inquiries set up by ministers.

The legislative process

The most important effect of this degree of government control has been to render the House of Commons incapable of adapting its procedure to keep pace with altered administrative practices. It is generally accepted that control systems have to be organized in parallel to the activities that they are intended to monitor. The procedures for legislation, for the scrutiny of expenditure and for raising taxation have been described to show how this worked in the Victorian period. By the 1970s, the legislative process had altered enormously, but the only changes in House of Commons procedure have been to make it less capable of controlling even the old pattern of legislation. Now legislation arises either from major political commitments made by the Cabinet (or earlier by the Shadow Cabinet while the party was in opposition), or it is of a more routine nature and comes from within the departments when they find their existing powers insufficient or inappropriate for the conduct of administration along accepted lines. Once it is agreed that legislation should be prepared, the civil servants consult with the outside pressure groups, they clear their ideas with other interested departments and negotiate any financial aspects with the Treasury. Sometimes, if a matter is difficult, a committee may be set up to gather facts and produce a report. The whole process will take months or even years if special problems are encountered.

When a bill has been negotiated in this way and drafted, it is then presented to the House for the first time. The old stage of asking the House for 'leave to introduce' a bill when the possibilities can be debated before any negotiations or drafting have been started has been abandoned. (The last remnant of this procedure allows MPs to have one short speech a day to introduce a 'Ten Minute Rule' bill.) Occasionally governments have opened up a discussion at this stage by publishing a 'Green Paper' which set out alternative possibilities, but this has been relatively rare. Thus the House receives what is, to all intents and purposes, a finished product. The Opposition state their view of the bill during the second reading debate. Then it is usually sent to a committee. During this stage, the government may accept amendments or amend its own bill if deficiencies in drafting come to light. Pressure groups that have narrowly lost points or who feel strongly opposed may brief members in the hope that with extra publicity and a show of support from friendly MPs, the government may relent during the passage of the bill. But on controversial bills, many of the amendments at the committee stage and the debates at the end of each clause on the motion 'that clause X stand part of the bill' merely give the Opposition a chance to reiterate its objections. This ground can be traversed again three times, at the report, Lords' amendments and third reading stages, all on the floor of the House. So the procedure is admirably adapted to permit the Opposition to make its case several times over, and for the government to explain the virtues of the measure an equal number of times. What the procedure does not permit is an exploration of alternative approaches, an understanding of the views of outside groups (unless they think it worth briefing MPs) and there is no scope for public opinion to form and react before the government has committed itself to a definite approach to the problem. With this process of legislation, any changes the ministers may want to make look like concessions to the Opposition. Government backbenchers are expected to be present at all stages and though they are entitled to speak for half the time available on the floor of the House, in committee they are expected neither to speak nor to move amendments but simply to keep voting for the government's proposals.

During the 1979 Parliament a very limited attempt was made to add to the flexibility of the committee stage. For a small number of less contentious bills, the normal proceedings of the standing committee were preceded by three sessions conducted on the lines of a select committee. Thus evidence was taken on the need for the bill and why it was proposed to deal with problems in a particular way. Members of the committee became much better informed. The quality of debate was improved. Time was saved in that it became less necessary to put down formal amendments designed to probe government intentions. This procedure is most suitable for bills that do not raise issues on which parties automatically disagree; to use select committee-type sittings on such a bill would be to provide further time for repetition of standard partisan arguments. The limited experiment was widely thought to have been successful. Yet the government is not keen to extend select committee-style examination of legislation, and it is not clear how far this process will be used in the future.

Authorizing public expenditure and taxation

In financial matters, much the same reduction in the capacity to scrutinize has taken place. As early as the 1880s, it was found that the Commons could not adequately examine and comment on the estimates. They were too complex for treatment on the floor of the House. Also the Opposition did not want to waste time on such minutiae, preferring to tackle the government on wider issues arising from the conduct of foreign or domestic policy. As a result, the scrutiny of the estimates in the Committee of Supply became a formal vote to reduce the money for this or that department by a nominal figure so as to permit a general attack on the government's policy in that field. Instead of these days being taken together in the spring when the estimates were published, 'supply days' (now numbering twenty-nine) were scattered throughout the session so that the Opposition, which is allowed to choose the subjects, could always have some time available should it wish to raise some immediate aspect of government policy. To meet this gap in the old 'circle of control', an Estimates Committee was appointed in 1912 and reappointed in every session, except during the two world wars, until 1960 when Standing Order No. 80 made the sessional appointment of the committee mandatory. At first, the committee was not very successful as it had no staff, and a body of twenty-four to twenty-eight members is not very effective for cross-examining witnesses. After 1945, the committee was allowed to divide itself into subcommittees, it gave up scrutinizing the estimates in detail and began to look at the way money was being spent in selected fields and how far government policy was being achieved. While this was useful and did hold the attention of members interested in the specific subjects being examined, the subcommittees moved from one area of expenditure to another each session so that they developed no expertise and could not follow up previous work. Thus House of Commons scrutiny of the estimates virtually ceased. Meanwhile, within the executive, the Treasury in 1961 accepted the Plowden Committee's proposals and began to plan public expenditure on the framework of a five-year rolling programme. Under this procedure, each summer a committee of officials called the Public Expenditure Scrutiny Committee (PESC) prepares a report forecasting public expenditure over the following five years. The figures for the first two years are easy as these decisions have already been taken, years four and five are merely projections on current assumptions while the hard decisions have at this stage to be taken for year three. At the same time a Medium Term Economic Assessment is prepared by the Treasury to show the anticipated resources available in the five years ahead. With the PESC Report and the Economic Assessment before them, a Cabinet committee of ministers with the same name (PESC) then decides the levels and share out of expenditure for year three. Only the conclusions or any outstanding disputes go to the full Cabinet.

But while Whitehall changed from organizing public expenditure on an annual basis to a five-year rolling programme, the House of Commons was still authorizing expenditure on the old twelve-month pattern. To complicate matters even further, the House only authorized annual 'supply services'. Charges on the Consolidated Fund (such as interest on the National Debt, the Civil List and certain salaries) do not require annual authorization and were not included. Expenditure by the nationalized industries and that of local authorities was not included. The PESC Report, on the other hand, covered the whole of public expenditure. Thus there was no House of Commons scrutiny of public expenditure and virtually no understanding of how the decisions had been reached. All that happened was a series of complaints when the results of the overall programme began to affect spending in a particular field. Occasionally, when there had to be a drastic reassessment of public expenditure, it became evident from the leaks and rumours of resignations that something important was going on in Whitehall during the summer months, but neither backbenchers nor the House in general were able to find out what was happening or to discuss the changes being made in expenditure plans.

Labour members of the Select Committee on Procedure obtained permission from the Chancellor of the Exchequer and the Chief Labour Whip to look at this omission in the 1968–9 session.

In July 1969, the select committee reported in favour of the publication both of the five-year rolling programme in the form of an annual White Paper with a full explanation of what changes had been made that year, and of the Medium Term Economic Assessment. The report called for a major debate each year on this White Paper and recommended the creation of a new Public Expenditure Select Committee to take the place of the former Estimates Committee. This was to be a body of seventy-two members divided into eight subcommittees each specializing in a particular field of expenditure and backed by adequate staff. The previous November, the government had assented to the idea of an annual White Paper on expenditure and a debate, the paper being published and the debate being held for the first time in the winter of 1969–70. It is interesting that the Treasury was only willing to publish the White Paper in the autumn of each year after rather than before the hard decisions for the third year had been taken, and made no commitment to publish the Medium Term Economic Assessment, actually refusing to do so in 1971.

The new Conservative Government after 1970 decided to accept the Select Committee on Procedure's recommendations and a Select Committee on Expenditure of forty-nine members (six subcommittees) was created in 1971. It had the right to examine policy and to question ministers and was organized into a general subcommittee which examined the whole PESC system and a series of specific subcommittees, each specializing in an area of expenditure. Once the general subcommittee had done its survey of the system, it turned to inform Parliament of the issues embodied (or concealed) in the annual expenditure White Paper, the first of these reports being the Fifth Report of the 1972–3 session. Meanwhile the various subcommittees reported on public expenditure in their fields.

The result has appeared unimpressive to some in that the issues embedded in the Public Expenditure White Paper remained obscure to most MPs and the annual debate did not become a major parliamentary occasion. On the other hand, more information did become available and there was more scrutiny of executive action. In 1979 the Expenditure Committee was replaced by a team of a dozen select committees. To each of these was allocated a major sector of government activity for inquiry and comment. Viewed in the long term, the importance of the Expenditure Committee was that it helped to persuade the Commons as a whole of the need for a more comprehensive effort to review the processes of public administration.

The functional select committees vary in the extent to which they pay attention to the expenditure proposals in departmental estimates. Some committees prefer to concentrate on broader issues of policy and administration. However, there is a strong feeling among many backbenchers that the select committee system should be used to enhance parliamentary supervision of public expenditure. In 1981 the Procedure Committee asked that eight days should be allocated in the chamber for the discussion of particular estimates; the estimates would be chosen by the liaison committee of chairmen of select committees, so this arrangement would provide a further opportunity of examining matters raised in committee inquiries. The government accepted the idea in principle but allowed three days for such debates – not eight. So since 1983 there has been a possibility that any estimate may be subjected to critical review by the House of Commons.

Estimates refer to proposals to spend money. The public accounts refer to money that has been spent. It was noted above that these accounts are audited by the Comptroller and Auditor General who reports to the Public Accounts Committee. In 1983 moves were made both to strengthen the powers of the Comptroller and to strengthen the links between him and the Commons. The National Audit Act, a private member's bill sponsored by Mr St John Stevas, provided that the Public Accounts Committee should have a decisive voice in the choice of the Comptroller – previously it had been a government nomination. This act also authorized the creation of a Public Accounts Commission composed of MPs to supervise the Comptroller's department, now known as the National Audit Office. The commission, subject to parliamentary ratification, approves staffing levels in the National Audit Office; as only one member of this commission is a minister, the Commons has made the National Audit Office remarkably independent of ministers. The Office examines the accounts of civil service departments for economy, efficiency and effectiveness. Its remit extends to the National Health Service and to many other public bodies more than half of whose income comes from public funds. Its scope does not include nationalized industries.

On the other side of financial procedure, that of authorizing taxation, the House is bound by a standing order of 1713 which prevents anyone, other than a minister, proposing a new or increased or varied form of taxation. Since 1966, debate has been founded on resolutions moved immediately after the Chancellor of the Exchequer's Budget speech. These are far-ranging debates on the state of the economy, though for some third of the time members have actually talked about taxation. The second reading of the Finance Bill follows and from 1969 the bill has then been divided, clauses and schedules which involve issues of principle being taken on the floor of the House while the more detailed clauses are sent upstairs to a standing committee. Here again the standing orders, which prohibit proposals to raise taxation or to provide relief if this would mean that other taxes would have to be raised, limit debate to general proposals about overall rates of VAT, supertax and corporation tax. The Speaker has to use his power of selection drastically, choosing about a quarter of the amendments put down but the discussions are extensive, the committee stage usually allowing some twenty hours of debate followed by a report stage and third reading.

It is probably in this area that the House of Commons has had most effect in persuading governments to modify their original proposals. Traditionally the Chancellor of the Exchequer relents in relation to some minor aspects of the tax proposals in the Budget. The reasons for this flexibility are that little party capital is made out of these alterations and since the Treasury fears forestalling, it is held that there can be no prior negotiations about tax changes with outside interests. Therefore these negotiations take place during the committee stage of the Finance Bill, so that besides their direct representations to the government, the various pressure groups often brief MPs individually and the Opposition as a whole. The issues are extremely complex and little understood by the public, so no great attention is fastened on these debates and concessions can be made without apparent loss of face. The ministers involved recognize that MPs are being well briefed and though they will not necessarily concede directly they encounter a good case, they will usually move the amendment themselves at a later stage.

The chief weakness of the House of Commons is in matters of taxation; the way in which it has not been able to keep pace with administrative developments is that it has no method of collecting information (other than the briefing from outside pressure groups already mentioned) on the social and other side-effects of a tax or of examining possible future departures in taxation policy. If this work is being done by the government or by outside agencies, it is arguable that the Commons should know what information has been collected and, if no work is being done, members should be in a position to insist that this be remedied. The Heath Government appointed a Select Committee on the Corporation Tax and the subsequent Labour Government appointed one on a wealth tax, but both refused a permanent subcommittee on taxation so that there is still no mechanism by which the House of Commons can know about or participate in investigations of taxation problems or possible developments in policy. In 1983 the Procedure Committee recommended drastic revision of parliamentary procedure on taxation. The annual Budget or Finance Bill now contains a wide mixture of items. Some adjust levels of existing taxes; some involve technical or administrative questions; a few may suggest wholly new forms of taxation. The Procedure Committee wanted these three categories to be kept apart. A new type of tax should have a separate bill. There should be an annual Taxes Management Bill to deal with technical alterations to tax law. The annual Finance Bill could then be greatly simplified and concentrate on changes to the rates of the main tax levies. Such reforms would greatly improve the quality of parliamentary supervision, but there is little sign that the government will accept these ideas.

As it is, Commons' scrutiny of public finance is defective. It is never possible to consider taxation and expenditure together: the rules of procedure insist that they be treated separately. A local authority can discuss whether particular items of expenditure be cut so that the local rate may be reduced. No such debate is possible in the House of Commons. Taxation and estimates are discussed on different days. Then the Commons have no powers in relation to borrowing. No parliamentary sanction is needed for the Treasury to borrow. Again, the Commons do not authorize public expenditure that is not included in the annual estimates, so the nationalized industries, the water authorities, the new towns and many other public bodies escape parliamentary review. Finally, MPs lack information about future economic prospects. The Procedure Committee has urged ministers to issue a 'Green Budget' in the autumn which would review the probable state of national revenue and expenditure in the coming financial year. The aim was to assist the work of the Select Committee on the Treasury and also to promote public discussion of economic affairs. Starting in 1982, an

Autumn Statement has been made, but it is less detailed than the Procedure Committee had intended.

Pressing the government from the floor of the House

Turning from the functions of legislating and authorizing both expenditure and taxation to the other traditional function of pressing the government, the procedures involved have also undergone change but there has been a greater effort made to keep this weapon sharpened and up to the armour it has to pierce. This is because, without some capacity to criticize, Parliament would be quite meaningless and because this capacity is of use to the Opposition, a point appreciated by ministers who may one day return to opposition. Formerly, the methods of control or influence were all concentrated on the floor of the House. Measures could be defeated or amended. Powerful speeches which had an almost visible effect on the House could lead to concessions without any vote being taken. So the great methods of exercising pressure were votes, speeches, the use of procedure to delay a measure and the demand for the relevant documents to be published or for the appointment of a select committee.

With the growth of party voting and the government's virtual monopoly of the timetable, the floor of the House has become much less important. However, attempts have been made to make up for this by the development of other devices such as question time, ten-minute rule bills and the practice of asking wide-ranging questions each Thursday when the business for the following week is announced. Also, since party loyalty is the first consideration when there are party battles and divisions on the floor of the House, the preliminary or supplementary debates within the parties have acquired a slightly greater measure of influence. In addition, there have been attempts to increase the influence of the House in a manner which escapes party divisions, particularly by the creation of more select or 'specialist' committees.

The methods by which MPs attempt to influence ministers from the floor of the House are by their speeches in major debates on government business, by calling for emergency debates under Standing Order No. 9, by the use of ten-minute rule bills, private members' bills and motions, adjournment debates, question time and abstention or cross-voting in divisions. It is hard to say whether speeches have any effect nowadays. A brilliant attack or defence (such as Iain Macleod's assault in 1950 on the then invincible Aneurin Bevan) can affect the career of an MP. A persistent and well-argued case has to be answered and this may eventually have some influence on a minister. But, on the whole, members either support their leaders, make constituency points or obtain some publicity for their rebellious views. But as the vote is a foregone conclusion (in outcome, if not in numbers), debates tend to be formalized occasions and, apart from the opening and the winding-up speeches, are attended only by the handful of MPs who wish to speak. Members who are invited to appear on television or who write newspaper columns can have a far wider public audience and a far greater impact, even on ministers who are fellow members, than those MPs who merely speak in debates.

With the tight government control of the timetable, it is barely possible for the House to switch to debate some urgent topic which is filling the press and current affairs programmes and thus occupying the attention of the public unless the Opposition choose this subcommittee for one of their supply days. Backbenchers can request an emergency debate 'on a definite matter of urgent public importance', but the decision on whether to grant the request rests with the Speaker. A series of restrictive rulings from successive Speakers almost caused this procedure to fall into disuse. However, since a report from the Select Committee on Procedure in 1966 a more liberal view has been taken. There are now about four emergency debates a year.

Private members' bills offer a major opportunity for backbench initiative. Members ballot for the right to introduce bills on Fridays allocated to this purpose. In the normal session, twenty members win a place in the ballot, but since only six Fridays are devoted to second readings of the balloted bills, only six members can be sure of a hearing. A controversial bill normally uses up all the available time on a Friday and other bills due to be considered on that day fail for lack of time. Since the great majority of members, other than ministers, enter the ballot, it follows that the chances of an individual member being successful are very low.

Nevertheless, some private members' bills have been important and become a focus for public attention. In particular, some bills have dealt with moral questions which as 'issues of conscience' fall outside the normal boundaries of party political argument. On such issues each member uses his judgement. There is no official party whipping. The outcome is thus less predictable. Major examples of such legislation are the acts on the abolition of capital punishment (1965), homosexuality (1967), abortion (1967), and divorce (1969) and the subsequent unsuccessful attempts to change the law on abortion and capital punishment.

Private members' motions and adjournment debates have very little effect. Many are simply propagandist and are the result of prompting by the whips, while half-hour adjournment debates, divided equally between the backbencher who raised the issue and the minister, are normally used to press constituency points. In the past, question time has been regarded as an effective method of pressing ministers. It developed simply because the old freedom to raise any issue in a short debate at virtually any time had disappeared. A fixed part of the Order Paper and a fixed time was first set aside for questions in 1869. As the numbers of questions asked grew, the procedures had to be tightened up, the number of oral questions rationed and members were in practice allowed only one supplementary question. In the 1930s and 1940s, question time was largely dominated by backbenchers, and those concerned with the point at issue were left to press their interrogation or were supported by others with a similar grievance. However, at all times questions have been asked for all sorts of reasons, ranging from the sheer desire for information to an attempt to trip up the Prime Minister on a major policy issue. By the late 1960s, members were putting down up to 300 questions a day and the Speaker attempted to reach more oral questions by speeding up the exchanges so as to cover forty to fifty questions in fifty or fifty-five minutes. As a result, it became very much easier for a minister to brush aside any interrogation, since not only was the original purpose of the question soon left behind, but also the frontbenches have tended to intervene to try and score broader party points to which the minister in turn makes the usual party retort.

The other and most publicized method of registering opinion is by abstention or cross-voting. As Philip Norton has shown, party discipline weakened steadily in the years before 1979. A defeat on a specific issue does not lead to the resignation of a government; it is no more than an expression of dissatisfaction designed to force the Cabinet to change its policy. When a government has a clear Commons majority such defeats are rare. In the 1979 Parliament Mrs Thatcher suffered but one major defeat; in December 1982 Right-wing Tories secured a majority of eighteen against plans for new immigration rules. (This revolt had no practical effect as the rules were subsequently passed in similar form.) MPs critical of their leaders are less unwilling to vote against them when the government's majority is assured, e.g. because the Opposition intend to abstain. Thus when Labour is in office, Left-wing Labour MPs can vote for cuts in defence expenditure in the certain knowledge that the Conservatives will not join them. It is also easier to defeat procedural motions rather than substantive ones, the Scotland and Wales (Devolution) Bill being effectively halted when the timetable motion (guillotine) was defeated by twenty-nine in February 1977. The object of these exercises was sometimes to try and get a change of policy, sometimes to indicate alarm should certain lines of policy be carried further and sometimes so that the critics can signal their feelings to sections of the party outside Parliament (Left-wing MPs, for instance, use this method to get support in the annual elections to the National Executive Committee of the party from activists in the constituencies).

The ultimate control over the government is the prospect that the Commons will refuse to pass a vote of confidence. Such an event must force either the resignation of the government or an immediate general election. It can only happen after a disastrous split in the majority party or when no party has a majority. In Britain, with its strong two-party system, a government defeat on a vote of confidence has long been regarded as a theoretical possibility rather than practical politics. However, in March 1979, the Callaghan Labour Government lost a vote of confidence by a majority of one and a general election followed. Previously this had not happened since 1924. The conditions in 1979 were exceptional. The government was elected in October 1974 with an overall majority of three. This majority disappeared by 1977 due to adverse by-election results. The government had been sustained in office from March 1977 to the autumn of 1978 by an agreement with the Liberals. Thereafter it lingered on with uneasy support from the Nationalist members who needed a Cabinet sympathetic to Scottish and Welsh devolution. When the referenda failed to produce the necessary 40 per cent vote in favour of devolution the Nationalists lost hope and saw no point in keeping the government.

The vote of no confidence was a final humiliation for a government that had been clinging to office. Had the Prime Minister called a general election in October 1978, as was expected, the Commons would not have had the opportunity to inflict a spectacular dismissal. Indeed, the lesson of 1979 may be that a government which cannot be certain of winning a vote of confidence in the Commons would be well advised to call an election. From the point of view of a Cabinet, if an election is inevitable, it is far better to hold it without a preliminary defeat in the Commons which gravely damages the prestige of the government and raises the morale of its opponents.

Pressing the government: upstairs and informal methods

Some writers have argued that since the parties became so strong, it was inevitable that the influence formerly exercised on the floor of the House should decline but that much the same influence is still exercised by the meetings of the parliamentary parties. On the Labour side, there is the Parliamentary Labour Party (PLP) which includes all ministers and Labour peers. It elects a chairman and a Liaison Committee. When the party is in opposition it also elects the Parliamentary Committee or Shadow Cabinet. The PLP normally has a meeting every Wednesday morning to discuss general issues and a meeting at 6 p.m. every Thursday to consider the next week's business. In addition it is divided into regional and subject groups which organize meetings on a wide variety of topics. Among the Conservatives, the equivalent is the 1922 Committee (since it was founded in that year) but it has its weekly meetings without ministers or shadow ministers present, dealing with the party leaders through an elected chairman. The Conservatives also have area and subject committees.

After the Labour victory in 1966 there was an attempt by Labour Left-wing MPs to push the government into certain policy changes, notably the abandonment of defence commitments east of Suez, by debates and votes at PLP meetings. The Prime Minister, Mr Wilson, reacted by saying that such votes were not customary; however, his presence and that of his senior colleagues on important occasions showed that importance was attached to these gatherings. The Labour Government also took the precaution of sending a special, private 'whip' or request to attend to all the 111 Labour ministers in both Houses. If most of what was sometimes called 'the payroll vote' attended, the critics would have to carry seven-tenths of the backbenchers and if this had ever happened, the press would have treated it as a total collapse of confidence in the government. In the early 1970s it became the practice to tell the press what had happened and whether any votes were taken.

With this publicity, the prestige of the leadership was clearly at stake. If this occurs in government, the Prime Minister can evoke the sentiment of party loyalty with much the same effect as when he faces opposition on the floor of the House.

In the 1922 Committee, there are no votes and less divisiveness but the opinions, as conveyed by the chairman to the party leader, may have more influence than the votes and debates in the Parliamentary Labour Party. This is certainly true of the subject groups. When the Conservatives are in opposition, the frontbench spokesman on each subject area is also chairman of the parallel party group, thus providing a direct channel of communication between backbench opinion and the Shadow Cabinet. Naturally, when Conservatives are in office, the opportunities for meetings between backbenchers and party leaders are more restricted. They also vary greatly depending upon the attitudes adopted by individual ministers. Mr Whitelaw when Home Secretary had weekly meetings with the officers of the Conservative Home Affairs group: Mr Pym, when Defence Secretary, had no meetings at all with the officers of the defence committee. Mrs Thatcher as Prime Minister has occasional meetings with committee officers, taking committees one at a time. Conservative party groups are better organized, better supported and are rather more effective than their Labour counterparts. Indeed, in 1976 the PLP set up a committee of eight backbenchers to study how consultation with the Labour Government could be improved. The report was highly critical of the backbench committees and noted that meetings frequently overlap or are cancelled and rearranged and that attendance was low. Although attempts were made to streamline the structure and to have fewer and better organized meetings, the position has scarcely improved. When Labour is in opposition the chairman of a subject committee is not the relevant shadow minister; instead the chairman is elected and the election is often another chance for conflict between opposing opinions among Labour MPs.

Besides these formal structures, each party has extensive methods of contacting its own leaders including deputations to the Prime Minister, casual conversation, the impression conveyed by the 'sense of the House' and messages relayed by Parliamentary Private Secretaries and by the whips. There is no doubt that the reactions of the parties do have some effect on the leaders, though probably this is a little more true in the case of the Conservative

Party. One reason for the difference is that the Conservatives are less committed to predetermined lines of action and are therefore more open to any positive case put by their backbenchers. Also Labour members have established positions on a Left-to-Right spectrum of opinion and more often put their own view than transmit the reactions of voters. As has been said above, the Prime Minister seldom worries if the Opposition is opposing – his fear is of losing those voters who usually support his party. If Labour MPs are known to have views which are not necessarily a reflection of the opinions of Labour voters, less attention can be paid to them. But Conservative MPs are much less easy to classify, they have fewer dogmatic positions to maintain and their criticisms of their own party's policies are therefore much less easy to dismiss in this way. If a Conservative MP X or Y, who has not been known to take ideological stands, approaches a minister or a whip and expresses grave doubts, this is viewed with considerable worry and it is assumed that these objections have been put forward by the MP only after the points have been put to him with equal or greater force in his constituency. For these reasons, the Conservatives are a little more responsive to widespread expressions of serious doubt on their own backbenches.

Standing and select committees

In addition to the activities of members on the floor of the House or in the parties, there has been an attempt to restore or increase the influence of the Commons by adopting new procedures, most of which involve the development of a new committee system. The reformers, until 1964 mainly outside the House, argued that since the public wished to vote governments in or out of power and since every serious vote had become an issue of confidence, it was no longer possible to restore freer voting in order to improve the independence and power of the House. But this did not mean that it was impossible for the House of Commons to exercise some influence. Here the problem was not so much party loyalty as the fact that parliamentary procedures no longer fitted into the timescale or permitted an understanding of current administration. The reformers argued that since departments built up their philosophies over a period of time and since new measures took a considerable period to negotiate, these processes should be opened up so that the informed public could make its reactions clear while principles were still being settled. For this purpose, they advised the creation of permanent or standing select (specialist) committees with powers of interrogation and investigation to watch over each area of government action. These select committees were not intended to be tied to producing particular reports, but were to collect information and let the House and the public know what disputes were going on and what agreements were being reached within ministries, between them and between civil servants and outside pressure groups. If this was done, the reformers argued, it would give the sections of the public concerned with these areas of policy a chance to react, and it would once again be worth the pressure groups' while to explain their points to the Commons before the precise details of forthcoming legislation were settled.

It is important to be clear about the distinction between these committees and the standing committees of the House (which include the Scottish and Welsh grand committees). The latter are legislative committees set up to take the committee stage of a bill and they have to reflect the division of party strength that exists on the floor of the House. With a chairman, two frontbenches and whips, these committees are microcosms of the Commons with no special facilities for fact-finding or for doing anything other than what would normally be done if the bill had been kept on the floor of the House. As far as government backbenchers are concerned, their instructions are to be present at these committees but it is hoped that they will be silent as each speech only adds that much longer to the proceedings. Opposition backbenchers, as in the House, make their general case against the bill. The select committees, in contrast, were to be investigating bodies where policy issues were not of first importance, the principal task being to find out what was happening inside the various government departments, to inform the House and the public, thus bringing public opinion to bear at an earlier stage while policy was still relatively fluid.

This type of committee was modelled on the Select Committee on Nationalized Industries which had been set up in 1956 because it was felt that Parliament could not adequately control the range of corporations it had created. The experiment, which had caused some worry, particularly on the Labour benches, was entirely successful. All shades of political opinion on the committee worked well together elucidating the policies of the industries. In 1966 the Labour Government agreed to establish two similar committees to examine specific areas of policy-making and administration – science and technology and agriculture. Later, further select committees were established on education, Scottish affairs, overseas aid and race relations; the Agriculture Committee was closed down.

These committees had a chequered history between 1966 and 1970. Mr Crossman had originally told the backbench parliamentary reform group of Labour MPs that the committees were to be permanent (so that they could indeed be 'specialist' committees) and two more would be added each session till all the main areas of governmental activity were covered. But he had only been able to get the proposal through the Cabinet on an experimental basis, with the life of each committee to be reviewed at the end of each session. Towards the end of the Labour Government the entire experiment was being reviewed; some ministers and civil servants had found the experience troublesome. The 1970 Conservative Government replaced the Estimates Committee by an Expenditure Committee with broader terms of reference; it had forty-five members and worked through subcommittees specializing in different areas of government activity. The Conservatives seemed rather more favourable to the prospect of scrutiny by backbench committees, perhaps because they felt that such a challenge would help to restrain public expenditure. The 1974 Labour Government created a further select committee to review European legislation with the task of recommending which EEC measures should be debated on the floor of the House.

In 1978 the Select Committee on Procedure urged the creation of a series of select committees specialized by function as a permanent feature of parliamentary life. A year later the essence of this proposal was accepted by the new Conservative Government. Twelve committees were established for agriculture, defence, education, employment, energy, environment, foreign affairs, home affairs, industry and trade, social services, transport, and the Treasury and the civil service. Two further regional committees were continued for Scotland and Wales but the committees for Europe, science and technology, race relations and the nationalized industries were discontinued as they would duplicate aspects of the work of the new committees.

Those who have urged wider activity by select committees were faced with some uncertainty about how MPs would react to this development. For the system to succeed, two conditions had to be satisfied. First, MPs had to be willing to devote considerable time and energy to the new committees. Second, it was vital that the proceedings should be conducted largely on non-party lines; if the committees merely offered another forum for party battle, then the government side would always win, the committees would have no effect whatever and no good purpose would be served. The slow evolution of select committee work has helped to ensure that both these obstacles have been surmounted. The non-party tradition of the Public Accounts Committee extended to the Nationalized Industries Committee, the committees established in the 1960s and the Expenditure Committee. With occasional exceptions the new departmental committees have worked in a parliamentary spirit as opposed to a party spirit. The non-party element is emphasized by the fact that not all the chairmen are government supporters. Committee energy can be shown by the extent of their activities in the parliamentary session 1981–2: the departmental select committees produced thirty-eight reports and met on average thirty-one times in the year. Members' attendance record was 73 per cent. However, the attendance figure is misleading. With three exceptions, these new committees are not allowed to form subcommittees, but some have done so on a *de facto* basis. This arrangement enables a committee to pursue two inquiries simultaneously; it is agreed that only certain members will go to certain meetings and that these will be concerned with a particular topic. In this way the scope of a committee's work is increased while limiting the amount of extra work imposed on MPs. But the attendance record ignores the informal agreement that some MPs should not go to some meetings.

The committees do not go about their work in a uniform way. There is no reason why they should. They appoint advisers to assist them to help with the choice of witnesses, the preparation of questions to put to witnesses and perhaps to help the clerk of the committee to frame the draft of a report. Some committees make more extensive use of advisers than others. Some committee clerks come to have an important role, especially when they work with the same committee and the same chairman for some time. Some of the inquiries amass substantial memoranda and take oral evidence from a wide range of witnesses, ministers, civil servants and other people thought to be able to make useful contributions. Such endeavour can last several months. Other inquiries deal with matters of immediate concern and will be completed in a couple of weeks. It is not possible to say whether a substantial report is more likely to make an impact than a slim report. It follows that the subject matter of these inquiries varies considerably. A committee may look at the rationale underlying a major aspect of policy, e.g. the investigation of the Treasury Committee into Monetary Policy. Alternatively, the subject may be much more limited and not be a problem for government, e.g. the report on the BBC and promenade concerts.

Without question, these select committees constitute a major development of the work of the House of Commons. Two questions emerge. What is the extent of their influence? And what is their effect, if any, on the atmosphere of Parliament?

Of course, it is impossible to measure influence in a precise manner. Government departments always respond to committee reports, but the form of the response varies. Major inquiries elicit a formal reply issued as a parliamentary paper available to all MPs and the mass media. On lesser occasions the reply will appear as an answer to a 'planted' parliamentary question or be simply a letter to the chairman of a committee. Often the contents of a reply are non-committal; it is said that points made by a committee are noted or that certain matters will be kept under review. Possibly a subsequent review stimulates action that would not have taken place but for the committee's initial probing. Even if the committees do not persuade ministers and civil servants to change what they do, their very existence makes Whitehall aware that any aspect of policy or administration may become the subject of more searching scrutiny than would be possible in the Commons' chamber. Another important element is the chairman: the chairman of the Treasury Committee is Mr du Cann and his stature, experience and ability have added greatly to the weight of this committee. Perhaps the clearest example of success has been that the Home Office was persuaded to repeal the 'sus' law by a critical report from the Home Affairs Committee. On other occasions committees have been generally in support of government action but have urged that it be undertaken more vigorously: the Defence Committee has been critical of the Ministry of Defence when it has spent less than the sums provided in the annual estimates. To be effective, a committee must be unanimous or virtually so; on the fairly rare occasions a committee divides on party lines, it is certain that its work will be ignored.

How far do select committees influence the general atmosphere in the House of Commons? Again, no exact answer can be given. But the non-party style of select committees involves more MPs than ever before. The number is now in excess of 300. Besides the fourteen committees discussed above that are concerned with the policy and administration of particular departments, there are further select committees on public accounts, privilege, statutory instruments, the Parliamentary Commissioner for Administration and others besides. Over half the backbenchers are regularly involved with select committee activity. They thus become used to working together with political opponents and often find common ground. It is not uncommon for a government backbencher to support his select committee as opposed to a ministerial view. So it is arguable that the select committees promote independence of mind among MPs and make them less willing to vote automatically as the whips would like. Certainly, as Philip Norton has shown, since 1970 MPs have been increasingly ready to go against the party line. Some party leaders and whips dislike the new select committees because they encourage an independent approach, but the system is now quite strongly established and is likely to continue. Yet it does not follow that there will be a constant growth of non-partisan tendencies among MPs, for much depends on the type of new MPs that will arrive at Westminster. If the newcomers have fairly extreme opinions, some towards the Right and some towards the Left, it will be more difficult for the select committee atmosphere to mould them into a team upholding the legislature as opposed to the government of the day.

Televising the House of Commons

One reform or change in Parliament's relations with the public was put to the House on a free vote. This proposal came originally from the First Report of the Select Committee on Broadcasting under Tom Driberg (later Lord Barking) that the proceedings of the House should be televised and the tape made available to the various television networks. The proposal for an experimental period was debated on 24 November 1966, and rejected by one vote, to the surprise of most observers. Subsequently the issue has been raised on a number of occasions. Until January 1980 the majority always rejected the admission of cameras. Then a ten-minute rule bill promoted by Austin Mitchell (the Labour MP for

Grimsby) produced a tie with 201 votes in favour and 201 against the first reading. The Chair then gave a casting vote in favour, following the tradition of the Commons that a casting vote shall always be used in a way that will allow an issue to be raised again. In fact, Mitchell's bill made no further progress as there is never any time available for opposed ten-minute rule bills. In April 1983 the same fate befell a similar bill initially accepted by 153 votes to 138.

Arguments for and against television can be summarized briefly. Those in favour assert that democratic government should be conducted with as much publicity as possible: the more electors are aware of the actions of their elected representatives the better. Opponents of television claim that the innovation would encourage exhibitionism and alter the intimate character of debate, elevate the stature of the frontbench performers and depress that of the less frequent backbench participants even further.

Since 1978 the Commons debates have been recorded on tape and so can be reproduced in extract on radio and television. A few very important speeches, such as the Chancellor's Budget speech, have recently been broadcast live. Initially the Prime Minister's questions were also broadcast live. Yet this caused adverse comment. Parliamentary question time is frequently noisy; the interchanges are more concerned to make debating points than to add to public enlightenment. Listeners were not pleased to learn that the Commons sometimes sounded like an undergraduate debating society and so these broadcasts of question time ceased. It was widely thought that the acceptance of sound broadcasting would soon weaken opposition to television. But to show pictures of major scenes in the chamber could well revive criticism of parliamentary manners. Further, now the debates are recorded, it cannot be said that the Commons attempt to remain aloof. Whether the tapes are used depends upon the broadcasting and television producers. Television could add to the drama but would not, in essence, increase public information.

Some reformers have attached considerable importance to televising the House and regretted its defeat. But in fact the degree of public attention paid to Parliament over the past century has varied directly with the institution's powers. If debates and votes in the Commons can be seen to affect British life, they will once again be the subject of great interest. While television programmes picking out the highlights in the House would fascinate the minority among the public who are deeply concerned about politics, it is unlikely to alter the general standing of the House of Commons with a public whose interest is not in how the machine works but in what actual effect it has on their lives.

The House of Lords

Almost all democratic states have a legislature composed of two Houses. The British second chamber is unique in that the majority of its members belong to it through hereditary right or accident of birth. Since the Life Peerages Act 1958 the hereditary nobility have been reinforced by a trickle of people, usually fairly elderly, whose titles do not pass on to their heirs. These life peers now play a major role in the day-to-day work of the Lords; indeed, their presence is essential for the great majority of hereditary peers rarely, if ever, attend. In practice, then, the Lords is tending to become a nominated chamber. The patronage is in the hands of the Prime Minister who may from time to time invite leaders of opposition parties to propose names. Thus many life peers are former members of the Commons.

The formal powers of the Lords are slight. They can delay a bill for a year by forcing the Commons to pass the rejected bill a second time in the following session. A 'money bill', one dealing essentially with financial matters, can be delayed only for a month. However, the Lords still have a complete veto over legislation designed to extend the life of Parliament beyond five years and over statutory instruments, an apparently minor point which was brought sharply to public attention when the Lords rejected the Southern Rhodesia (Sanctions) Order in 1968. It is impossible to deny that the Lords do useful work by clearing up minor points on government legislation and often having the major discussions on non-controversial measures and private bills. The Lords are also active in their scrutiny of EEC business. They hold debates on a wide variety of topics, some of which are squeezed out of the Commons programme through lack of time.

The objection to the House of Lords is that it is not a democratic institution. It imparts a bias into the constitution as there is a permanent Conservative majority. The Lords are more likely to interfere with Labour legislation than Conservative legislation. Admittedly the Lords have been cautious and, apart from Rhodesian sanctions, have avoided a head-on clash with Labour when a Labour Government had a clear majority in the Commons. There are also two recent examples where the Lords have blocked particular clauses of Conservative measures. In 1980 a provision in the Education Bill was defeated which would have given local authorities the power to charge for transport to school. In 1983 the Lords deleted a clause in the Housing and Building Construction Bill which gave tenants of charitable housing associations the right to buy their homes.

In 1967 there was an all-party conference on the future of the Lords, the objectives being to retain these useful minor functions while ending the hereditary basis of membership, the built-in Conservative majority and the delaying powers of the Lords. The solution proposed was a two-tier system by which government-appointed peers would have the right to vote, hereditary peers being allowed to speak but not vote while the delaying powers on legislation would be cut to six months. Though agreed between the parties, these proposals were bitterly attacked by some Conservatives as destroying the traditional upper House and by a few Labour members as creating a large new area of patronage for the Prime Minister. As a result, the measure was abandoned.

Labour's 1983 election manifesto pledged the party to 'take action to abolish the undemocratic House of Lords as quickly as possible and, as an interim measure, introduce a bill in the first session of Parliament to remove its legislative powers – with the exception of those that relate to the life of a parliament'. The final phrase seems to recognize that the Lords have some merit as a residual guardian of the constitution. If there were no House of Lords, there would be nothing to prevent a majority in the Commons from postponing an election by extending Parliament beyond the limit of five years. The Lords serve to protect the electorate against the possibility that the Commons might prevent the electorate from using their present rights. The Labour Party has not yet decided how it can stop a single-chamber Parliament from abusing its position. There is another problem about getting rid of the Lords. They perform minor but useful functions: how far can these be absorbed into an already overcrowded schedule in the Commons? One way out of the dilemma would be to change the composition of the second chamber by having it elected in some form. But the Labour Party dislikes this prospect, and avoided it in 1967 because of the fear that an elected House might feel entitled to challenge the supremacy of the Commons. Thus an elected second chamber could be a much stronger barrier to the achievement of socialist ideals than the present House of Lords.

The influence of Parliament

It is hard to estimate the effect of Parliament on the other sectors of British government, though its role is best understood by regarding it not primarily as a check on the executive but as one of the institutions through which the government operates. Broadly speaking, the support of Parliament for any government with more than a nominal majority can be taken for granted and ministers come to the House to explain their policies, put through their bills, counter opposition propaganda and keep their supporters happy. For most members, supporting their frontbench is normal and the occasions when they rebel are rare and cause them some heart-searching.

It is impossible to be precise over how much influence Parliament exercises over government policy. There may be cases where there is parliamentary disquiet over a ministerial proposal and then the minister has a change of mind. Whether pressure from MPs was crucial can be a matter of doubt. Ministers may claim that the final decision was influenced by some other considerations than the objections of MPs. Yet there are some cases where it is clear that the views in the Commons were decisive. In 1969 the Labour Government was forced to abandon both the bill to reform the House of Lords and its projected Industrial Relations Bill, while in 1980 the Thatcher Government limited economic sanctions against Iran as a result of dissatisfaction in the Commons.

Of course, a Cabinet that does not have an effective majority in the Commons is in a quite different position. The situation which existed between March 1977 and March 1979 was unique in modern British politics. During this period it was impossible for the government to introduce legislation that was unacceptable to both Liberals and the Nationalists. Government backbenchers effectively destroyed the Devolution Bill by insisting on the 40 per cent rule in the devolution referendum. The 1978 Budget proposals were amended. Government defeats ceased to be unusual. Yet the government survived until March 1979 because it always managed to win any vote of confidence.

Party discipline in the Commons is less severe than it was. The party 'whip' has not been formally withdrawn from an MP for over twenty years. In the 1960s and 1970s abstention and cross voting became less unusual. But the truly independently-minded MPs are the sort of Conservatives who turned out Neville Chamberlain in 1940 and whose mutterings in the Smoking Room could affect Conservative premiers, and the kind of Labour members with the outside income or the zeal who saw through the European Communities Bill. But this kind of MP is becoming relatively rare. The Conservative local associations are turning increasingly to young men of professional or business backgrounds for whom Parliament is a career, while Labour Party ranks are being filled by further education lecturers, men and women with professional training with much the same outlook on politics as a profession as the younger Conservatives. For these MPs there is both more restiveness over the aimlessness of life on the backbenches and a stronger motive for not annoying the leader on whose patronage a ministerial career depends. In addition to these changes within the Commons, the public are now beginning to appreciate the small extent of Parliament's influence and its prestige is falling. The alienation of groups among the younger voters has perhaps received too much publicity but it is an attitude which is shared to some degree by other sections of the community. This attitude, together with the frustrations experienced by the abler and younger men coming into politics, may in time lead to a decline in the quality of political leadership available, at least in comparison with the capacity of those setting the pace in other sectors of British life.

When it is argued that because the British Parliament is now under the control of the executive, nothing should or can be done to alter the situation, this denies the capacity of politicians and the public to remedy defects in their own institutions. In fact, the chief restriction on British politicians is imposed by their own and the community's view of what is proper and desirable and if the former, supported by some public opinion, are convinced that changes are needed, there is every reason to think that effective reforms can be carried through. Nothing stops a British government removing or reducing the Opposition's freedom to attack the government for roughly a third of the parliamentary session except the belief that this would be undesirable and would hamper both parties in the long run. Similarly no party today would, without some adequate and agreed substitute, abolish the Public Accounts Committee and the right of the Opposition to nominate its chairman. If there was a widespread desire to alter the degree of influence exercised by Parliament and to make the life of a backbench MP an attractive prospect in its own right for public-spirited men and if this could only be done by the acceptance of some new countervailing powers, this would be no harder for successive governments than, for example, accepting the limitations involved in joining the Common Market. But it could only be done if there was this general agreement about the direction in which democracy in Britain should develop and about the role which Parliament should play.

11 Governing through the Whitehall departments

A highly centralized country

In addition to Parliament, the other principal agency or institution through which the political leadership operates is the administrative machine. Though local government is important in Britain and there is some decentralized administration, the chief impetus and the major decisions all come from the central departments of state based in Whitehall. Britain has always been a highly centralized country. Wales was conquered and subjected in the middle ages, Scotland's parliament and administration were absorbed in 1707, Ireland lost all but local administration in 1801 and the British upper classes reacted in horror at the prospect not of Irish independence but of an element of internal self-government when it was proposed by Gladstone in 1886. The intensity of their feeling was due not just to fear that the landed interest might suffer but to the affront caused to a governing class centred on London and the Home Counties by the notion that those living in the provinces might prefer a degree of local autonomy. It has remained the accepted practice that all important governmental decisions emanate from the central departments in Whitehall, a practice which is of great help to the political leadership as it collects all the levers of policy-making and administrative control into one, compact, signal box.

The convention of ministerial responsibility

The structure and methods of the Whitehall departments, the system of organization and the practices and outlook of the civil servants are determined by a number of historic decisions and constitutional conventions governing the relations between the administration and the other institutions. Of these, by far the most important is the convention of ministerial responsibility. Whitehall departments are pyramids whose apex is the minister and the whole governmental machine is a larger, all-inclusive pyramid with the Prime Minister at the top. Everything focuses on this control from above. An instruction from the minister is the final word within a department, an excerpt from the Cabinet minutes conveying the decision of a committee of the Cabinet or of the full Cabinet outranks all other orders and is the source of direction for all the policy decisions taken lower down in the government.

The various departments' relations with Parliament, with outside bodies and professions are all governed by the same consideration that the minister is in charge and that he can be attacked (in or out of Parliament) for anything that happens or fails to happen in his department. So civil servants have to establish that negotiations with outside bodies will be in secret, or else they will not be able to explain and consider alternatives in case the arguments they deploy in favour of an option, not eventually chosen, may later be quoted against their minister. For the same reason, civil servants above a certain level cannot take an overt or active part in politics in case it could be said that their opinions influenced the minister.

This convention of ministerial responsibility also enforces a vertical organization on the departments. Everything that is done must be subordinate to some official who reports up to a member of the administrative class, who is under an assistant secretary who then puts the matter to the permanent secretary, he being the adviser to the minister. It is not possible to take separate sectors of administration, appoint an official to be in charge, give him a budget and let him get on with it, because if anything is raised in the press or in the House about this sector, there must be an immediate channel of communications to and instructions from the top. For these reasons also, it is hard to fit in any check points at intermediate levels in the hierarchy.

Somewhat the same difficulty arises when outside bodies wish to deal with the civil service as such. For instance, when select or specialist committees of the House of Commons have called officials as witnesses, the latter have often been uncomfortable. The older civil servants accept that they can put facts before parliamentary committees and explain the grounds on which ministers took certain decisions but, if asked for their own opinion, they feel they must decline in case their arguments are later used against the minister. Younger officials have tended to feel freer to express opinions and when the Association of First Division officers gave evidence to the Fulton Committee, it noted that officials called before parliamentary committees 'are excused from answering questions on matters of policy, but this does not, in practice, exclude very much'. However, the doubts as to just how far the old practices can be put aside do remain. They arose over the work of the parliamentary commissioner (the ombudsman) when he found that there had been maladministration in certain Foreign Office decisions about compensation due to men kept in Sachsenhausen concentration camp. The Foreign Secretary, Mr George Brown, denied any error but changed the decision to which objection had been taken. The Committee of the House appointed to review the work of the parliamentary commissioner wished to interview the official who had taken the decision in order to find out what the Foreign Office had done to prevent such errors recurring. The Foreign Office refused to allow the official to give evidence and sent the Attorney General who said that to call anyone below the rank of permanent secretary was a breach of the collective responsibility of the department. The committee refused to accept this but the dispute was not resolved and no further case of this kind has as yet arisen. In a milder way, the doctrine of ministerial responsibility also inhibits the mass of able and highly trained and experienced men in the civil service from contributing fully in their own professional associations and academic conferences, in case their opinions or comments on their own work or methods might catch a headline or embarrass a minister. The doctrine of ministerial responsibility is thus a major explanation for the isolation of Whitehall departments, for their inward-looking nature and for their constant emphasis on keeping within the policy bounds set from above.

It may be wondered why this doctrine is retained, but it has great advantages for both the major groups involved – the ministers and the civil servants. The original point of the doctrine has disappeared. It was devised in the mid nineteenth century, at a time when the Commons had considerable direct power over the government, the purpose being to ensure that the Commons could exercise control over officials by pressing the appropriate minister. Then, this method was effective, forcing ministers to watch over everything that might cause trouble and forcing officials to be punctilious about every major step they took. Since the decline of the Commons' direct powers to censure ministers, they have not felt obliged to resign if faults are revealed in their departments. It is true that Sir Thomas Dugdale insisted on resigning over the Crichel

Down case in 1954 but he was not pressed to go. Certainly, it is ridiculous to expect a minister to resign because a civil servant makes a mistake, even if the error be very serious. Government departments are now so vast that it is unrealistic to expect a minister to know all about matters of administration. If a minister is in trouble over policy the tendency is for the Cabinet to rally round in support, at least in the short term. Ministerial resignations were out of fashion until 1982 when there was a sudden change. Mr Nicholas Fairbairn, the Solicitor General for Scotland, left office in a hurry after widespread criticism of his comments about a rape case. The Falklands crisis led to the resignation of three Foreign Office ministers, Lord Carrington, Mr Humphrey Atkins and Mr Richard Luce. In the Scottish rape case it was the personal action of the minister that caused indignation. In the Foreign Office case it was felt that the responsible ministers should have been more alert to the possibility of aggression by Argentina. So while the practice of resignation has been re-established, it is still true that ministers are not expected to suffer for the shortcomings of their staff.

Thus ministers no longer feel that the doctrine exposes them to special risks in the House but, by confining all the advice of the departments to ministers, it does ensure that they are so much better informed and briefed than their critics. As a result, the public, the press and MPs are often starved of the material with which to make up a counter-argument. The ministries are staffed by very able men who have spent years on these particular issues. They can put the case for the minister's decision, copy his style, anticipate hostile points and leave him feeling at a great advantage in any conflict. If the doctrine was broken and officials could explain their views freely in public, then ministers would have the much more formidable task of making their case against men who were seized of the key counterpoints and who knew that their arguments were accepted by many in the ministry. It is clear why ministers, who lose only a little and gain a great deal from the doctrine, should want to keep it going.

For civil servants, the advantage is that the doctrine leaves them utterly free of any repercussions arising from their advice and thus greatly adds to their freedom and power. Consider, for instance, the position of the men in the Ministry of Employment and Productivity who advised Mrs Barbara Castle to press for sanctions against unofficial strikers in 1969. If their names were known, large sections of the Labour Party would be baying for their blood. Under the working of the doctrine, they can tell the minister what they believe to be proper and still meet the TUC on good terms. The experience of a recent Governor of the Bank of England, Sir Leslie O'Brien, a quasi-civil servant, is a constant reminder to senior Treasury officials of their good fortune. When Sir Leslie commented publicly on policy in a manner disliked by the Left in the Labour Party, there were immediate motions calling for his removal, yet there is no doubt that some Treasury chiefs said much the same with no unpleasant repercussions. In addition, the doctrine reinforces civil servants' positions as 'insiders'. They know what is going on, their advice is the best informed and they know how difficult it is for ministers to rely on outsiders for other opinions. The outsiders (such as Professor Kaldor or Lord Balogh) are named and known and are therefore the targets for just the kind of attacks which the civil servants escape.

Thus ministerial responsibility is the main principle moulding the structure and outlook of the senior civil service and it is retained because it does much to reinforce the special position and powers both of ministers and of civil servants.

The Northcote–Trevelyan principles

The second main body of principles governing the civil service derives from the Northcote–Trevelyan Report of 1853 which was put into full operation in 1870. The first idea on which the report was based was that the home civil service (the foreign and colonial services were not included) should be organized as a single body of men with a common system of recruitment based on academic ability. This latter task was allotted to a semi-independent Civil Service Commission which would conduct examinations for men in two age groups, 19 to 25 and 17 to 21, the one on the level of final examinations at a university, the other at approximately school-leaving standards. Once recruited on this basis, the candidates would be allocated to departments. Though promotion from one class to another was possible, it was across a wide gulf as the distinction between classes was held to be the distinction between mechanical and intellectual activity. It was accepted that some specialists and a class of supplementary clerks would be needed, but they did not fit into the overall scheme.

This system has remained in broad outline. The administrative grade, recruited from top-quality university graduates, prepares policy advice for ministers. The executive grade undertakes a wide range of management tasks and is drawn from both graduates and the more able school-leavers. The clerical grade undertakes routine duties. The unity of the service has been encouraged by movement from one department to another. Training has been 'in-service' rather than before entry, and the highest posts have not gone to specialists but to broadly educated men and women who have specialized only in administration. Thus administrators have tended to live a relatively insulated life of their own, lacking close connections with those doing similar work for private organizations or in professional life. As a result the service has produced administrators with a distinctive approach and outlook. Accustomed to the doctrine of ministerial responsibility, used to the idea that they are the repository of the collective wisdom and experience of their departments, accepting that they must handle outside agencies and pressure groups as well as the vagaries of the politicians and the press, they operate with caution but also with great confidence knowing that they alone are in possession of all the facts and that without their activity the whole machine would come to a halt.

Departmental organization and the Treasury

Besides ministerial responsibility and the Northcote–Trevelyan principles, a third determining feature has been the organization of the service on a departmental basis. Being highly centralized, the British system has not been to have powerful centres outside London from which groups of services can be conducted for that area, but to administer each of the important functions of government from Whitehall for the whole of the country. The exceptions are Northern Ireland, Scotland and Wales, experiments with regional offices and controllers in England having done nothing to alter the fact that both policy and much of the details of administration are still controlled from Whitehall.

The first of the special cases mentioned is Northern Ireland which (until the imposition of direct rule in 1972) had a devolved system based on the 1920 Government of Ireland Act. This act allocated agriculture, health, home affairs, education, housing, roads and indeed all internal administration to a local executive and civil service responsible to the Stormont parliament. In Scotland and Wales, there are regional ministries under a secretary of state, the

Scottish Office having five departments (education, development, home and health, agriculture and fisheries, and economic planning) while the Welsh Office has housing, roads, local government and certain aspects of development.

England is administered by centrally-based functional departments, while such functions as the supervision of employment and productivity, the work of the Departments of the Environment and of Health and Social Security also extend over Scotland and Wales. Given this pattern, the task of controlling and co-ordinating these departments at the centre is of major importance. This is undertaken by the Cabinet, the Cabinet Secretariat and then by the Treasury.

The central role of the Treasury dates from a minute of 1860, when it was decided that all funds for the government should be released by the Treasury to the various ministries. These ministries had to ask permission for all major items of expenditure within the total sum voted and had, at the end of the year, to account to the Treasury for the detailed expenditure of their allocation of funds. The permanent secretary in each ministry became the accounting officer responsible to the Treasury for the expenditure of the money allocated to his ministry. Besides this control through the finances of a department, new activity usually means more staff and this requires the sanction of the Treasury. The constant oversight of the Treasury is now maintained not only by its control of the normal disbursement of money, but by the fact that each year forward estimates of public expenditure have to be put by the departments before the Treasury and Public Expenditure Scrutiny Committee and agreed upon there. The Treasury employs sections which monitor the expenditure of the various departments and go over their estimates, the role of the Treasury being to insist on certain overall policies and ceilings on expenditure while the spending departments tend to argue in favour of certain policy objectives or programmes, hoping that if these are accepted, the necessary funds will be forthcoming. The Treasury never likes to get involved in considerations of which aspects of departmental policy are more or less desirable, as the only result would be to commit the Treasury to the financial consequences. Yet in fixing the allocations between departments, they have to take into consideration the policy of the government and what each department proposes to do with the money.

Criticisms of the civil service: its relation with ministers

Given this framework and governing principles, the civil service has operated without many upheavals over the last century. Recently, however, there has been some criticism and some arguments about its structure, in addition to the more long-standing discussion of how far ministers can dominate their departments and how far civil service practices and attitudes have proved too much for the politicians. The criticisms have fallen into certain categories, one general line being that the service has failed to adopt modern methods of management, that it has been slow in understanding the use of statistical information and of specialized knowledge of the social services, and that it does not think ahead enough or organize its planning on a sufficiently systematic basis, in part because officials spend too much time on routine departmental work. A second theme has been a particular criticism of the Treasury and of its economic policies; in particular that too much emphasis has been placed on the balance of payments or prevention of inflation, while the need for economic growth was neglected. There have also been attacks on the 'generalist' or 'all-rounder' in administration, combined with the argument that the civil service is too isolated, complacent and insulated from outside pressures.

The post-war governments, both Labour and Conservative, have shown that a minister with coherent, workable policies and reasonable energy and capacity can get loyal co-operation from his or her civil servants. Moreover, for such a minister, the ideal is not a department without a policy or officials without positive ideas as to what needs to be done. If there is a vacuum of this kind, far from the field being clear for political decision-taking (as Ramsay Muir suggests), the minister is lost because there are no properly prepared and documented alternatives from which he can choose. On the other hand, from the civil servant's angle what is wanted as a minister is not a malleable man who can be moulded or pushed into particular views. The officials want and respect a minister who can pick up a problem quickly, select from among the alternatives the line most in accord with the outlook of his Cabinet colleagues and his party, who is courageous and can win any necessary battles with other departments outside or inside the Cabinet, and who can explain the policy well in public. Above all, they want a minister who, having taken a decision, does not constantly alter it every time some pressure is brought to bear.

But though the relationship, when satisfactory, is relatively straightforward and works as would be expected when any large organization is taken over by a new and competent managing director, there are other cases where problems can arise. For instance, Cabinets are not chosen on grounds of administrative competence. This is a factor in selection, and all Cabinets have some first-class administrators, but there are other, political reasons for appointments and it is possible that in any Cabinet of twenty, a half would not have been chosen if the only grounds had been the capacity to run a large department. Second, parties new to power have on their frontbench men selected for their oratory and their critical faculties and these may not be associated with the administrative and constructive capacities needed for government. And the longer a party is in opposition, the fewer of its leaders who have had a chance to develop these abilities. After thirteen years in opposition, only two of the Labour frontbench in 1964 had had experience of a previous Cabinet. Finally, the reasons for moving ministers frequently have little to do with ability and the time spent in any particular office is often too short to allow the minister to master the subject and the department.

Senior civil servants can scarcely be blamed for thinking of their political masters as relatively temporary and likely to move on before fully understanding departmental problems and the merit of traditional policies. It is notorious that ministers are overworked. They cannot concentrate wholly on matters put before them by civil servants because they have to deal with parliamentary duties, party business and constituency cases. An exhausting schedule of appointments means that ministers have too little time to think. What happens is that having to serve on many Cabinet and other committees, anyone other than a top-grade and experienced minister tends to use the brief he has been given. And before most ministerial committees an equivalent official committee meets and goes over the points, so that the meeting can proceed without a hitch to an agreed conclusion, provided none of the ministers wishes to interject a personal note. The author recalls an able Treasury minister who, after resignation, became a convinced and cogent parliamentary reformer, explaining that as a minister he had had no time to work out this aspect of policy and therefore, since the Treasury was opposed to more specialist committees of the House of Commons, he used the brief they provided and he had been a formidable opponent of these reforms at the Cabinet Committee level. One source of official strength is to take time. Civil servants are in the same department for many years, if not for life, while the minister lasts only two to three years. It is understandable that a civil servant takes longer to negotiate or work out a solution over which he is unenthusiastic, the result being that by the time the work is complete, there is a new minister who is more ready to see the weaknesses of this line of action. In addition, to argue with able, patriotic, experienced men is tiring and some ministers have found that it is best to conserve their energies for major issues. Finally, a strong departmental philosophy is hard to resist. In the 1950s the Home Office persuaded successive Home Secretaries to support the death penalty. In the 1960s the Foreign Office successfully urged the case for joining the EEC. Overall, civil servants are loath to disturb good relations with well-established bodies that can sometimes be useful.

There is no doubt that senior civil servants exercise great influence. If a minister lacks ability, experience, knowledge or, perhaps, the time to become confident of his own judgement, then the departmental view tends to prevail, and this may be desirable, for a country cannot be policyless on major issues. But when a government sets its mind to a change of policy within the limits of feasibility, this can be achieved. Exactly how far civil servants are prepared to go in order to thwart ministers is a matter of some controversy. Left-wing critics allege that civil servants restrict or delay the availability of information to ministers if it does not fit easily with departmental views. Briefs can be presented in a way which suggests a particular conclusion. Ministerial instructions may be modified or evaded by clever drafting of documents. In an extreme form this analysis would suggest that the senior civil servants constitute an effective and permanent ruling class forced to make adjustments to their policies from time to time because of the intervention of ministers.

No doubt, that picture is an exaggeration. Nevertheless, when ministers are short of ability and determination, competent officials are able to offer opinions as to the proper policy, though these can be moulded by ministerial views. And if the ministers do lack opinions or energy, the departments can at least maintain sufficient continuity and activity to keep government going.

Criticisms of the civil service: its administrative methods

Turning to the criticisms of the administrative machine through which the political leadership operates, the pattern was set in the early 1960s by Professor Brian Chapman's *British Government Observed*. He argued that Britain had failed to make 'a reasonable proportion of right and wise decisions in matters of major policy', and that other nations had done better. The specific weaknesses of British government which Chapman alleged were first that the ministries, though expected to take all key decisions, were not expected to act – to build roads, run hospitals, train teachers and so on. This always had to be done by another agency so that British government became 'a rich Byzantine structure' of boards, local authorities, commissions and joint committees. As a result, he argued, responsibility is hard to pin down, action becomes desperately slow, planning is inadequate and too many wrong decisions are made. In part, this is because the civil service is a closed corporation, over-specialized in 'general administration' and London-based to the point of becoming parochial. In part it is because training is in-service and little emphasized and also because so much of government is secret, information being deliberately kept from Parliament and the public. Further evidence of these weaknesses is the way governments, faced with difficult problems, do not turn to the departments (or to the Commons) but set up commissions and inquiries manned by distinguished outsiders to investigate and pronounce.

This was a formidable catalogue of sins, but many of the ideas became generally accepted and to some extent underlay Mr Wilson's thinking in 1963 when he talked of the Conservatives' period in power since 1951 as 'thirteen wasted years' and promised that in the first hundred days of dynamic government after a Labour victory at the polls a new atmosphere would pervade Whitehall. However, it was not until 1966 that a committee under Lord Fulton was appointed to 'examine the structure, recruitment and management, including training, of the Home Civil Service'. The report appeared in 1968. It asserted that 'the structure and practices of the Service have not kept up with the changing tasks' and found six major faults. The first was the 'cult of the generalist' or 'all-rounder' which the Fulton Committee said was 'obsolete at all levels and in all parts of the Service'. Then the division into classes was held to be an impediment and a cause of frustration. The report alleged that many scientists, engineers and other specialists were not given the opportunities they should have and too few civil servants were skilled in the techniques of modern management. There was not enough contact between the service and the world outside Whitehall while, in general, promotion depended too much on seniority and too little on merit.

Before considering the Fulton Committee's proposals to remedy the situation, these assorted criticisms of the public service have to be examined. In general, the Fulton Committee's critique was overdone in that it was attacking a caricature of the service which was never wholly true, and certainly underestimated the changes that had taken place since the late 1950s. The two further major reservations that must be made are first that the service is moulded chiefly by the doctrine of ministerial responsibility with all that flows from it – anonymity, one collective viewpoint, secrecy and a degree of isolation from the rest of the community. The Fulton Committee was not, by its terms of reference, allowed to look at the relationship with Parliament but, as a result, it blamed the service itself for many characteristics imposed on it by virtue of this relationship. The second was that this was the very difficult period when, as Dean Acheson said, Britain 'had lost an Empire and failed to find a role'. Inevitably, policy failures were attributed to the government and its officials, when the blame lay more widely with the whole of the community and in particular with the strong British dislike both for rethinking an entire situation and for the radical changes that might have to follow from such a reconsideration.

Given these two reservations, some of the detailed criticisms contain an element of truth but others are superficial. For instance, the attack on the 'generalist' is overdone and for most specialists, the training that counts is what they learn after they start work. After ten years in a department working, for example, on housing, the fact that one man's undergraduate degree was in philosophy and another's in sociology will make little or no difference; what will matter is the capacity and experience they have developed at the task. It is true that over a decade when the senior civil service was moving from being primarily regulatory in outlook to being primarily managerial, there was a lack of research, of assessment of situations before action could be properly planned. It is also true that the service is still obsessed with the idea that it should, if possible, not act itself but should operate through some external agency. Thus when the officials think they must do something to stimulate tourism, plant trees or preserve the countryside, instead of acting themselves, they float a tourist board, a forestry commission or a countryside commission. This has its merits and has been the practice in Sweden, but it is of value only if the central government departments then restrict themselves purely to planning, thinking and regulating. In Britain, however, because of ministerial responsibility and because of the suspicion that the appropriate ministry could do the job much better than a new, inexperienced board (which usually has a lower calibre of staff), the ministries concerned have their own sections on tourism, forestry and the countryside which go over everything the board in question proposes, giving authorizations, suggestions or exercising a veto. The result is delay, duplication and frustration. The ministries become bogged down in detail when their energies and resources should be concentrated more on overall policy, and the *ad hoc* commissions grow disillusioned and frustrated because they are not allowed to get on with the job.

To solve the problems it diagnosed, the Fulton Committee recommended a number of changes which amounted to an attempt to introduce the modern (largely American) techniques of business management into the civil service. The main principle involved is the delegation of responsibility for budgets and for staff to accountable units each with defined objectives and one person responsible for the performance of the unit. Control is exercised by financial techniques and revision of the objectives set for each unit. This permits both an effective method of assessing ability and achievement with the minimum of day-to-day interference. The weakness of this approach in terms of the British civil service is that it ignores the force of ministerial responsibility. At present, no minister could answer a parliamentary question by saying that whatever his views on the matter, responsibility had been allocated for this function to Assistant Secretary Brown and it was up to that official to take whatever course of action he thought best to achieve the set objectives.

Thus the aspects of the Fulton recommendations that could be put into practice were those compatible with ministerial responsibility. They included the abolition of separate classes in favour of a unified grading structure, the foundation of a civil service college, the establishment of planning units and the devotion of more resources to career management. The independent Civil Service Department suggested by Fulton was also created but was brought to an end in 1981. All the changes that were made underlined trends already evident before Fulton reported and none made any basic difference to the civil service.

Since 1979, the civil service has been under renewed pressure to reduce administrative cost. Mr Heseltine, Secretary of State for the Environment 1979–83, made great efforts trying to streamline the operations of his department by insisting on a continuous review of its objectives and priorities. More generally, efforts were made to reduce staff by limiting state functions or by privatization, i.e. by passing over some tasks to private contractors. Other more drastic proposals were ventilated but never put into practice. They included the abolition of one of the senior grades, that of under secretary, to reduce the steps in the administrative hierarchy, and also to remove the inflation-proofing of civil service pensions. In 1981 conflict over pay settlements led to an unprecedented civil service strike. The demise of the Civil Service Department may have been due to a feeling by ministers that it was too conscious of the interests of staff. The position of public servants must be uneasy when the Cabinet is zealous to prune expenditure.

The civil service and Parliament

The fundamental problems, which any proper review of the service ought to have tackled, are its relationships with Parliament, with the public and with the organized interest groups which constitute so much of what the civil service must regard as public opinion. Once the parameters which condition the existence and operation of the service have been agreed and set out, its internal organization can be arranged on lines which give the maximum efficiency compatible with these conditions. First, is it desirable that civil service departments should deal directly with the public? If no suitable local elected authority can be found, should the central department run a service itself through officials in the regions? Is it intrinsically more desirable for local nominated hospital boards to run the hospitals or would this be better done by regional sections of the Ministry of Health? In part, the answer depends on the size and capacity of the local government units to be established. But if the principle is accepted that any services not operated by local government should be conducted directly by the central ministries (perhaps through their regional offices), this would lead to a tremendous simplification of administration and probably to much greater efficiency.

Then there is the question of whether the civil service should deal directly with pressure groups, reach agreements, embody these in draft legislation and only then tell Parliament, or whether Parliament should be brought in at a formative stage so that the pressure groups would be encouraged to lobby MPs as well as departments. If the objective of a democratic legislative process is to inform the public about the issues, to let them know what pressure groups are saying on their behalf and to allow the civil service to assess public reaction before rather than after the government is committed to a line of action, then both the pressure groups and the civil service ought to explain their proposals to Parliament which, in practice, would mean to committees of the House of Commons.

Finally, if Parliament is to exercise its ancient function of scrutinizing both legislation and departmental policy-making, it has to be able to deal directly with the civil service because ministers do not, in fact, make all policy decisions. These changes would require the destruction of the principle of ministerial responsibility, a principle which is such a comfort to both officials and ministers. But to do so would not only help to achieve better relations between the civil service on the one hand and Parliament, the public and the pressure groups on the other. It would also make all the Fulton reforms in management possible. If it could be accepted that ministers made overall policy but that the working and effectiveness of subsections within departments, which operated under certain policy directives, was not the responsibility of the minister but of the civil servant in charge, this would make an enormous change. The civil servant would cease to be anonymous. He would be allowed to explain and defend his subsection's conduct in public. The minister would only be blameworthy if the subsection failed to achieve its objectives or overspent its budget to no purpose and the minister then failed to take the appropriate action.

If this pattern were adopted, Parliament could develop departmental specialist committees which would watch over these subsections of the administration and offer their heads a platform for explaining and defending their policies. Because control was being exercised through the investigations and comments of a parliamentary committee, the pressure groups would once again find it worthwhile to spend some of their time pressing their case on MPs, some of whom would be members of the specialist committee concerned while others could raise points in the normal course of debate.

But not until ministerial responsibility has been abandoned will it be possible to end the pyramidal structure of the civil service, to diminish anonymity, to decrease secrecy and to open up the processes of public administration to public discussion and accountability. Also it is almost certainly the case that in terms of pure efficiency, it does any administration good to have to explain and defend its policies against every variety of argument and pressure which interest groups and an informed representative assembly can bring to bear.

The case for political advice

Any basic change in the executive branch of British government will need something more than the type of structural reform of the civil service proposed by the Fulton Committee. It would require an injection of supporters of the ministerial party, divorced from the tradition of the non-political career public servant. There are two ways in which such an adjustment might be achieved. A group of people politically sympathetic to the government of the day could be appointed to each department to assist ministers with advice that would have a political content. Thus ministers would have alternative briefing to that provided by civil servants. The alternative would be to ensure that top civil service posts were held by political supporters of the government: such people would have to lose their jobs if ministers lost office.

The idea that a minister should have a political associate to assist him is not new. Each senior minister appoints a Parliamentary Private Secretary (PPS) who is a backbench MP. There is no payment; the arrangement is purely personal. The functions of a PPS vary. Some ministers use them largely to keep in touch with parliamentary opinion on matters affecting their own departments. Other ministers find it useful to consult with them more broadly on political questions. Since 1964 some ministers have appointed political advisers to make policy suggestions that reflect their party's viewpoint. This support need not be related to departmental business: in her diary entry for 4 March 1976 Barbara Castle, then Secretary of State for Health and Social Security, bewails the fact that she had no briefing for the Cabinet discussion of the defence review because her political adviser, Jack Straw, was out of action because of a family bereavement. Lord Crowther-Hunt, who has had experience both as a policy adviser and a minister, records in his book, *The Civil Servants*, that the permanent staff tended to isolate advisers by excluding them from official committees and by reducing the information available to them.

Clearly, if the party input into the development of policy is to be significant then something more than an isolated individual is needed to make the system effective. Mr Brian Sedgemore, formerly PPS to Mr Benn, has suggested in *The Secret Constitution* that these political offices should be staffed 'by whoever the Minister wanted – industrialists, academics, journalists, trade unionists, shop stewards, may be MPs'. However, there is a serious difficulty about adding to the number of MPs linked to the government. Ministers cannot vote against the government in the House of Commons; nor can a PPS. Were more MPs to be drawn into the Whitehall web, then all independence on the government backbenches would be eliminated. Ministers could expect to have a parliamentary majority whatever they did. But the crux of the issue is whether it would be good for ministers to receive more partisan advice. Pressure for this development comes from both Left- and Right-wing sources. Sir John Hoskyns, head of Mrs Thatcher's Policy Unit 1979–82, and thus a temporary and political civil servant, favours drastic change as much as Mr Brian Sedgemore. On leaving office he argued that the top level of the civil service needed an injection of fresh blood. It was too much of a closed circle. It lacked the confidence and energy that came from success. Indeed, the concept of success could scarcely apply since it worked to no clear objectives. Ministers are too overburdened with engagements to think out effectively what they want to do. The tradition of the non-political civil service demands that ministers should be helped to put their ideas into practice, while being made aware of the pitfalls; but impartial civil servants should not put political ideas into ministers' heads. This analysis led Sir John Hoskyns to support both the concept of political 'think tanks' to assist ministers and the nomination of some senior civil servants on a party political basis.

The contrary view is that such outsiders, fired with enthusiasm but lacking in experience of the realities of administration, would tend to produce ideas possibly admirable in theory but which would not work in practice. Indeed, the permanent staff can argue that a cautious approach is in the best interests of the minister and his party for, if an unorthodox scheme is tried and fails, the result is politically damaging. On this basis it is arguable, perhaps with some truth, that ministers need protection from their friends.

The weakness of a political office must be that it would lack the knowledge and experience of traditional civil servants. A way to avoid this difficulty might be to put the political team on top of the bureaucratic hierarchy instead of in a separate box at the side of it. This suggestion is truly drastic. It means that, as in the USA, a change of the party in power would mean a complete change of those holding the most senior posts in government departments. Continuity would be lost. The permanent staff would lose the prospect of promotion to the highest rungs of their career ladder. Damage to their morale would be severe. The civil service would have great difficulty in recruiting and retaining those with the highest abilities. Even if its policy advice role were reduced, the nation still needs managers of the best quality to run the public services. And the idea of placing party enthusiasts in command of policy advice is likely to appeal only to those who are keen or extreme supporters of the party in power. Temporary advisers, especially those with a secure job to which they can return, need not feel a great sense of responsibility. They may be too keen to indulge in social experiments. If things go well, it is fine; if things go ill, it is goodbye, but at little personal cost. The arguments against temporary appointments at the top of the civil service pyramid are overwhelming.

It is highly unlikely that any formal moves will be made to politicize senior civil service appointments. When a vacancy occurs for the top post in a department, the tradition is for the vacancy to be discussed by the head of the civil service with the secretary of state. The Prime Minister is also consulted. As can be seen from the Crossman Diaries, the personality and ability of possible candidates are reviewed, but not political opinions. The assumption is that senior civil servants are non-partisan and serve ministers loyally irrespective of politics. It is reported that Mrs Thatcher has been keen to ensure that those promoted are sympathetic to her scale of values or are not unwilling to break away from the style of middle-of-the-road consensus policies that have predominated in recent years. Such a development could have most serious consequences.

If there is a change in the party in power and the new Cabinet feels that their senior civil servants are personally attached to the policies of the previous Cabinet, then there would be a serious breakdown in confidence. To resolve the matter smoothly might well be impossible. If the new ministers took no action they would feel, perhaps with justice, that they did not get the quality of cooperation they were entitled to enjoy from their most senior staff. But if permanent secretaries were dismissed or persuaded to retire *en masse*, then the cry would go up that the new ministers were engaging in a new and improper extension of patronage. The new Cabinet could claim that they were faced with a dilemma not of their own making. Whatever the outcome the long-standing, unwritten code of behaviour that governs relations between ministers and civil servants would be gravely battered.

12 Government outside Whitehall

The purpose of this chapter is to describe the rest of the machinery through which the political leadership operates outside Whitehall and this includes more than just the system of local government. In the late nineteenth century, all administration was grouped at two levels – central and local – so that at each level, decisions could be subjected to the scrutiny of an elected body. Since then, central government departments have established regional offices. Many essential services are now operated by public bodies organized on a regional basis; leading examples are gas, electricity, water and the hospitals. Numerous *ad hoc* bodies have been created to run specific functions such as broadcasting and television, the ports, industrial training schemes and the administration of government property. Such a proliferation of bureaucracy is an inevitable consequence of the expansion of the activities of the state.

These organizations are sometimes described as fringe bodies but more often the acronym 'quango' is used. The word is a shorthand form for 'quasi autonomous non-government organizations'. Exactly how many quangos exist is not known. Different studies produce different figures depending upon the categories included. Certainly the total runs to hundreds. They have been a very popular means of dealing with a wide variety of functions which ministers want to encourage, to finance and to guide, but which would not fit easily into the structure of a government department. To create a separate agency for a particular task helps to remove it from the political arena. Ministers do not have detailed responsibility for the decisions made. An increase in the number of civil servants is avoided – and that is politically popular. The growth of quangos fits in with the idea that the burden on ministers could be eased if government departments concentrated on the development of policy and 'hived off' large blocs of routine administration. Nevertheless, quangos are financed from public funds, so there is a problem of public accountability. The boards and commissions that run these organizations are commonly appointed by ministers and so provide an increase in ministerial patronage. It can be argued that they also produce an increase in civil service patronage in that senior civil servants generally advise ministers about the appointments, and quite often important chairmanships are awarded to recently retired civil servants. So there has been criticism of the growth of patronage and of the extent to which bodies which are paid for by the taxpayer are not fully accountable to Parliament for their actions. Public trading organizations, the nationalized industries, should, in theory, cover their own costs, but do not always do so.

The Thatcher Government has been critical of the growth of quangos. They represent a growth of public expenditure and activity which Conservatives wish to curtail. So some quangos and advisory committees have been eliminated. Yet they still operate a substantial if ill-defined fringe of functions provided by the state.

The nationalized industries

When these various bodies were created, the question of control did arise, most acutely in the case of the nationalized industries. These were created or taken over by the state at various times since the first examples under the 1906–14 Liberal Government, but the largest group of Nationalization Acts covering coal, road and rail services, gas, electricity and iron and steel came under the 1945–51 Labour Government. At that time the old doctrines of the need for democratic control were still strong and an argument arose between those, such as Mr Aneurin Bevan, who favoured total subordination to Parliament (with a minister for each industry on the lines of the Post Office), and those led by Mr Herbert Morrison, who wanted to leave the industries a measure of independence to operate as fully commercial undertakings. The latter approach prevailed and though the various Nationalization Acts differ in detail, the main points were the same. A board was nominated to run each industry as a viable commercial enterprise. The minister can change the board and give the board directions of a general character which have to be observed. He has to be consulted on any substantial capital outlays and be provided with a full report of the board's activities. In practice, the minister has only once had to issue such a directive (when the Conservatives after 1951 stopped any further action by the Iron and Steel Board) as these reserve powers are quite sufficient to make the boards listen carefully to any suggestions made in a less formal manner by the minister. Parliament, however, has a far weaker position. It is entitled to see (and debate, if necessary) the annual accounts and report of each industry but it can only question the minister on those aspects of the industry's activities for which the minister is responsible. In practice, this means that censure motions are possible and questions can be tabled on the general issues where it could be held that the minister ought to have issued a directive. But on day-to-day issues or on detailed matters where the minister would not be authorized to intervene by the relevant act, however much he might discuss these points on an informal basis and influence the actions of the board, Parliament can do nothing.

In practice, the nationalized industries are subject to Whitehall and civil servants often re-examine the major management decisions (and some minor ones) in case points of principle arise, in particular considering whether investment and pricing policies are satisfactory from the ministry's point of view. Also, ministers are often prepared to get answers on detailed questions for MPs, though the Commons decided that such letters were not 'proceedings in Parliament' and were therefore not protected from actions alleging libel. It is scarcely surprising that when the Select Committee on Nationalized Industries examined this problem it found a 'lack of clarity and certainty and purpose' among what it called the sponsoring government departments. The result was a 'lack of understanding and in some cases, a breakdown of mutual confidence between boards and ministries'. The select committee then went on to recommend very much the same principles as the Fulton Committee wanted to see adopted widely in the civil service. It argued that government control should be 'strategic guidance' and should be exercised as far as possible in the same way for all the industries by the use of economic and financial criteria, and that this should be done by one minister and one department. Other aspects which concerned the public such as the need to retain certain uneconomic railway lines, the use of coal to prevent too fast a rise in unemployment in areas dependent on mining or the case for airports on remote islands in Scotland, could then all be urged from outside on the individual industries and on the Ministry for Nationalized Industries without confusing these social objectives with the normal criteria of operation. These recommendations (made in 1968) have not been adopted.

The major method of ensuring public accountability is through select committees of the House of Commons. Originally, in 1955, a select committee was appointed to give specialized attention to the nationalized industries: when a full range of select committees were established in 1979, the Committee on Nationalized Industries was discontinued and its responsibilities transferred to the appropriate functional committees, e.g. energy and transport.

There has been a continuous tendency for governments, both Conservative and Labour, to intervene in the affairs of the nationalized industries in order to promote immediate political objectives. Often the purpose has been to encourage wage restraint; the size and shape of investment programmes have been the subject of ministerial concern; in the past the National Coal Board has been dissuaded from closing uneconomic pits. The scale and importance of the nationalized concerns are so great that ministers are not prepared to give their managers a free hand.

At the same time there has been strong pressure from MPs to allow the House of Commons to play a more effective role in these matters. The new select committee system has strengthened parliamentary scrutiny over government departments: why should there not be a similar advance in relation to nationalized industries? In 1983 Mr St John Stevas promoted a private member's bill, The National Audit Bill, which sought to give the Comptroller and Auditor General access to the accounts of nationalized industries so that his staff could investigate them as they do the accounts of government departments. The chairmen of the nationalized industries were greatly alarmed by this proposal. The government also objected and, ultimately, these provisions were dropped from the bill. The controversy was quite fierce and embarrassing for Conservative ministers. They were as keen as their backbenchers for the nationalized industries to be efficient and cost effective. But such was the resistance from management, it was feared that it would become impossible to recruit top-quality personnel from the private sector if they were going to be subject to oversight from the Comptroller. Further, the original theory of nationalization put forward by the Attlee Government after 1945 stressed that corporations should be free to take commercial risks in a way that would be inappropriate for government departments. Thus it is arguable that the traditions of the Comptroller's Department do not fit the task of examining commercial accounts. Scrutiny by the Comptroller could also reveal more fully the extent of ministerial influence over nationalized industries and could provide fuel for parliamentary criticism of ministers.

Since 1979 there has been some contraction of nationalized industries. Conservative policy is to 'privatize'. Public concerns that are profitable are being sold.

Local government: its structure and weaknesses

Local government was reformed in England and Wales in 1972 and in Scotland in 1973. A system with historic origins which had been made democratic in the nineteenth century was reorganized on a two-tier basis after a series of reports. In order to appreciate some of the present problems and the need for a reform, it is necessary to examine the pattern of local government as it stood before the 1972 act. This pattern dated originally from the Middle Ages when the towns were able to purchase their right to self-government by paying an impecunious Crown for a charter. The latter gave the right to self-government and self-taxation to all living within the town walls or boundary, leaving the surrounding rural area under the control of the aristocracy. This division between town and country became hardened by the end of the nineteenth century into fifty-eight county councils and eighty-two county boroughs in England and Wales. While these county boroughs looked after all their own local government, in the counties there were subordinate, partially self-governing bodies; namely 270 non-county boroughs, 535 urban district councils and 473 rural district councils, these last being further subdivided into some 7500 parish councils. Thus the administrative map of England and Wales looked like a cloth with patches on it, the patches being towns governed by borough or urban district councils with the entire surrounding area administered by a county council. County boroughs totally opted out of the surrounding county council's affairs, but for the other types of subordinate authorities the situation was complicated because they performed some functions for themselves while other functions in their areas, such as education, were run by the county council. Thus the councillors for non-county boroughs, urban districts and rural districts had a limited range of responsibilities; separate elections were held to choose county councillors. Similarly, the rates paid by the citizens in these areas had to be shared between the two levels of local authority.

In Scotland, the structure was very much the same except that the number of people resident in the various categories of local authorities tended, on average, to be smaller and there was no third tier equivalent to the parish council. The actual structure consisted of thirty-one counties and four cities, with the counties divided into twenty-one large burghs, 176 small burghs and 198 district councils.

This system of local government had much fine work to its credit but it was generally accepted that its structure had not changed enough to keep pace with the changing social pattern of travel to work, shopping and holiday areas. Nor were the levels of resources available enough to pay for the increased skills needed for the more complex requirements of local administration. These weaknesses appeared in many forms. Perhaps the most fundamental was the great variation in the size and resources of units all supposed to perform the same tasks at roughly the same standards. Thus Rutland with a population of 28,000 was supposed to provide a full range of county services of the same standard as Lancashire with a population of 2.3 million. Among county boroughs the range was also extreme: Canterbury had only 33,000 souls while Birmingham had 1.1 million citizens.

These variations had arisen from political unwillingness to change boundaries in the period between 1888 and 1972. The consequence was that many authorities were too small and too poor financially to provide a good standard of service to employ the requisite staff and provide the necessary specialized units.

Besides these limitations of area and size, finance added another dimension. Traditionally, local government provided services for property owners – paved streets, lighting, water, sewerage and police – and so the main local government tax has always been a rate levied on property values. But this meant that the areas with most problems are usually those where property values are low and where there are therefore fewest resources available to pay for remedial services. Second, while many other tax sources are buoyant, property assessments only rise slowly and so more revenue means raising the tax rate and this always causes trouble as the tax is regressive, weighing more heavily as a percentage of total income on those in the lower income ranges.

These weaknesses as administrative agencies partly explain the suspicion of local government in the central departments and among many politicians and others in all walks of life. In part, these feelings sprang from the tremendously centralized tradition of British society and administration. It was felt by many politicians and officials that local government, in its recent form, was slow and inept so that the departments dealing with local authorities either developed a mass of controls to enable them to watch over local authorities or actually withdrew services from the local authorities. They also developed a series of financial controls through the grants made to local government. All was underpinned by the widespread belief that local councillors were not likely to take a progressive view on educational policy, such matters as the arts or the preservation of historic buildings, and that local authority officials were less competent than their counterparts in Whitehall.

The results were evident at many levels. One was the withdrawal of such functions as running hospitals, manufacturing gas and electricity and the distribution of national assistance (now known as supplementary benefits) from local government. A second was the elaborate controls over local authority activities. These developed from the legal concept of *ultra vires* (beyond the strength) which, since the mid nineteenth century, had prohibited local councils from doing anything for which they could not show precise legal authority. As a result the law relating to local government had become very detailed. Councillors have come to feel very dependent on legal advice and the top official of a local authority has normally been a lawyer. Legal controls have been supplemented by financial controls, especially over capital expenditure. In the nineteenth century limits were imposed on local borrowing to ensure that councils would not default over their debt liabilities, for any such default would have undermined financial confidence in public authorities and had a serious effect on rates of interest. Today, the government wishes to control local borrowing as part of the attempt to limit the total of public spending.

Another powerful financial weapon is the annual decision made by the government on the amount of grant to be given to local authorities to aid current expenditure. The accounts of local authorities are subject to scrutiny by government appointed auditors, the district audit. Further, some local functions, notably education, police and the fire service, are subject to inspection by government appointed inspectors. In the case of some functions Whitehall has the power to take over the duties of a local authority if it fails to carry out its statutory obligations. Examples of the use of this ultimate sanction are few. The most recent case was in 1973 when the government appointed a commissioner to take over the housing responsibilities of the Clay Cross Urban District Council because that council refused to operate the provisions of the Housing Finance Act 1972 and charge higher rents to council tenants.

The wide array of central controls has necessarily created tension between central government and local councillors. Ministers and perhaps civil servants may think of local authorities as useful agents for carrying out policies decided nationally in government departments and approved by Parliament. Councillors feel that the fact that they have been elected gives them a right to some independence. They can claim to represent local public opinion; such a claim cannot be made by those who serve on public bodies as a result of government nomination. However, ministers are not impressed by the democratic mandate claimed by local councillors. A national election victory gives a stronger moral claim to rule than a local election. The turnout at a local election is also on average little more than half that at a general election. Nevertheless, local elections are fought increasingly on national issues. Often the local results reflect the unpopularity of the national government. The longer a party has a majority in the Commons, the greater the number of local authorities likely to be captured by its opponents. Thus the political message of local elections provides another motive for ministers to deny their importance.

Meanwhile the strong element of central intervention ensures that one local authority cannot be very different in its policies from all the others; citizens can travel round the country to places under different party control without detecting any very noticeable variations in the quality of local services. This encouraged apathy about local affairs and a poor turnout at local elections. The management of council business was organized on a time-consuming basis with a separate committee to look after the detailed operation of each local authority function; it was argued that this system reduced the willingness of able people to serve as local councillors.

Ever since 1945 it had been widely accepted by students of local affairs that there was a need to reform local government to bring greater efficiency and more vigour into the system. However, the lack of any popular interest in the subject, and the opposition of the local authority associations and of councillors who often hold posts in the constituency organizations of their parties, prevented any action. Ultimately the pressure for reform came from the Whitehall ministries because they had to use local government to execute many of their plans, particularly for local economic development and urban renewal and they found that the machinery was simply ineffective.

The spate of reports on English local government began with the report by Professor Allen of *The Committee of Inquiry into the Impact of Rates on Households* (Cmnd 2582) in 1965. The Report on the *Management of Local Government* chaired by Sir John Maud came out in 1967 as did the report on *Staffing of Local Government* prepared by a committee under Sir George Mallaby. Then in 1969, the two royal commissions reported, the Scottish Commission presided over by Lord Wheatley and the English by Lord Redcliffe-Maud. The Labour Government's reaction to the Royal Commission Report emerged in two White Papers (Cmnd 4276 and Cmnd 4310). After the Conservative victory at the 1970 general election a further White Paper (Cmnd 4584) outlined the policy of the new administration. There followed the Local Government Act 1972 dealing with England and Wales and the Local Government (Scotland) Act 1973 and the National Health Service Reorganization Act 1973. None of these studies dealt with London, whose government had been considered by a royal commission under Sir Edwin Herbert between 1957 and 1960, the main proposals being enacted in the London Government Act of 1963.

The chief weakness of all this work was that the fundamental questions were not tackled first. It was assumed rather than argued that all government should be under some form of democratic control. But, having made this decision, the two royal commissions on local government were not allowed to consider how the vast range of central, local and intermediate government agencies could be supervised or scrutinized in a democratic way. Rather than face this, the royal commissions were limited to 'the structure of local government . . . in relation to its existing functions', so that there was no serious discussion of what should or should not fall to local government as opposed to central government or of the financial problems facing local government.

Given these limitations, the two commissions proceeded in a very similar manner. The Redcliffe-Maud Commission began by considering each of the existing functions of local government in turn. Evidence was heard from many sources but great weight was placed on the views of the central government departments. They gave minimum population figures, arguing that below these there were not the financial resources or flow of work to permit the employment of a highly specialized staff and thus a proper service could not be run. Some departments gave estimates of optimum figures but most of the evidence merely tried to fix a minimum. The result was a broad agreement that the major services required a unit consisting of at least 250,000 people and, without much evidence, Redcliffe-Maud fixed a ceiling of a million beyond which, it was said, administration would cease to be local.

Then each service was examined and it was found that there were clear interconnections. Planning involved transport and the wider aspects of urban redevelopment but all these were tied up with housing. Then the social services of health, education and welfare were best administered together but these also had close connections with housing. The result was that the Redcliffe-Maud Commission found itself turning towards unitary authorities of between 250,000 and a million in size performing all these functions and the commission finally recommended fifty-eight such bodies in England. This excluded London, and the commission also named three metropolitan areas where, it argued, planning and the environmental services would have to stretch over an area including far more than one million people, the result being that the personal services would be too remote. For this reason a second tier administering education, housing, social and health services was recommended in these metropolitan areas. The commission accepted that there were broader aspects of physical planning which the fifty-eight unitary authorities could not handle and, for this purpose, they recommended provincial councils but these were to be indirectly elected and were to have no executive powers. The provincial councils were simply to co-ordinate planning for the unitary authorities, and it was thought that they might also undertake the preparation of wider schemes in the fields of further education, the education of handicapped children and in cultural and recreational matters. Finally, the commission proposed local councils with no powers but with the right to put forward the views of local communities (the boundaries probably being the same as those of the present unreformed local government units) to the unitary authorities.

The Wheatley Commission on Scottish local government proceeded in a similar way but concluded that there was sufficient difference between the sizes of authority needed for the broader services and the more immediate local functions to merit the retention of a two-tier system. However, the second tier proposed by Wheatley had nothing like the powers recommended for the second tier in the English metropolitan areas, being confined to local planning, local amenities and minor regulations. In fact, the distribution of population in Scotland would have made two unitary authorities possible, one based on Aberdeen and the other on Dundee, but the Clyde Valley is a major conurbation while the Highlands and Borders both lacked any appropriate urban centre. As a result, Wheatley proposed seven regional authorities with an average of 755,000 people and a second tier of thirty-seven district authorities averaging 143,000 inhabitants.

Despite this attempt to revitalize local government, the government decided to abandon any idea of restoring the hospital service to local government and thus to democratic control. It also found it very hard to propose the unification of the three arms of the service, the hospital, the general practitioner and local authority services, as had long been advocated by reformers. A Green Paper, *The Future Structure of the Health Service,* published in 1970, proposed area health authorities which would coincide with the unitary authorities and metropolitan authorities of Redcliffe-Maud and with groups of London boroughs. These health authorities would be responsible for services that are primarily medical, taking over, for example, the school health service from local government. On the other hand, the home help service would be left to the local councils. Thus the divisions within the health service would remain, though the shares would be altered, the area health authorities administering the hospital and general practitioner services and taking over from local authorities ambulances, family planning, health centres, health visiting, home nursing, maternity and child care and preventive medicine. The new unitary local councils would retain the services dealing with the elderly, handicapped and homeless, the children's services, family case work, day centres, residential accommodation for those needing care, unsupported mothers and the home help service. The Green Paper made proposals for sharing staff in an effort to bridge this gap between the health authorities and the local councils. Also the area health authorities are regarded as too small to plan overall hospital and specialist services, to organize postgraduate medical and dental education, to deploy senior staff or to run training schemes or the blood transfusion service. To supervise these functions, fourteen or more regional health councils were recommended to follow the areas of the present regional hospital boards.

The Conservatives, in opposition, had objected to the unitary authorities and came out for a two-tier system which was explained, after they had won office, in a White Paper, *Local Government in England* (Cmnd 4584) published in February 1971. Their scheme was for thirty-eight counties and six metropolitan areas. The counties were divided into about 300 second-tier districts which were to handle housing, aspects of planning and development and local amenities. The six metropolitan areas contained thirty-four districts. This plan was put into the Local Government Act 1972 (thirty-nine counties with 296 districts; six metropolitan areas with thirty-six districts), the only change being a slight increase in district powers. Wales was divided into eight counties and thirty-seven districts.

This scheme was far from the Redcliffe-Maud proposals and solved few of the weaknesses noted earlier in this chapter. The authorities are still too many and too small and it is ironical that while land-use planning had been in the hands of some 150 authorities, it is now shared among 380 while there is no one (except Whitehall) to look at planning at the regional level. In the metropolitan areas, the districts are often too weak and it will be hard to establish rate equalization schemes, whereby the richer districts aid the poorer, as the consent of every district is necessary. Also the boundaries of the metropolitan areas have been tightly drawn so that there is no room for expansion and the unsatisfactory separation between the town and the country is preserved. Some district boundaries are highly artificial and the split between the functions of the two tiers is by no means clear; it will still be necessary to have joint committees. Although the act was supposed to bolster the strength of local government, in the process of reform, water, sewage disposal and some sewerage functions are removed and given to new regional water authorities while the local authority health services were allocated to the new area health boards.

As a result, the relations between central and local government have not been materially altered and the system of detailed central government controls remains virtually intact. The Conservatives had condemned too much dictation to local councils on local issues but their Housing Finance Act 1972 gave Whitehall the power to determine and enforce local authority rents. Later, in 1976, the Labour Government took powers to force all local education authorities to make their schools comprehensive. In 1972 the

Labour Opposition denounced Conservative policy on council house rents as a monstrous interference with the democratic rights of local authorities; in 1976 the Conservative Opposition denounced Labour policy on compulsory comprehensive secondary education as a monstrous interference with the democratic rights of local authorities. The situation illustrates perfectly the old adage: 'where you stand depends on where you sit'. When in office each major party wants to enforce its views irrespective of local opinion; in opposition, it is convenient to uphold the right of local councillors to make their own decisions.

This central issue of the extent of local authority independence was also at the heart of the Report of the Layfield Committee on *Local Government Finance* (Cmnd 6453) published in 1976. The committee had been established two years earlier by the Wilson Government in response to widespread indignation about rate increases imposed by the new councils in 1974. Local rates are politically more delicate than other forms of taxation because they are the most visible. Cash or a cheque has to be produced to pay a rate demand; in contrast, VAT is absorbed in the price of a commodity or service and most people pay income tax through a PAYE system which means that money is deducted before it is received. But a rate increase cannot be concealed. The distribution of the burden of rates is arguably less fair than that of income tax, so the Layfield Committee was expected to study the possibilities of reforming local taxation. Indeed, in 1974 the Conservatives promised to abolish the rating of residential property, but never explained how the loss of rate revenue would be replaced.

After a full examination of the problem, the Layfield Committee recommended, not that the local rate should be abolished, but that rates should be supplemented by a local income tax. It argued that some extra form of local taxation was needed if local government was to preserve its separate identity. Without new taxing powers, local authorities would come to depend more and more on help from the National Exchequer and, since he who pays the piper calls the tune, the result must be even stronger central influence over local decisions. If a local income tax were introduced, then the amount of national subsidy could be reduced and local councillors would be in fuller command of local affairs. Greater local power would mean greater local responsibility and more public interest in local government. The prescription was logical but totally unacceptable to the government, and there were two major objections to the Layfield proposals. First, a local income tax would be complex and therefore expensive to administer. Second, income tax has long been regarded as a tax of central importance in government management of the economy; it is a major financial and psychological weapon in securing the success of the Cabinet's economic strategy. The introduction of local income tax would allow local authorities to undermine the budgetary plans of the Chancellor of the Exchequer.

So no action was taken on the ideas of the Layfield Committee. On the contrary, the weight of central supervision over local authorities becomes ever stronger because of the steady decline in our economic fortunes. In 1976 the Labour Government was forced to impose curbs on public expenditure in order to obtain assistance from the International Monetary Fund. Inevitably, local government could not escape from this policy and the rate support grant was trimmed back from 66 per cent of local authority expenditure to 61 per cent. Thus local authorities, faced with this reduction in aid from the national taxpayer, had either to reduce their services or increase local rates. At this time a new Central Council for Local Government Finance was established, composed of representatives of the government and of the local authorities. Its formal purpose was to strengthen consultation between Whitehall and town and county halls. To put the matter into more realistic fashion, the aim was to try and get local councils to understand and accept the implications of national economic policy for local government.

The Thatcher Government, inspired by monetary theories of economic management, was even more insistent on the need to cut back local expenditure. This reaction was not simply another facet of their economic philosophy. There had been deep disappointment in the Conservative Party with the results of their own reform of local government. In 1972 it expected that the new system of fewer and larger local authorities would prove more efficient. Economies of scale and the use of computers were expected to reduce administrative costs. Big was beautiful. There would be fewer committees, streamlined methods of decision-making, more delegation to officers and thus less delay. Somehow this ideal was never achieved. The larger size of authorities has produced complaints about remoteness from rural areas. Further, larger authorities are felt to have increased the influence of officials and – very important from a Conservative viewpoint – this influence has not helped to reduce expenditure. Indeed, the cost of local government has risen sharply since 1972; much of this increase is due to inflation, but the number of staff employed by local authorities has also risen. The 1972 reform strengthened the local professional bureaucracy and a bureaucracy that is made stronger is unlikely to resist any opportunity to grow.

So since 1979 the Conservatives have made a determined effort to curtail local expenditure. No major changes have been made in the responsibilities of local government. Somehow local authorities are expected to perform the same range of duties more cheaply. Targets for reductions are issued but each local council has to decide for itself how to meet the targets. Some councils refuse to co-operate. New legislation, the Local Government and Planning Act 1980, changed the basis of financial aid to local government. Previously the rate support grant had been distributed to authorities on the basis of a complex formula which took account of a number of factors, including levels of local prosperity, which influence the need for local services. The details of the formula were varied, sometimes year by year, but the formula was then automatic in its operation (it is true that the government had a reserve power to withhold grant from a particular authority, but this power was never used). The 1980 act changed these arrangements. The rate support grant was replaced by a block grant to be calculated separately for each authority, so a council which displeases the central government by failing to co-operate with its economic policy can be penalized by a reduction in grant. A council faced with such a threat would be forced to choose between cutting services to satisfy the government or imposing an even higher rate on the occupiers of property.

To promote simpler and cheaper administration the Conservatives have removed a large number of detailed administrative controls over local government. The relationship between district and county planning authorities has also been modified with the same objective. However, the net result of the Local Government and Planning Act 1980 will be to give local councillors less freedom, not more. Controls over capital expenditure are made more extensive and the implied pressure on current expenditure from the new block grant system shows firm determination to weld local government into a national programme of economic management. It is a moot point whether one can now fairly speak of *local government*; local councillors and local government officers are now mainly engaged in the administration of policies decided in London.

Regionalism and devolution

The growing weakness of local government in terms of making decisions has been more than counterbalanced by the increasing weight of government departments and the influence of civil servants. Yet this trend has also stimulated resistance. There have been complaints that central departments are inefficient because they are overburdened; the Fulton Committee on the Civil Service urged the 'hiving-off' of units dealing with routine administration which were little concerned with major policy issues. The development of semi-independent quangos was noted at the start of this chapter. In the 1960s it was also argued that government departments dealing with domestic questions should be decentralized so that civil servants who had a powerful voice in matters of economic planning could be kept in touch with regional and local interests. In 1966 regional planning was applied to the whole of England which was divided into eight regions for this purpose. Each had a board of civil servants to bring together local representatives of central departments related to economic development. Each region was also given a Planning Council nominated from prominent local figures. The task of these boards and councils was to draw together the planning and administration of the area, to produce comprehensive studies setting out regional priorities and to link the efforts of central government and local authorities. It cannot be claimed that this machinery was very successful and the Thatcher Government rapidly did away with it. The Conservative view was that economic development should not be fashioned by the state but should rise from the natural operation of a free market economy.

Scotland and Wales enjoy separate administrative systems operated by their own government departments which are headed by ministers with seats in the Cabinet. The Scottish arrangements were well established by the end of the nineteenth century; in Wales the pattern has evolved since the 1950s. The Scottish Office, often known from the name of its Edinburgh offices as St Andrew's House, deals with local government services, including education, housing, social services and roads, economic development, agriculture and fisheries, health and Home Office functions including police and probation. The Scottish Office does not cover functions which are felt to require uniform standards throughout the country, e.g. social security. The Welsh Office is similar although it has fewer devolved powers.

These regional ministries operate as a normal part of the Whitehall machine except that they are located in Scotland and Wales, and they have the normal right to membership of any Cabinet committees dealing with matters for which they take responsibility in their areas. Although one object of having such ministries is that they can deal with problems in a manner specially suited to conditions in Scotland and Wales, the fact that the ministers belong to the UK Cabinet and are responsible to the UK Parliament means that there is considerable pressure for uniformity. In the case of Northern Ireland, the pressure for uniformity came from the majority of the electorate who want to be as well treated as British citizens are in England or Scotland. In Scotland and Wales there is the same pressure for equal treatment but it comes in the first instance from MPs who will pounce on any discrepancies and ask why England (or Scotland and Wales) is receiving special treatment. As a result, it is an established convention that the Scottish and Welsh Offices consult their Whitehall opposite numbers (and vice versa) before proposing any action which could be the thin end of an undesirable wedge for the other ministry. In financial arrangements, neither of these offices approaches the Treasury with a request for a single budget for all their functions. They allow the English ministries to make a case for an overall allocation for housing, health, roads and so on, the Scottish (and, where relevant, the Welsh) departments putting in a bid for a share of these functional budgets based on the special needs of Scottish or Welsh housing, roads or water resources. The reason for accepting this approach rather than asking for a 'block allocation' is simply the conviction that the summation of functional budgets produces a larger and more defensible total.

In England it has often been disputed whether there is any regional feeling and obviously there is nothing of the quasi-nationalism evident in Scotland and Wales. There may be some sense of cohesion in the North-East, Yorkshire, Lancashire, or the South-West, but even if this sentiment is totally lacking in the rest of England, it can be argued that these areas would be better administered by a series of regional ministries. However, most national politicians and local councillors share the civil service preference for the functional and centralized system based on Whitehall.

In Scotland and Wales public pressure developed for more independence than could be gained from decentralized administration. The most extreme nationalists wanted complete separation from England. Before 1966 these claims were not widely supported and carried little political weight. Then in July 1966 the Welsh Nationalists won a by-election at Carmarthen and in November 1967 the Scottish National Party overturned a 16,000 Labour majority to win a by-election at Hamilton. These results were backed by solid gains at local elections and it became clear that the Nationalists had made substantial inroads into the Labour vote, at any rate between general elections. Until this point, the structure of government outside Whitehall had been merely a matter which worried civil servants who wished to see their departmental policies executed more rapidly and efficiently, though some Liberals, some academics and sections of the 'quality press' had shown a passing interest in the subject. For most of those in political life, the existing pattern of local government (through which numbers of politicians, particularly in the Labour Party, had graduated) was quite satisfactory and there seemed to be little point in tinkering with it. Most politicians, in any case, are not interested in the machinery of government; their absorption is with the end product, the pensions, houses, levels of income and foreign policies that come out of the machine. Added to this, MPs and ministers have in a special degree the conviction that central government knows best and that any devolution from London must mean giving powers to authorities that are poorer, weaker, slower, perhaps corrupt, perhaps more reactionary (for Labour members) or perhaps more reckless with public funds (for Conservative members).

But the advent of the Nationalists, though hard to analyse, did suggest that there were votes to be won or lost, at least in Scotland and Wales, on the public's sense of remoteness from decision-taking or its lack of knowledge of the existing degree of devolution to the Scottish and Welsh Offices and on the general confusion as to which body was responsible for what. Both major parties were seriously worried by the situation. The Labour Party saw its strongholds in Scotland and Wales endangered and some of the younger members elected in 1964 and 1966, who had been interested in devolution and governmental reform long before the nationalist challenge arose, saw this as their chance to press for a degree of devolution to an elected all-Welsh or all-Scottish council. But the older MPs from these areas saw these efforts as merely concessions to the Nationalists. On the Labour side, these members were the products of the 1930s when the main issue in politics was insufficiency. For them, the task was to win power at the centre and then to distribute wealth more fairly. Talk of regional governmental or elected assemblies seemed pointless eyewash, a sign of weakness in the face of the nationalist challenge; a policy designed to lead either to a call for total independence for Scotland and Wales or to a permanent loss of authority by Whitehall and therefore a diminution in the competence of Scottish and Welsh MPs.

The Conservatives likewise were aroused by the prospect of a weakening of Labour's hold on Scotland and Wales, as the Conservatives had had a constant majority at every post-1945 general election in England; it was the Celtic fringe that tilted the balance in favour of Labour. Also some Conservatives were genuinely interested in decentralization. In August 1968, the Conservatives established a Scottish Constitutional Committee, which behaved like a royal commission, under Sir Alec Douglas-Home. It reported in early 1970 recommending a Scottish elected Assembly of some 125 members which would take all but the last or Third Reading stage of Scottish bills and would debate the Scottish estimates and general topics. The flaw in this idea was that the Assembly was to have no executive powers and no powers to make or unmake ministers. It would be expected to advise the Secretary of State for Scotland who would still be in the UK Cabinet and responsible to the UK House of Commons, a situation which would be intolerable to its members, resented by Scots MPs and bound to lead to conflict.

Inside the Labour Party, the conflict as to how to react was acute, those opposed to any concessions finally triumphing with the well-known formula of putting the matter to a royal commission which could not report till after the forthcoming general election. This was the Commission on the Constitution asked to look at 'the present functions of the central legislature and government in relation to the several countries, nations and regions of the United Kingdom'.

When the Nationalists won only one seat at the general election of 1970, the tension went out of the argument. But the Kilbrandon Commission reported in 1973, a majority of its members recommending legislative devolution for Scotland and Wales. The issue suddenly came alive again with the Scottish National Party

(SNP) winning seven seats and the Welsh Nationalists three in February 1974. The Labour Party promptly changed its position and in October 1974 (when the SNP won eleven seats with 30 per cent of the Scottish vote) promised to bring in legislative devolution setting up a Scottish Assembly with most of the functions of the secretary of state in the hands of a separate Scottish executive responsible to that Assembly. The Welsh were offered a scheme of executive devolution only.

The 1974 Labour Government produced a White Paper in late 1975 entitled *Our Changing Democracy* outlining its proposals for devolution. A devolution bill in the parliamentary session 1976–7 failed because of backbench Labour objections: the government was unable to carry the guillotine motion to curb debate which was essential if the bill was to reach the Statute Book. In the following session separate bills for Scotland and Wales were issued. A guillotine motion was carried and, after amendment, the bills were accepted. Labour objectors did not change their minds but they feared that the loss of the bills could undermine the future existence of the Government which was depending on Liberals and Welsh and Scottish Nationalists for its survival. Further, some opponents hoped that, even if the bills passed through Parliament, they would still be lost at the subsequent referenda. This wish was ultimately fulfilled.

It is easy to make a case for devolution in terms of democracy and participation. The Commission on the Constitution had argued that opinion in Scotland and Wales resented government being conducted far away in London. A more accessible regional assembly would have a better idea of the problems and aspirations of people in Scotland and Wales. No doubt all this is true, but the difficulties emerge immediately attempts are made to produce precise plans to deal with the situation.

In other parts of the world there have been cases where it was desired to combine a system of local independent governments with a unifying central administration which would provide strength especially for foreign affairs and defence. The solution has been a federal system. Leading examples of this form of government can be seen in the United States, Canada, Australia and West Germany. Why not adopt this arrangement for the United Kingdom to meet the claims of Scottish and Welsh Nationalists? The simple answer is that there is no evidence that the inhabitants of the United Kingdom want a federal system. Only in Scotland is there significant support for federalism and even there it is far from the majority view.

So the Devolution Bills proposed something less than federalism. In Scotland the Assembly would have had limited powers to pass legislation on domestic affairs while in Wales the Assembly would have been restricted to the approval of Statutory Instruments. The Assemblies had no taxing powers or independent source of revenue. Their funds would come from a grant by the National Exchequer – an obvious source for constant friction. The bills contained complex provisions to control the extent of the devolved powers. The remainder of this paragraph relates to Scotland where devolution was to be greater. Local government was devolved, but not the police. Transport was to be devolved, but not the railways; how could an overall plan for transport be administered? Education was included, but not universities. Nor was agriculture, so what would happen to agricultural education? Functions of the Scottish Development Agency were to be split; those relating to the environment were devolved, but not those relating to industrial investment because Whitehall was determined to keep command over questions of economic management. Clearly, there would have been conflict and confusion over what had and had not been devolved. If the Secretary of State for Scotland felt that the Scottish Assembly had exceeded its powers, he could refer any Scottish act or order to the Judicial Committee of the Privy Council for a ruling on its legality. In addition, the Secretary of State could override or veto any decision of the Scottish Assembly if it affected a matter reserved to the Westminster Parliament in a way which the Secretary of State felt was contrary to the public interest. A veto of this kind would, of course, be subject to challenge and approval at Westminster. It is also likely that a veto would produce severe strains in the relationship between Edinburgh and London.

Devolution would also create serious problems within the Westminster Parliament. Under the terms of the Scotland Bill, MPs representing England, Wales and Ulster would have no rights over matters devolved to Scotland. Yet MPs representing Scottish constituencies would be entitled to vote on all matters affecting other parts of the United Kingdom. This anomaly became known as the West Lothian question as it was continuously raised by Tam Dalyell, the Labour Member for West Lothian and a firm opponent of devolution. To attempt to meet this situation the Commons passed an amendment by a majority of one and against the wish of the Labour Government. The amendment, originally moved by Lord Ferrers in the House of Lords, required that if any Commons vote on a matter devolved to Scotland was passed by the votes of Scottish MPs, then a second vote on the matter would have to be taken two weeks after the first. In the interval there would be pressure on Scottish MPs to abstain at the second vote on the ground that their constituents were not affected. Of course, the wider implication is that a Cabinet might lose its majority if Scottish MPs do not vote. Since Labour normally holds a large number of Scottish seats, a Labour Government with a small majority could find its authority undermined in moral terms if not in actual fact.

The anomaly highlighted by the West Lothian question is further aggravated by the existing distribution of seats in the House of Commons. On the basis of size of population, both Scotland and Wales were already overrepresented at Westminster. Scotland has seventy-two MPs; *pro rata* with England it should have but fifty-eight. The parallel figures for Wales are thirty-eight and thirty-two. Of course, this problem could be eased by reducing the number of constituencies in Scotland and Wales, but since Labour has overwhelming strength in Wales and majority support in Scotland, the idea of cutting down their representatives in the Commons did not appeal to a Labour Government. The plain fact is that any move to split up the political system of the United Kingdom would increase the chance of having Conservative Government in England.

No doubt that was one reason for the deep-rooted Labour hostility to devolution, and there were other reasons. It was feared that devolution would produce economic advantages for Scotland. The North of England thinks it is in competition with Scotland for industrial investment. If Scotland gains favours from the government, then the North fears the loss of opportunity and so Labour MPs from Northern constituencies were uneasy. A further cause of tension is that devolution does not fit the concept of democratic centralism favoured by many Left-wing MPs. This theory is that socialists should seek to capture power by winning control of a central legislature and use this position to impose their plans and policy on the whole community. Any divisions in a political system, in the form of federalism, devolution or strong, independent local authorities, make it more difficult, perhaps impossible, for the central legislature to impose a socialist programme. So Left-wing Labour MPs were aware that devolution could make yet more obstacles to the achievement of their long-term aims.

A quite contrary type of criticism of the Devolution Bill came from those who felt it did not go far enough: the existing degree of administrative devolution in Scotland required a genuine, federal assembly even with taxing powers. Others claimed that the constitutional complexities of the bill could make it unworkable. The original author of this book commented in the House of Commons, 'Seldom have I seen the House or the Government in quite such a mess . . . as we are in over this Bill . . . this House does not contain a majority for this Bill. As a person who has supported devolution for 20 years, I would rather see the House have the courage of its convictions and reject the Bill. It should be thrown out and the electorate should make their views known at a general election so that the Government can come back with a better Bill at a later stage.' But the bill was passed. John Mackintosh then argued strongly, right up to his death, for a 'Yes' vote in the referendum on the grounds that only a Scottish Assembly, however imperfect, could sort out the anomalies with Westminster.

The resistance to devolution was so strong that the government was forced to accept that the bills should be ratified by referenda. Later the government agreed that orders should be brought before Parliament to annul the legislation if less than 40 per cent of the electorate in Scotland and Wales supported the proposals for their respective countries. In Scotland 32.5 per cent voted 'Yes' while 30.4 per cent voted 'No'. Thus the vote, while in favour, was far short of the 40 per cent target required by Parliament. In Wales the support for devolution amounted to a derisory 11.8 per cent. So the legislation died.

At the 1979 election the Scottish Nationalists lost all but two of their seats in the Commons. The electorate was consulted and gave an answer, although the response was possibly not that which John Mackintosh had in mind. Nevertheless, it should not be assumed that the devolution issue is dead, at least in Scotland. If the economic situation in Scotland continues to deteriorate, that could lead to greater disenchantment with the two major parties.

To return to England, the proposals for devolution to Scotland and Wales inevitably raised the question – why should England be left out? If decentralization produced benefits, why deny them to the majority of the population of Britain? Faced with this challenge, the Labour Government issued a consultative document in 1976, *Devolution: the English Dimension*, which outlined arguments for and against the establishment of elected regional authorities in England. Such bodies could ease the burden on central government and so help it to concentrate on matters of national importance. They could take over the duties of nominated bodies, for example those for hospitals and water, and so make these services subject to democratic accountability and, in general, it is argued that they would strengthen popular interest and involvement in public affairs. On the other hand, elected regional bodies should not be able to damage the power of ministers to sustain their policies. There would be problems about fixing the boundaries of regional authorities and providing them with finance – a regional rate would scarcely be popular. Finally, there is no enthusiasm at all in local government circles for elected regional assemblies because it is feared that the regions would ultimately take over existing local government functions.

The Consultation Paper failed to provoke any public excitement for the idea of regional government beyond the Liberal Party and a few academic writers. Local government reform had raised expectations followed quickly by disillusion. The public mood seemed to be that more organizations mean more bureaucracy, complexity and expense. So with neither national nor local government in favour, the prospect for elected regional councils in England is bleak.

Northern Ireland

Northern Ireland poses quite unique problems. There is general agreement about the principle of allowing some measure of independence to the province. The problem is the enmity between Protestants and Catholics and the prospect for the Catholic minority of permanent subordination to the Protestant majority since the political parties are almost entirely based on religious affiliation. Thus most Ulster Catholics want Ulster to be merged with Eire in a united Ireland; Ulster Protestants vigorously oppose such a policy and stress their loyalty to the British Crown. Extremists on both sides resort to violence. The consequence is an apparently endless flow of death, injury and destruction of property.

The original devolution arrangements for Ulster were set out in the Government of Ireland Act 1920, supported by several conventional arrangements. A bicameral parliament at Stormont near Belfast was given control of domestic policy on matters that did not affect other parts of the United Kingdom. The financial arrangements were that the Northern Ireland government received 2.5 per cent of whatever was raised by UK taxation and could raise a very limited amount in taxation on its own account. Out of this it was agreed that services (unemployment relief, pensions, education, etc.) were provided at a similar level to those in Britain and if there was any money left, an 'imperial contribution' was paid towards the cost of common services such as the armed forces and the cost of conducting foreign policy. In return for the element of subsidy in this system, the Treasury was consulted about any expenditure which was abnormal by British standards. Thus Northern Ireland enjoyed the same standard of services and endured no greater taxation than the rest of the UK. In most fields, the Stormont government aimed to follow British practice in so far as this benefited its citizens but to act separately when special local conditions required separate treatment. Normally London left Stormont to get on with these policies, only intervening in 1969 at the time of the civil rights movement when there was a clear danger of a collapse of law and order due to disputes between Catholics and Protestants over local government, over the allocation of houses and of jobs and over the conduct of the Royal Ulster Constabulary and of the armed 'B' special reserves.

From 1969, the British government pressed certain reforms on the Stormont government, while the British army was deployed in Northern Ireland to try to separate inflamed areas and to preserve law and order. As the situation deteriorated, it was felt that some further evidence of the British government's determination not to allow the majority to lean on the minority was needed. In March 1972, the Stormont parliament and executive were abolished and direct rule was applied. After much discussion but no evident diminution in the communal struggle, the British government brought out a White Paper in March 1973 proposing a return to a modified Stormont system. The modifications were statutory proportional representation with 'power sharing' in the Cabinet and in the committees of the assembly, similar to those of Stormont except that control of security and law and order remained with the UK government. Elections were held in June 1973 but the assembly was first paralysed by the Protestant-led 'workers' strike' and then prorogued by Parliament. A constitutional convention was elected in May 1975 to try to agree on a new form of government but it too ended in failure, leaving the province under direct rule from Whitehall, through the Northern Ireland Office and the continued presence of the army.

Later attempts to solve the political deadlock have failed. The British government, whether Conservative or Labour, wants a solution that provides some safeguard for the Roman Catholic minority. Protestant politicians resist such restraints as impediments to democracy, defined as the will of the majority. The path least likely to cause trouble appears to be the continuation of direct rule from Westminster. However, this policy is unpopular with British ministers and civil servants, with Ulster Catholics and many Ulster Protestants. Reasons for this dislike are varied. Official circles in London would dearly like to be rid of Irish problems. The Catholic community objects to any part of Ireland being ruled from London. Most Protestants want to return to the days of Stormont when they could control the internal policies in Northern Ireland. In 1982 a fresh attempt was made to find a political solution by the establishment of a new assembly for the province. At first its role was to be consultative. The hope was that the assembly would come to be accepted by both religious groups; unanimity was not possible but the objective was to achieve a fairly broad consensus. The assembly can ask the Westminster Parliament for powers to be transferred to it provided that such requests are supported by 70 per cent of the assembly. Proposals failing to meet the 70 per cent target will still be considered if the Secretary of State for Northern Ireland believes that they enjoy support in both religious communities.

However, the Catholic parties have refused to take the seats they won in the assembly elections. Sinn Fein, the political wing of the IRA, will not co-operate because to do so would be to recognize the partition of Ireland. The Catholic Social Democratic and Labour Party (SDLP) will not co-operate because the assembly does not offer them the opportunity of power-sharing which they gained in 1973. Accordingly, the outlook for further progress through the assembly is not promising. Meanwhile, the number of seats for Northern Ireland in the House of Commons has been increased from twelve to seventeen, so it is now represented *pro rata* with the rest of the United Kingdom. This move weakens the case for a separate legislature at Stormont.

Democratic processes are difficult to operate in Northern Ireland for two basic yet related reasons. Political consent cannot be obtained in a community where a large minority deny the legitimacy of the state. Nor can democracy be expected to work smoothly in a society with rigid divisions, producing a permanent majority and a permanent minority. In a democratic system political parties expect to alternate in office. The minorities of today are kept happy by the prospect of a brighter tomorrow: the present majority is restrained from abusing power by the thought that it will be defeated at some subsequent election. These restraints do not apply in Northern Ireland. At present, it is hard to see a way forward.

13 The direction of change: the attitudes of the parties

Away from the Westminster model towards what?

At the end of Chapter 3 it was pointed out that the 1960s had seen a series of reform proposals in British government and that by 1980 most of these had been carried out in some form though the question of devolution had still to be settled. But these reforms failed to coalesce into a coherent system because there was no prevailing political doctrine which could provide answers to such questions as, how much power or influence should the House of Commons exercise or how far is it ˙desirable to have some democratic control over local and regional administration? The doctrine that is usually referred to in the opening pages of these royal commission or ministerial committee reports is a watered-down version of the late nineteenth-century belief in democracy which inspired the system described as the Westminster model. Genuflections are still made towards these old gods. Thus every time a nominated board is established to perform some administrative function, it is felt that some sort of democratic check is necessary and as elections cannot be run for each *ad hoc* board, another nominated body is created called an 'advisory council', the idea being that this acts in lieu of democratic control. In fact, these advisory councils neither have the strength conferred by expert knowledge, nor the experience of full-time work in the field, nor the responsibility conferred by direct election, but they cover up for the assumed need for some outside, popular supervision of these administrative agencies. At the same time, this adherence to the remnants of old political beliefs can add to the complication of government. For example, in the interests of efficiency, there should be amalgamations of the many regional and local authorities responsible for planning, development and the major environmental services. One solution, to do all this from Whitehall, which is allegedly under the scrutiny of the House of Commons, is impossible because of the extent and variety of the work. To hand the work over to elected local authorities covering an extensive area would be to set up bodies with a genuine degree of independence and power, and this is suspect. The result is the present multiplicity of bodies producing confusion both at the administrative level and on the part of the electorate, who are left wondering where and by whom decisions are actually taken. The same problems inhibit reform of the Commons. If it were possible to be clear about what power or general role the House should have, the relations between MPs and the executive could be adjusted accordingly. At present the fiction that each MP acts on his own judgement and takes a discriminating part in legislation is preserved by insisting that members must be present and pass through the lobbies night after night, though in fact such activity makes no material difference, but seriously impedes MPs in their task of keeping up to date with their special interests and with their constituency work.

It would be perfectly possible to recast the system of democratic supervision so as to restore a considerable part of the power of the Commons and to provide a devolved system of regional and local elected councils, which would mean that every important administrative body was subject to checks and examination at one or other of the three levels – national, regional or local. At the same time, the doctrine of ministerial responsibility could be limited, the degree of independent influence already existing in the civil service openly recognized, the Fulton reforms on management implemented and the Commons given powers of direct scrutiny of these subsections of the public service. The reason all this has not happened has not been because of technical problems but because there is no clear view of how government should be organized or controlled. The public are not very interested in such issues. They are used to politicians listening with some care to their demands, and the evidence of this attention and the obvious impact of general elections is usually sufficient to make them feel that the old maxims of the Westminster model still have some meaning.

If the present drift in ideas and in practice was recognized and accepted, the British political system could openly be established on a popular plebiscitary basis, with a quinquennial election to put one party or the other in power checked only by 'advisory committees' at certain levels – the Commons in the centre and similar nominated or elected bodies at suitable subordinate points in the administration. But though the machinery of government is developing in this direction, there is insufficient willingness to face the facts, to give up some of the pretences left over from the old period of vigorous, participatory democracy in order to remove the anomalies and rationalize the system.

The political parties and the community

If some clarity of purpose and coherence of action is to take the place of this drift, the ideas and energy ought to come from the political parties because, in theory, they are supposed to provide the driving force in political development. Yet the parties are rooted in the community. The old view of the party organizations dating from Ostrogorski's great work, *Democracy and the Organisation of Political Parties* (translated by F. Clarke in 1902), was that these bodies had a life of their own. They were organizations which could operate on the one hand on the electorate and on the other on the MPs, thus directly influencing policy. In fact, this is to elevate a small group of officials or 'caucus', as Ostrogorski called them, into a prominence they do not deserve. In Britain, the party machines are relatively weak and only hold meetings, choose candidates, run election campaigns and hold conferences. But the parties are also deeply influenced by the two ends of their operations, the one end being in the constituencies and the other in the Cabinet or Shadow Cabinet. The parties' greatest area of freedom and influence lies in the local constituency activists' power to choose the candidate for a parliamentary election. This is normally a once-and-for-all choice as it is unusual for the sitting MP to be refused renomination. But in making the choice, the selection conference in the case of the Labour Party, and the constituency executive in the case of the Conservative Party, are not easily moved by pressure from outside and even the leaders of the parties have found it hard to get close friends and political associates nominated. Senior party figures (such as Creech Jones on the Labour side after 1951 or Christopher Soames on the Conservative side after 1966) have found it almost impossible to be selected. Thus this is one important way in which the parties must reflect the opinion of the more active local members, a necessity which keeps the parties tied fairly closely to their local connections.

At the other end, the parties are tied to promulgating the views of the parliamentary leadership. In the Conservative Party, the organization is directly under the control of the leader while in the Labour Party, the organization serves the National Executive which is elected by the annual conference. In practice, being elected to the National Executive does give its members a degree of power and position. Some are elected because of their independent standing in the party and because of specific positions they have adopted on certain issues. A combination of the loyalty of trade union members, of the distribution of ministerial posts among MPs on the executive and of personal persuasion by the Prime Minister and senior colleagues helps to keep the Executive and the party leadership together, though there can be tension and even open conflict as occurred in 1976–82.

These two ends of the parties, in the constituencies and in the Cabinet, are brought together at regional and national conferences where the activists meet and exchange views with their leaders in the company of their MPs. On such occasions, there is a process of mutual education and stimulation which can at times descend to mere manipulation of the delegates by the leadership and can also rise to a high level of discourse about the basic problems confronting the nation. The activists are usually to the Left, in the case of the Labour Party, and to the Right, in the case of the Conservatives, of their parliamentary leaders. But there is a recognition by both activists and leaders that the party's task is to win an election and this means carrying the less opinionated sectors of the electorate with them. On the other hand, the leadership appreciates that it cannot indefinitely trample upon the deeper convictions of the solid party supporters.

Rooted in this way in the community, the parties are not organizations apart from British society which can, as it were, operate on society from outside. The parties are collections of those most actively concerned with the political aspects of government and, by long association, these groups of activists develop their own slogans, atmosphere, myths and methods. While Professor R. T. McKenzie was right to argue that the common purpose of winning elections and of maintaining a government in power imposes or produces an almost identical power structure in the parties, it is wrong to infer from this that the atmosphere within the parties is the same. A visit to the annual conferences of the two major parties should convince any observer of the deep contrasts, and this is as evident in the case of the minority parties such as the Liberals and Social Democrats, and the Scottish and Welsh Nationalists.

In the past it has been common wisdom that a major party will not suggest extreme policies, for to do so is to invite electoral defeat.

The winning side is that which holds the centre ground of politics. Often it has seemed that there was not too much difference between the major parties. Today the situation may be changing. After the 1979 Conservative victory, it is less clear that a party will suffer if it advocates policies which are a clear break with the past. Many people may not vote on the basis of a judgement of the party manifestos. They may not know what is in these documents; even those who do may not understand the implications of the proposals. Instead, it seems likely that voters choose on the basis of their experience, particularly of recent events. So the crucial question is not whether party programme A is preferred to party programme B; the issue is whether we want to keep the same government for the next five years or whether we want a different one. Is the devil we know better than the devil we don't know? If the government's record has been unsatisfactory, then some voters may not examine too closely the nature of the alternative devil. Should voters behave in this fashion, the contents of the Opposition's election manifesto become less significant in deciding the result. Occupation of the centre ground may not be essential for success. The major political parties may move further apart. In the following sections it is shown how the parties have developed their ideas and attitudes.

The Labour Party

Looking first at the Labour Party, its doctrine or beliefs are now by no means as clear cut as when the party constitution was adopted in 1918. Clause four declared that the objective of the party was 'to secure for the producers by hand or by brain the full fruits of their industry, and the most equitable distribution thereof that may be possible, upon the basis of the common ownership of the means of production and the best obtainable system of popular administration and control of each industry and service'.

Underlying this was a mixture of beliefs and of desires to remedy particular situations. British society was condemned by the early Labour leaders as being selfish and cruel. There was too much poverty, and hardship fell on those with the fewest reserves and resources. The accepted explanation was that the capitalist system of production was based on selfishness since only some in the community could prosper, as their prosperity had to be at the expense of others. This was because these capitalists lived in part or in whole out of the profits which should have been shared with all those who had helped in the process of production. The solution was to end the capitalist system by turning to public ownership, where community interests could be considered first, where profit would be eliminated and where work and reasonable prosperity could be guaranteed to all. But there was also a strong democratic element in the doctrine. The early Labour leaders supported votes for women, home rule not merely for Ireland but for Scotland and Wales, and were deeply concerned about the respect that should be paid to individuals, about the sense of freedom that was lacking in the nineteenth-century employer–employee relationship.

In the 1930s, the emphasis changed. The misery of the inter-war years in the areas of declining heavy industry left their mark, while the intractable nature of the problem was revealed by the failure of the first two Labour Governments. As a result, Labour thinking began to lay more stress on state control, on the need to take over at the centre and then to redistribute wealth and plan for the whole country. This drift of thought was emphasized in the 1940s by the Beveridge Report recommending a comprehensive pattern of welfare organized on a national basis, by the new emphasis on Keynesian planning and by Herbert Morrison's concept of the large national corporation as the best method of organizing nationalized industries. The populist element in the party's thinking remained, but focused more on the party conference than on the degree of scope to be given to the House of Commons or to local government. On the whole, the Labour Party took the old radical view that the task of Parliament was to enact the legislation foreshadowed or promised in the party's election manifesto. A Labour majority in the House of Commons should rally round the executive and protect it against the array of hostile capitalist forces, the Conservative Opposition being merely the front-line troops for the captains of industry, the financiers and the press barons.

These ideas came together and were put into operation by the 1945–51 Labour Government. Some of its politicians were backward-looking in that their major objectives were to remedy inter-war problems. The older, declining industries were nationalized, the Beveridge plans enacted, a National Health Service started and full employment maintained, the emphasis all being on the results of these policies, on their effects on people's lives.

When the Conservatives, after 1951, managed to retain most of the benefits of Labour rule with fewer controls, no rationing and an increasing standard of living, this helped to precipitate a flare-up inside the Labour Party. The dispute was over a mixture of issues, the Left or Bevanites being somewhat anti-American, opposed to rearmament, opposed to charges being introduced into the health service and, it was assumed, in favour of the traditional public ownership approach of the party. Later some of the Bevanites, though not Mr Bevan himself, added opposition to nuclear weapons to their list of policies.

When Mr Wilson was elected to the leadership in 1963, these doctrinal disputes were smoothed over and the Labour Party entered office in 1964 committed to a more rapid rate of growth, improved welfare benefits, more expenditure on schools, houses, roads and health and one major measure of public ownership – the renationalization of the steel industry. Mr Wilson had also said a good deal about modernizing the machinery of government. He had proposed a more extensive No. 10 staff, a smaller Cabinet and many of the modern techniques of business management in the civil service which were later elaborated in the Fulton Report. In 1966, he went further and proposed two new select or investigatory committees in the House of Commons. But after four years of difficulty and unpopularity, the attitudes of the Labour Party were more mixed. In economic affairs, fiscal controls were being practised by the Treasury to try and maximize the advantages gained by the 1967 devaluation of the pound. The new Ministry of Technology, on the other hand, was using more positive methods of intervention, injecting public money into industry, encouraging mergers and pushing technological innovation. At the same time, welfare benefits were increased but this did produce complaints about 'idlers' and 'scroungers', across-the-board welfare payments were becoming increasingly expensive and some Labour Party members began to press for more selective methods of eliminating poverty.

By the early 1970s, it remained true that the Labour Party was identified with the interests of the working classes, with the need for a reduction in class barriers and for the maintenance of the welfare system. But there was less confidence that rapid growth could be ensured and less assurance that the gaps between the really poor and the better-off workers could be narrowed by the traditional remedies. There was some evidence that Labour's emphasis on regional development had reduced the contrast between the prosperous Midlands and South-East and the older industrial areas. But it would be hard to identify a coherent or clear-cut Labour or socialist philosophy in the sense in which such philosophies had existed before 1914. The democratic element in the party's thinking was mainly a conviction that 'the people must be right', but popular views were indicated by the act of choosing every four or five years between the two major parties.

But the party fell into the hands of those who saw it as the spokesman of the organized workers in politics, a view which combined the Left and Centre. This was embodied in what was called 'the social contract' with the unions. When Harold Wilson retired in March 1976, the candidate of the radical Right, Mr Roy Jenkins, got only fifty-six votes and soon left British politics for the chairmanship of the European Commission. The Left-wing of the party continued to fight for the adoption of socialist policies. Meanwhile the actual direction of the party under Mr Callaghan, aided by Mr Foot, was in the hands of those who believed that its main task was to represent the interests of trade unions. Even this concept was strained as the wish of the Labour Government to restrain inflation clashed with the unions' desire to return to free collective bargaining. This conflict led to industrial unrest in the winter of 1978–9, the breakdown of the Government's pay policy and the Conservative election victory in 1979.

In opposition, the fratricidal strife within the Labour Party became stronger. This tendency was predictable. Whenever Labour has lost office there has always been strong pressure within the party to press for more extreme policies. The years 1931, 1951 and 1970 each provide evidence of such a movement; notably in the early fifties the Bevanites provided a challenge to the Labour leadership. But after defeat at the 1979 election, the feuding within the Labour Party was more severe because it was more highly organized. Various groups within the party were formed to try and achieve particular objectives. The most important were the Campaign for Labour Party Democracy (CLPD), the Labour Co-ordinating Committee (LCC), Militant and the Rank and File Mobilizing Committee (RFMC), which was an attempt to get the other Left-wing groups to work together. To try and counteract the influence of the extremists, the moderate wing of the party launched a Labour Solidarity Campaign in 1981. Thus the Labour Party became a battleground for its own warring factions. The conflict was regularly reported in the mass media and had a serious effect on public confidence in the party.

The LCC was first established in 1978 to campaign on policy issues, especially withdrawal from the EEC, more nationalization and stronger efforts to reduce unemployment, a package often known as the alternative economic strategy. The CLPD was founded in 1973 and became influential during the period of the Callaghan Government, urging constitutional changes in the Labour Party in order to make party leaders and MPs more responsive and responsible to opinion within the party. Support for these changes grew as many active members became more and more dissatisfied with the performance of the Labour Government between 1974 and 1979. In their defence the party leadership could argue that they had been hampered by the lack of a parliamentary majority; the choice had been hanging on by the skin of one's teeth or of giving up and holding an election in the face of adverse opinion polls. But the Left-wing were not satisfied and sought to ensure that the next Labour Government would do what the party wanted. So the CLPD pressed for three major reforms. The party leader should not be chosen by MPs alone. MPs should be subject to a process of re-selection between general elections. The party policy at an election, the manifesto, should be decided by the National Executive Committee on the basis of resolutions passed at the annual conferences. On the first two issues the CLPD was successful. Only the preparation of the manifesto stays unchanged and is a joint responsibility of the National Executive Committee and the Parliamentary Labour Party. Even here the practice altered, for there was much fuller consultation about the preparation of the 1983 manifesto than had previously been the case.

The CLPD secured remarkable success by the tactics of lobbying influential trade unionists and local party members and also by drafting model resolutions carefully designed to promote its aims, which could then be proposed by supporters at a wide variety of meetings. The Labour Solidarity Campaign also achieved success by discreet lobbying among leading trade unionists; among constituency parties there was little to show for its efforts. As a result of trade union voting power, the Left-wing lost control of the National Executive Committee and this paved the way for a fresh conflict between the NEC and Militant.

The Militant Tendency is an organization of Labour Party members whose views are far to the Left of traditional Labour doctrines. Militant believes that basic reforms in society cannot be achieved without victory in the class struggle. Workers must defeat employers and take over power. Class consciousness must be encouraged through industrial strife. Parliament is an inadequate means to secure change; there must be mass protest on the streets. Violence is not ruled out as a political weapon. Clearly, these views are incompatible with the Labour Party's acceptance of the parliamentary system. However, the conflict between the NEC and Militant has not been conducted in terms of an argument over policy but has developed as another constitutional wrangle. The NEC decided that Militant did not satisfy the criterion that any group within the Labour Party must be open and free to any members. Militant runs its own newspaper, has a substantial number of full-time employees and its financial basis is mysterious.

Friction within the Labour Party died down in the period before the 1983 election: all sides knew that further exhibitions of unbrotherly animosity would be disastrous for the party at the polls. Yet it is certain that tensions will re-emerge. Many local Labour Parties, particularly in London, are controlled by Left-wing supporters. Labour MPs with moderate opinions will come under increasing constituency pressure. The moderates' main support at party conferences comes from the voting power of trade unions where union delegations command massive block votes that may or may not reflect the views of the members they represent. One might expect the CLPD to challenge the way in which trade union power is exercised. The difficulty is that to open up arguments about how trade union votes are cast is to invite parallel arguments over the case for 'one person, one vote' in constituency Labour Parties that could undermine the influence of local Left-wing activists.

It used to be said that the Labour Party was a 'broad church', as it managed to contain such a wide range of opinion. Today that is less true, as many of the middle-class, Fabian-style intellectuals have departed. The Labour Party is largely a trade union party in which unions from the public sector play an increasing role. There are also many active individual members, deeply dissatisfied with the record of recent Labour Cabinets, who are determined to ensure that any future Labour Government shall carry out socialist policies and be responsive to the views of active party members. Whether this kind of Labour Party is capable of winning a general election is open to doubt. Due to higher unemployment, trade union membership is falling. Even more significant are the reports of opinion polls which show that less than half of union members fully support Labour Party policy.

The Conservative Party

The Conservatives, in contrast, have always been a party more accustomed to government and less interested in theories, but they have been equally class identified. Although the party had a strong aristocratic and agricultural interest, by the 1930s it was becoming closely connected with industry. Conservatives strongly held the Victorian belief that there were large areas of social organization in which it was simply improper for government to meddle. The government did not have to concern itself with the balance of payments (which was always expected to be favourable or self-adjusting), free trade meant that there was no need for elaborate connections with industry, the level of employment had to be left to the supply and demand for labour, and all that the government should do was elementary regulation in the interests of those sections of the community unable to defend themselves. With this view, the Conservatives in the inter-war period were for small-scale government and low taxes – the less done by government, the better and cheaper. At the same time, those public health, welfare and property protection services, which the central or local government did provide, should be efficiently administered. Thus, though Neville Chamberlain personified the Conservatives' connection with industry and with these *laissez-faire* ideas, he was a most effective and efficient Minister of Health from 1924 to 1929. In addition, the Conservative Party was closely identified with Britain's overseas empire, with the armed forces and with a foreign policy resting on a balance of power in Europe and elsewhere on the use of appropriate force to defend British interests.

In the 1930s, this Conservative outlook (rather than philosophy) did not face any very serious challenge from the Labour Party's ideas but events did inflict certain serious blows. The first was the pressure for independence or at least for a measure of internal self-government in India. But more serious was the alarm and despondency caused by the 1929–33 slump in which the confidence of British industrialists, already sapped by the doldrums of the 1920s, was seriously shaken. Some of the beliefs in the limited nature of government activity were abandoned. The Conservatives turned to protection disguised as imperial preference in 1933, and adopted a series of state measures to aid the reduction and consolidation of the declining heavy industries. This whole experience was so shaking that though the Labour Party had failed in both its minority governments and had shown no sign of making radical changes when it was in office, the Conservatives were seriously worried by the possibility and consequences of losing office. This sense of self-doubt also had some part in convincing Conservative leaders that neither Britain nor western society could survive another trauma of the seriousness of the First World War and thus, for the only time in history, the party abandoned its usual reliance on strong defences and the balance of power in Europe, adopting a policy towards Nazi Germany known as appeasement.

Although Conservative morale rallied under the pressures of the Second World War and first accepted and later was thrilled by the leadership of Winston Churchill, some of the other aspects of the war constituted a serious challenge to Conservative ideas. Wartime experience seemed to show that the government could control industry, produce full employment and higher output and then share the available produce more fairly. Also the movement of people involved in wartime adjustments, the identification of the Conservatives with appeasement and the 'fair shares' aspect of rationing all helped to undermine *laissez-faire* doctrines. As a result, the Conservatives found themselves badly defeated in 1945.

In response to the early activities and enthusiasm of the Attlee Government, the Conservatives mounted little challenge. Their older emotional attachments suffered with the decision to grant independence to India, Burma and Ceylon, but the new post-war MPs who came into the party (particularly at the 1950 election) were more exclusively concerned with domestic policy. In part, they developed the traditional Conservative view that government was inherently inefficient and undesirable, particularly fastening on the record of the nationalized industries. They were also protagonists of greater parliamentary supervision of the nationalized industries and supported the creation of the select committee on these industries against Labour resistance in the mid 1950s. But the Conservatives are also by tradition believers in a strong executive. They have felt this was necessary to conduct proper policy and, while in power, they trusted their own leaders. For most Conservatives, there was no need for elaborate control systems built into Parliament. Normally, having chosen a leader, they were prepared to leave everything to him. If there was trouble and they became unhappy, a direct visit to the leader or the Chief Whip would usually suffice. So there was no need for specialist committees, or reformed local government. As for the civil service, it has to be cut down to the lowest level necessary. But if a service was necessary, for example at the Ministry of Defence, then it should be supported against interference, particularly by a parliamentary committee which might well contain several busybodies, ultra Left-wingers or just cranks. Thus the Conservatives wanted a smaller, efficient and cheap executive but were then ready for a strong executive. And each time there was a surge forward in governmental activity, for instance during the war or under the post-war Labour Government, they were prepared to extend their view of what was necessary to cover some if not all the machinery which had been established.

But new problems appeared which required a more positive approach on the part of the government, and this threw the Conservatives into some disarray. One issue was 'the two Britains', the problem of regional discrepancies in the different levels of wages, unemployment and emigration north and south of a line drawn across England at about York. Gradually this forced the Conservatives into ideas of planning and influencing the location of industry, special plans being brought out for Scotland and for the North-East of England. Then the effort to locate industry in new areas and to build new towns showed up the weakness of local government as an executive agency and the first talk of reform began in Whitehall. In the early 1960s, it became fashionable to criticize British institutions and to say that this country was lagging behind its European competitors in many aspects of modern life from trade union structure to central heating, from the capacity to sell and provide after-sales service abroad to playing football. Devising and enacting appropriate remedies fitted more easily into the Labour Party's outlook than into that of the Conservatives and they produced few very positive ideas for reform or change. On the other hand, the disengagement from empire was completed, and then the Conservatives decided to apply to join the European Common Market in 1961.

After Labour won the general election of 1964 and 1966, the Conservatives were on the defensive, until the consequences following on the deflation of July 1966 began to make the Labour

Government unpopular. But, unlike the last years of the Attlee Government, the Conservatives developed no critique of the form or extent of government. Rather, they called for tax reductions, firmer enforcement of law and order and legislation to reduce the number of unofficial strikes. Thus, Conservative views had changed very little since the 1950s. There was a willingness to accept most of the new social and economic measures but to administer them as tightly as possible and to cut the cost of government. Within this framework, the Conservatives wanted to retain a strong executive and to strengthen similarly the hands of private authorities, particularly the employer in dealing with the unions. Some Conservative leaders when in opposition said that they would like to improve the Commons' capacity to scrutinize public expenditure and to appoint some more select or specialist committees, but this ceased to be their policy once in office again in 1970. The Expenditure Committee was made permanent but the atmosphere was no longer favourable to reform as it had been in the mid 1960s.

Mr Heath's Government was chiefly preoccupied with his attempt to restore the economy after Labour mismanagement. Time was spent undoing Labour measures on price and income controls but the main effort was put into a new Industrial Relations Act, a new Housing Finance Act, into tax cutting and the reduction of public expenditure on industry and alleged welfare extravagances. Unfortunately, the hoped-for investment boom did not materialize. Unemployment rose to a million and inflation got worse, so the government had to reverse many of its policies. It came to the rescue of Rolls-Royce and of Upper Clyde Shipbuilders and negotiated an incomes policy with the unions. It enlarged the money supply in order to reduce unemployment. The latter part of the Heath Government was taken up with the enforcement of its incomes policies and when the miners, having defeated the government in 1972, challenged again in late 1973, the government resisted while trying to find a formula for concession. In the end the miners called a strike and the government called an election. Unfortunately again for the Conservatives, the stern measures taken by the government added to its unpopularity, not to that of the miners and, after a series of mistakes or misfortunes in the campaign, the Conservatives just lost.

Two election defeats within a year had a major effect on the party. In 1975 Mrs Thatcher replaced Mr Heath as leader and the common assumption was that the Conservatives were moving towards more Right-wing policies. There was fresh emphasis on rolling back the frontiers of the state, that government should do less, that the way towards prosperity was to make more room for private enterprise to expand. Public expenditure was to be cut, except for defence and the police. Taxation was to be cut to stimulate personal initiative. Parts of state enterprise would be sold. After the 1979 election this programme was put into operation, a domestic break from consensus politics.

Certainly there are many influential Conservatives who are doubtful about this approach. Some would like their party to ensure that it commanded the centre ground of politics by introducing a form of proportional representation; this device would exclude all possibility that a future Cabinet would introduce socialist measures. There is also unease about monetarism. The control of the money supply to control inflation had a depressing effect on economic activity and increased unemployment greatly. Inflation and unemployment are often treated as alternative evils, but in the 1980s we have both. Whether political and social pressures will force changes in Conservative policy is unclear.

The SDP, Liberals and Nationalists

The SDP was launched on 26 March 1981, by the 'Gang of Four': Mr Jenkins, Mrs Williams, Dr Owen and Mr Rodgers. All of them had held office in Labour Cabinets. It marked the most dramatic rift in a British political party since Ramsey MacDonald and his associates left the Labour Party fifty years earlier. The immediate cause of the split was the constitutional changes taking place in the Labour Party; it was not that the Gang of Four and their sympathizers objected to reforms which improved internal party democracy, but they opposed the particular type of reform which was designed to strengthen the position of Left-wing elements in the Labour movement. But behind these technical issues there were profound policy differences which became steadily greater as Left-wing influence increased in the Labour Party. The Gang of Four were all keenly·pro-Europe: Labour policy was to leave the EEC. Their new Social Democratic Party favours multilateral disarmament as opposed to unilateral nuclear disarmament. The SDP favours the welfare state and state action to reduce unemployment but argues that government control of the economy must include an effective incomes policy if ruinous inflation is to be avoided. The SDP opposes further nationalization, believing it to be inefficient. It favours social equality but accepts that economic equality is an unrealistic objective. It strongly favours reform of the electoral system.

Thus there are major differences between the SDP and both the two major parties. Yet the degree of difference with the Liberals is virtually non-existent. Without too much difficulty the SDP formed an Alliance with the Liberals to fight national and local elections. One may well ask why the Gang of Four chose to start a new party instead of joining the Liberals. To have separate parties urging effectively identical policies seems absurd and is quite contrary to British political traditions. However, there were psychological and tactical advantages in forming a new organization. It was easier for Labour MPs and other party members to move to a new organization than to transfer to another party; the SDP could stand for the memory of Attlee, Morrison and Gaitskell, and argue that the present-day Labour Party had moved away towards more extreme policies. It was also true that the Gang of Four would obviously lead a new party whereas their position within the Liberal organization would have been uneasy and uncertain. The creation of a new party was also a more exciting enterprise which was expected to have a greater effect on public opinion: for the first twelve months – until the Falklands crisis arrived – the SDP gained much favourable publicity and appeared to be potentially successful. Twenty-eight Labour MPs joined the new party and two gains were recorded at by-elections.

The 1983 election proved to be a near disaster for the SDP. The party won only six seats in the Commons and all but five of their former thirty MPs were defeated. Mr Jenkins and Dr Owen were successful, no doubt greatly assisted by the publicity they enjoyed during the campaign. Mr Wrigglesworth almost certainly survived at Stockton South because his Conservative opponent was shown to have had fascist connections that had been concealed. After the election Dr Owen replaced Mr Jenkins as leader with almost indecent haste. The central issue now is whether the SDP can continue as an effective, separate party.

As noted already, the policy differences between the SDP and the Liberals are slim. Voters tend to link the two parties together and see them jointly as holding the middle ground between the extremes of Toryism and Socialism. If the parties joined together there would be some saving on administrative expenditure.

Awkward disputes about which party should contest which seat would also be avoided. At the 1983 election the SDP and Liberals agreed to share candidatures equally between the parties, but this arrangement inevitably caused some local irritation, especially among Liberals who had much stronger organization at local level. A vigorous constituency party that cannot put forward its own candidate at a parliamentary election will be seriously frustrated. Yet it would be political suicide for the SDP and the Liberals to fight against each other. The way out of this dilemma could be for the two parties to agree on local joint selection of a candidate representing the Alliance. Liberals favour this solution; the SDP does not, probably fearing that the Liberals would do better under such an arrangement, which could tend to lead to the absorption of the SDP by the Liberal Party.

The Liberal Party was replaced after 1918 as a major political force by the Labour Party. In the period after 1945 the Liberals were at a very low ebb and had significant support only in rural areas of Scotland, Wales and South-West England where industrial development was largely absent and so there was little trade union activity. Religious nonconformity remained strong in these areas and combined with the anti-landlord, anti-aristocratic feeling which was the basis of historic liberalism. More recently, this pattern has altered. There has been an emergence of fresh support curiously scattered around England. Some of this support has emerged in suburbs of owner-occupied housing of modest dimensions. Sometimes it is linked to particular local circumstances or an individual, e.g. Mr Stephen Ross (Isle of Wight) and Mr Cyril Smith (Rochdale). And in Liverpool the Liberals have replaced Conservatives as the main opponents of Labour at local elections.

Between 1945 and the 1983 election Liberal strength in the Commons has fluctuated between six and fourteen. Of course, this is grossly disproportionate to their strength in terms of votes. In 1983 the Liberal/SDP Alliance secured 26 per cent of votes cast but won only twenty-three seats or 3.5 per cent of the 650 constituencies. With 28 per cent of the vote Labour won 209 seats. The reason for this fantastic disproportion is that the Labour vote is heavily concentrated in industrial, mining and inner-city areas, whereas Alliance support was widespread across the country, but rarely sufficient to actually win a seat. Indeed, to an extraordinary degree any Alliance victory depended on the reputation of an individual candidate. The sayings commonly quoted in the 1950s that 'A candidate cannot be worth more than 500 votes' or 'I would vote for a pig if the party put one up' are simply no longer true.

It is not surprising that the Liberals and their SDP allies urge the need for a fairer electoral system. They are also keen on other schemes of institutional reform which enable people to take a more active role in public affairs. Thus, during the Lib-Lab pact with the Callaghan Government the Liberals urged on the cause of devolution for Scotland and Wales. The most active Liberal associations are keen on stirring up interest in purely local issues – a process known as community politics. The Liberals are free of links with class interests. Essentially they are the party of the centre ground, the middle way. Their weakness is explained by two major factors. Unlike the Conservative and Labour Parties there are no powerful economic forces to subsidize and support them. And they are treated harshly by the form of the electoral system.

The main plank of the nationalist parties in Scotland and Wales is a solution to the problem of local government, albeit an extreme one in that they advocate total independence. In practice, these parties have gained support through disappointment at the economic performance of the government in London combined with irritation at remote and impersonal bureaucracy. In Wales, the desire to preserve the Welsh language is another major factor and the Welsh Nationalists (Plaid Cymru) are strongest in North-West Wales where the language is still in common use. It is doubtful how many of those who work for the nationalist candidates truly want full independence. The nationalist cause prospered in the 1970s but is now in decline.

Conclusion: no clear direction

The major cause of division in British political opinion is based on class. People who regard themselves as working-class generally vote Labour; those who regard themselves as middle-class tend to vote Conservative. Yet there are also many who do not fit this model. The decline in support for the major parties suggests that class matters less than it did. Society is less class conscious because of greater economic equality in terms of income, because of the spread of home ownership and through the erosion of social distinctions, for example in relation to dress. Wage levels in some traditional working-class occupations are higher than salary levels in some traditional middle-class occupations. Nevertheless, it remains true that the South of England, relatively prosperous and content, elects Conservative MPs while the industrial North elects Labour MPs.

A feature of political life which has intensified since the early 1960s is a willingness to challenge those in authority. Democrats can welcome the trend as a flowering of the independence of spirit. The movement has had institutional recognition and acceptance through the establishment of commissioners to hear complaints about local and national administration. Planning inquiries into development proposals encourage public participation by inviting the expression of opinion. Victorian-style deference is in decline. Each man and woman is held to be as good as his or her neighbour, even if the neighbours have more money, and naturally this mood affects politicians. Their actions are viewed more critically and they enjoy less automatic respect. Similarly, political parties stimulate less enthusiasm and more cynicism.

One consequence of this mood is that people who have a cause, who wish to see change, tend to join a pressure group rather than a political party. The pressure groups flourish. They seem well able to recruit volunteers who provide energy and money. Some of these bodies have become well-known and constantly press their views on ministers and MPs. Leading examples are CND, Shelter, the Child Poverty Action Group, Friends of the Earth, and the League Against Cruel Sports. In the case of abortion opposing organizations exist to put both sides of the argument. In addition to these groups pressing a particular issue there are many long established, financially powerful bodies with permanent staff that exist to protect certain interests. The CBI, the TUC, the BMA, the NFU and the associations of local authorities fall into this broad category. As a result ministers are forced to spend much time considering the views of interested parties whenever a review of law or policy is being undertaken.

It is now often said that we live in a pluralist society in which no party or group is wholly dominant. Political victories are won through a coalition of interests. The coalitions are ever changing so there is no total success and no total defeat. Sometimes the trade unions win; sometimes the employers win. Sometimes the advocates of better social services win and sometimes not. Sometimes Mrs Whitehouse wins and then she loses. This model of politics can produce a picture of the government doing little more than deciding which group of interests has assembled most weight on a particular occasion and then adjudicating in their favour.

Of course such a view is grossly exaggerated. Governments have views and are in a powerful position to put them into effect. However, they do not always succeed. Mr Callaghan was unable to secure acceptance of his incomes policy in 1978. And governments do not have a policy on all issues. In such areas, the interest groups are very powerful. The tobacco industry has fought a remarkable campaign to prevent prohibition of the advertisement of their products. Similarly, the connection between alcohol and ill-health, crime and road accidents is beyond question. No new action is taken to impede the consumption of alcohol. Inaction can be defended as upholding individual liberty, but no parallel tolerance is shown to other drugs, possibly less harmful, which are not supported by strong commercial interests.

Are governments too weak when faced with opposition from pressure groups? Is the nation's economic decline largely the fault of timid and ineffective political direction? Support for the idea that what is needed is stronger government can be found in all parts of the spectrum. What is lacking is any consensus on the objectives that tougher leadership should follow. Right-wing opinion wants stronger action against trade unions and against crime; the Centre favours the imposition of some form of incomes policy; the Left wants more state intervention to limit the inequalities of capitalist society. Those who speak of the need for the smack of firm government are likely to be the first to complain if the type of firm government they get is not to their liking.

A different theory to explain the shortcomings of state action was set out in a White Paper *The Reorganisation of Central Government* (Cmnd 4506) issued by the Heath Government soon after taking office in 1970. The argument here was that government action is not always successful because government tries to do too much. If ministers intervened less in the affairs of the nation, then their actions could be more fully considered. If the state does less, there is more scope for personal initiative and individual freedom. Such a philosophy is acceptable to Conservative and Liberal opinion, but not to socialists. It is a view shared by Mrs Thatcher's Government even more strongly than that of Mr Heath. Yet, in practice, it runs into difficulties. Businessmen who are fervent supporters of private enterprise are keen to limit the role of the state, but if their own industry gets into difficulties they are not averse to seeking state aid either in the form of investment grants or restrictions on imports to ease the pressure of foreign competition. Liberals, too, face a dilemma. They are the strongest advocates of the value of membership of the EEC, yet the European Commission is always trying to impose common standards throughout the Community which require fresh laws and regulations in this country. The path of those who advocate less government is not smooth.

Conservatives favour the combination of stronger government and less government. Psychologically this is an awkward marriage. The Thatcher Government is in favour of reducing central controls over local authorities. It also wants local authorities to spend less as part of the national campaign to spend less and cut down on the scale of public sector activity. So, many minor administrative controls over local government are removed but, at the same time, the method of central subsidy is changed to exert greater influence over local expenditure. These changes can be described as firm government and, in a sense, less government; but local authorities do not enjoy more freedom.

The result of this discussion is inconclusive. It does not answer the question of how British government is likely to develop in the next decade. It shows that the community has not gone through dramatic experiences (or rapid industrialization, defeat in war, or class or race conflict) which would produce a powerful political philosophy, a philosophy which would then provide the answers to the major problems of political organization. There are remnants of old beliefs, a new hedonism, and interest largely in the outcome of government, an impatience with authority, a dislike of élite assumptions, all mixed together. As a result it is likely that the solutions adopted will be mixed but will, on the whole, confirm the present drift towards centralized executive power. At the same time there may be increasing doubt as to whether politics and politicians matter as much as we used to think. Leaving aside the question of war, how far do governments make a difference to our daily lives? Labour supporters are deeply disappointed with the performance of recent Labour Governments. The key phrases of the past, the 'technological revolution' of the 1960s and the 'social contract' of the 1970s seem, in retrospect, to have had little meaning or little effect. Mrs Thatcher's Government had a firm Commons' majority and was expected to make some changes that would reverse the previous direction of affairs. Public expenditure was to be reduced; in fact, it has grown although the distribution between services has been slightly adjusted. Taxation was to be reduced; except for the rich this has not happened. Great emphasis was placed on improving law and order; the outcome was more crime. Monetary restraint produced lower inflation but this did not, as intended, greatly improve economic conditions. Instead, there was a massive rise in unemployment to a figure which, even a few years before, would have seemed quite unacceptable from a political standpoint. But in 1983 many voters seemed to agree that unemployment was unavoidable, so the government should not be blamed for it. In relation to economic and social behaviour there is a growing feeling that there are limits to what the state can do, or should try to do, to alter existing patterns. Of course, not everyone shares this view. But that such a mood exists at all is a startling contrast to the universal expectation aroused after 1945 that state action could make a major and positive contribution to a better life.

Further reading

It is inevitable that books on British government become out of date. Listed below are some of the more recent and most valuable contributions to the literature. However, to keep abreast of current events this reading should be supplemented by quality newspapers and journals of opinion, such as the *Economist* and the *New Statesman*.

Bagehot, W., *The English Constitution* (Fontana 1963)
Beer, S. H., *Modern British Politics* (Faber 1969)
Beer, S. H., *Britain Against Itself* (Faber 1982)
Beloff, M. and Peele, G., *The Government of the United Kingdom* (Weidenfeld & Nicolson 1980)
Birch, A. H., *Political Integration and Disintegration in the British Isles* (Allen & Unwin 1977)
Bogdanor, V., *Devolution* (Oxford University Press 1979)
Bogdanor, V., *The People and the Party System* (Cambridge University Press 1981)
Brown, R. G. S. and Steel, D. R., *The Administrative Process in Britain* (Methuen 1979)
Butler, D., *Governing Without a Majority* (Collins 1983)
Butler, D. E. and Stokes, D., *Political Change in Britain* (Macmillan 1975)
Chapman, L., *Your Disobedient Servant* (Chatto & Windus 1978)
Chapman, R. and Dunsire, A. (eds.), *Style in Administration* (Allen & Unwin 1971)
Crossman, R. H. S., *Inside View* (Cape 1972)
Finer, S. E. (ed.), *Adversary Politics and Electoral Reform* (Wigram 1975)
Finer, S. E., *The Changing British Party System* (AEI 1980)
Gilmour, I., *The Body Politic* (Hutchinson 1971)
Headey, B., *British Cabinet Ministers* (Allen & Unwin 1974)

Heclo, H. and Wildavsky, A., *The Private Government of Public Money* (Macmillan 1974)

Hill, M., *The State, Administration and the Individual* (Fontana 1976)

Johnson, N., *In Search of the Constitution* (Pergamon 1977)

Kavanagh, D. (ed.), *The Politics of the Labour Party* (Allen & Unwin 1982)

Kellner, P. and Crowther-Hunt, N., *The Civil Servants* (Macdonald & Jane's 1980)

McKenzie, R. T., *British Political Parties* (Heinemann 1964)

Mackintosh, J. P., *The British Cabinet* (Stevens 1977)

Marquand, D. (ed.), *John P. Mackintosh on Parliament and Social Democracy* (Longman 1982)

Minogue, M. (ed.), *Documents on Contemporary British Government* (Cambridge University Press 1977)

Morgan, J., *The House of Lords and the Labour Government 1964–1970* (Oxford University Press 1975)

Norton, P., *The Commons in Perspective* (Martin Robertson 1981)

Punnett, R. M., *Front Bench Opposition* (Heinemann 1973)

Richards, P. G., *The Local Government System* (Allen & Unwin 1983)

Robinson, A., *Parliament and Public Spending* (Heinemann 1978)

Wade, H. W. R., *Administrative Law* (Oxford University Press 1961)

Walker, P. G., *The Cabinet* (Heinemann 1972)

Walkland, S. A. (ed.), *The House of Commons in the Twentieth Century* (Oxford University Press 1979)

Walkland, S. A. and Ryle, M. (eds.), *The Commons Today* (Fontana 1981)

Index

Aberdeen, Lord 16, 147
Acheson, Dean 190
administrative tribunals 132–5
agriculture 12, 112, 113, 125, 133,
    218; 1947 Act 113
Allen Report (1965) 206
Alliance *see* Liberal Party; Social
    Democratic Party
alternative economic strategy 233
Appropriation Act 139
Armstrong, Sir William 72
army: and law enforcement 137–8; in
    Northern Ireland 137–8, 222, 223
Army Act 138
Atkins, Humphrey 182
Attlee, Clement (Earl) 27, 59, 60, 68,
    76, 78, 79, 90, 98, 240

Bagehot, Walter 16, 19, 127, 128; *The
    English Constitution* 126
balance of payments 27, 42, 186, 235
Baldwin, Stanley (Earl) 48, 51, 52, 76,
    95, 100, 101
Balfour, A. J. (Earl) 29, 100, 150
Balogh, Lord 183
Bank of England 27, 183
Basnett, David 92
Beer, Professor Samuel, *Modern
    British Politics* 84
Beith, Alan 117
Benn, Tony 50–1, 106, 120, 137, 195
Bentham, Jeremy 31
Bevan, Aneurin, Bevanites 36, 59,
    66, 162, 199, 231, 232
Beveridge Report (1942) 26, 230
Bevin, Ernest 68, 76, 78
Bill of Rights 129, 131–2
Birch, Nigel 77
Bonar Law, Andrew 48, 69
Boundary Commission 110
Brand, Speaker 150
British Broadcasting Corporation
    (BBC) 12, 27, 90, 93, 94–5, 171
British Medical Association (BMA)
    90, 243

British Rail 90, 133–4
Brittan, Leon 77
Brixton riots (1981) 140
Brown, George (Lord) 49, 50, 77, 78,
    79, 181
budgets 25, 148, 159, 160, 173, 176
Butler, David and Stokes, Richard,
    Political Change in Britain 55, 57,
    115–16
Butler, R. A. (Lord) 52, 70, 71, 146
Butt, Ronald, *The Power of
    Parliament* 145–6, 147
by-elections 20, 38, 61, 74, 99, 115,
    116–17, 164, 215, 240

Cabinet 62, 72, 83, 227, 228;
    agenda 69; Cabinet Office 68,
    72; Cabinet Secretariat 68, 69, 185;
    Central Policy Review Staff 89; and
    civil service 87, 185; committees
    68, 69, 70, 72, 78, 156, 188, 214;
    dismissals and resignations 16, 70,
    77, 80; and electorate 41–2;
    functions and organization 11, 16,
    79–80; and House of Commons 16–
    17, 20–1, 29–30, 85, 153, 176; 'inner
    cabinets' 69, 82; and media 94,
    95; meetings of 78, 79–80;
    nineteenth-century 16–18; PES
    Committee 156; power of 36, 37,
    38, 39; and Prime Minister 16, 38,
    39, 67–72, 76–82, 98; and referenda
    120; selection of members 16, 76–7,
    78, 187; Statistical Office 68
Callaghan, James 49, 50, 59, 60, 61,
    69, 73, 76, 77, 78, 79, 81, 83, 85, 107,
    116, 117, 124, 164, 232, 233, 242, 244
Campaign for Labour Party Democracy
    (CLPD) 232, 233, 234
Campaign for Nuclear Disarmament
    (CND) 88, 243
capital punishment 115, 163, 188
Carlisle, Mark 77
Carrington, Lord 78, 182
Castle, Barbara 70, 80, 81, 182, 194–5

Central African Federation 75
Central Council for Local Government
    Finance 211
Central Policy Review Staff 67, 89
Central Statistical Office 67
'Chalk pit' case 133
Chamberlain, Austen 100
Chamberlain, Joseph 42, 149
Chamberlain, Neville 75, 76, 101–2,
    146, 177, 235
Chancellor of the Exchequer 70, 77,
    156, 211; Budget speech 159, 173
Chapman, Brian, *British Government
    Observed* 189
Chief Whip 63, 64, 65, 74, 81, 150,
    151, 156, 237; *see also* Commons,
    House of
Child Poverty Action Group 243
Churchill, Randolph 42, 149
Churchill, Winston 59, 60, 68, 76, 79,
    101, 102, 106, 115, 236
Civil List 156
civil rights 129–30, 135–7
civil service 12, 18, 27–9, 40, 153, 179–
    97, 237; accountability 189;
    anonymity 190, 193; appointments
    to senior posts (promotion) 88, 190,
    196; centralization 179, 184, 189;
    Civil Service Commission 183; Civil
    Service Department 68, 185, 191–2;
    criticisms of 186–92;
    decentralization 213; doctrine of
    ministerial responsibility 179–83,
    184, 190, 191, 193, 194, 226;
    expenditure, control of 185, 192;
    Fulton Report on reform of 28, 34,
    180–1, 189–92, 194, 213, 226, 231;
    and government 34, 39, 40, 86–9;
    impartiality 18, 21; management
    34, 189–90, 191–2, 193, 231; and
    ministerial control 39, 179–83, 186–
    8; and nationalized industries 200;
    Northcote–Trevelyan principles
    183–4; number of civil servants 27;
    and ombudsman 136, 181; and
    Parliament 190, 192–4; and party
    manifestos 106; pay settlement
    conflict (1981) 192; and political
    advisers 194–7; and pressure
    groups 28–9, 113–14; and Prime
    Minister 38, 41, 67, 72–3, 86–9,
    112–13; and the public 112–14, 192–
    4; and quangos 199; recruitment
    to 18, 31, 34, 183–4, 189; and
    regionalism 213; role 27–9; Select

Committee 169; structure 34,
    184–5, 189, 194; training 184, 189,
    190
class, social 231; declining role of
    242; of Prime Minister 58–9; in
    voting behaviour 54, 55–6, 57
Clay Cross UDC 204–5
coalition government 26, 51–2, 53,
    110
commissioners, nineteenth-century
    17
Common Market (EEC) 37, 120, 174,
    178; British membership and
    applications 12, 39, 60, 61, 63, 68,
    70, 76, 85, 108, 115, 118, 188, 233,
    237; and financial contributions to
    61; and Labour Party 83, 108, 118,
    120, 121; Liberal-SDP support for
    239, 245; referendum 118, 120, 121;
    Select Committee 169; tax
    system 12
Commons, House of: adjournment
    debates 161, 163; backbenchers *see*
    Members of Parliament; bills,
    passage of 18, 80–1, 148, 151, 152,
    153–5, 168; and Cabinet 16–17, 18,
    20–1, 29–30, 85; civil and military
    estimates 148; and civil service
    192–4; committees 66; cross-
    voting 161, 163–4, 177; debates
    30, 143, 148, 149, 150, 159, 161–3;
    and devolution 218–19, 220;
    divisions, party 29, 149, 152, 161,
    168; emergency debates 162;
    financial control 18, 32–3, 148–9,
    155–61; governing through 39, 40–
    1, 84–6, 142–78; guillotine 81, 150,
    152, 164, 217; influence and power
    31, 42–3, 145–6, 161–7, 176–7, 225–7;
    'issues of conscience' 162–3;
    Leader of 79, 150, 151; and
    legislation 153–5; and ministers
    16–17, 143, 151; National Audit
    Office 158; and nationalized
    industries 200–1; nineteenth-
    century 16–22, 146–7, 148, 152;
    Order Papers 163; parliamentary
    procedures 33, 34, 161–5, 167;
    pressing the government from
    floor 161–5; pressing the
    government: upstairs and informal
    methods 165–7; private member's
    bills 19, 151, 158, 161, 162–3, 201;
    Question Time 19, 31, 143, 161,
    163, 173; relations with Lords 11,

19, 32, 174–6; role 142–7;
Speaker 30, 150, 159, 162, 163;
Standing and Select Committees
168–72; Standing Orders 29, 150,
155, 158–9, 161; and taxation 158–
60; televising 172–4; 'Ten Minute
Rule' 154, 161, 172–3; timetable
29–30, 41, 63, 147, 150–2, 161, 162,
164; voting procedure and
abstentions 161–5, 177; whipping
system 63–5, 66, 85, 149, 151, 163,
166, 172, 177; *see also* Chief Whip;
MPs; Opposition; Select Committees
of House
Commonwealth constitutions 14–15
Comptroller and Auditor General
148–9, 158, 201
Confederation of British Industry 90,
243
conscription 12, 26
Conseil d'Etat (France) 134–5
Conservative Party 20, 24, 26, 53, 54,
227, 235–9; Annual Conferences
24, 83–4, 228; appeasement 75,
236; area and subject committees
165, 166; backbenchers 144, 149,
163, 166–7, 177; by-elections 117;
constituency parties 227; and
devolution 216; and electors 56,
103–4, 105–12; 'Fourth Party' 149;
governments 26, 27, 33, 57, 58, 76–
80, 83, 85, 89–90, 169, 231, 236–7,
238; Home Affairs group 166; and
House of Lords 174–5;
leadership 39, 59–61, 75, 76–80, 97,
100–2; leadership selection 45, 47–
9, 51, 52; and local government 33,
62, 122, 206, 209, 210, 211–12;
manifestos 105–9; and mass
media 93–6; mineworkers'
confrontation with 56, 91, 124; and
nationalized industries 201, 202;
1922 Committee 165, 166; and
opinion polls 115–16; party
loyalty 62, 64, 66, 75, 76, 100;
patronage 66; policies and beliefs
235–9; Policy Unit 195; and
pressure groups 89–92; sacking of
leader 97, 100–2; selection of
candidates 227; and trade unions
56, 60, 69, 89–90, 92, 238; and two-
party system 53–5; whips 64, 85,
166
Consolidated Fund 156
constituencies 20, 24, 53–5, 144, 216–

17, 227–9
Constitution, British 11–15;
Commission on 117, 216, 217
Corrupt Practices Act (1883) 32
Council of Europe 66
Court Line affair 136–7
Court of Appeal 131
courts: constitutional role 130–2; law
enforcement 137, 138, 139; in
Northern Ireland 138
Crichel Down case (1954) 133, 134,
181–2
crime 103, 130, 140; and law
enforcement 137–41
Cripps, Sir Stafford 76
Crosland, Anthony 69, 80
Crossman, Richard 66, 80, 81, 106,
169, 196; *Inside View* 94
Crown 13, 16, 19, 129, 202;
constitutional role 11, 19, 51–3, 126
Crowther Commission 33
Crowther-Hunt, Lord, *The Civil
Servants* 195
Cunningham, George 63
Curzon, Lord 51

Dalyell, Tam 218
Day, Sir Robin 94
decentralization *see* local government;
nationalist parties; regionalism
decision-making 37, 67–8, 80, 186
defence: Cabinet Committee on 70;
expenditure 164; Minister of
Defence 70, 166; nuclear
disarmament 57, 82, 231; policies
12, 25, 26, 37, 60, 69, 70, 82, 87, 165;
Select Committee 169, 171
democracy, evolution of 13–14, 225–7
Denning, Lord 131
devaluation 40, 60, 69, 77, 79, 231
devolution 215–21, 225, 242;
referendum 63, 85, 118–19, 121,
176, 217, 220
Devolution Act (1978) 63, 217
Devolution Bill (1976–7) 146, 164,
176, 217, 218
Devolution: the English Dimension
221
Dilhorne, Lord 48
direct action 124–5, 139
Disraeli, Benjamin 42, 105
dissolution of Parliament 19, 65, 71
Douglas-Home, Alec (Earl) 40, 48,
52, 71, 76, 95, 100, 117, 216
Driberg, Tom (Lord Barking) 172

Du Cann, Edward   171
Dugdale, Sir Thomas   181–2

East of Suez   60, 68, 69, 70, 165
economy   26, 27, 28, 37, 56, 58, 60–1,
    72, 79, 80, 85, 116, 186, 244;
    alternative strategy   233; Cabinet
    Committee on long-term strategy
    70; free market   213; Medium Term
    Economic Assessment   156, 157;
    monetarism   88, 171, 211, 239; *see
    also* public expenditure; taxation
Eden, Sir Anthony (Lord Avon)   59,
    68, 95, 101; *Full Circle*   71
Edinburgh, Philip, Duke of   126
education   25, 27, 104, 105, 112, 126,
    131, 169, 207, 209, 218;
    comprehensive   209, 210
Education Bill (1980)   175
Edward VIII, King (Duke of
    Windsor)   126
'electoral pendulum'   57, 58
electoral system   109–12, 241–2; by-
    elections   20; extension of
    franchise   14, 23, 28, 32;
    manifestos   83, 105–9; nineteenth-
    century   19–20; Prime Minister's
    right to choose date of election   58;
    proportional representation   19–20,
    111, 112, 239; redistribution of seats
    (1983)   110; secret ballot   32; single
    member constituencies   20; two-
    party system   53–5, 164
electorate: and civil service   112–15,
    192–4; disillusionment with politics
    122–4; effect on political parties   12;
    expectations   25, 27, 42, 43, 58, 87,
    91, 103–5, 108–9, 122–4; and law
    enforcement   137–41; leadership's
    relations with   41–2, 43, 103–41;
    legal disputes   130–5; and legitimacy
    of government   125–9; mass   23–6,
    27, 28, 42, 67, 127–9; MPs' relations
    with   23–4; ombudsman   135–7;
    opinion polls   115–16; party
    loyalties   41–2, 57, 116; personal
    freedom   129–30; referenda   118–
    22; voting behaviour   12, 42, 54–8,
    110–12; *see also* by-elections; general
    elections
Elizabeth II, Queen   48, 52
Ellenborough, Lord   147
Employment Act (1982)   125
Employment and Productivity,
    Ministry of   182–3, 185

Employment Policy (1944)   26
European Coal and Steel Community
    37
European Commission   232, 245
European Communities Bill   177
European Economic Community *see*
    Common Market
European Parliament, elections to   83,
    109, 111
Exchequer and Audit Departments
    Act   148
executive: and legislative relations   16,
    29–31, 126, 142, 145, 146–7, 226, 237;
    how control of parliament was gained
    by   147–53; *see also* government

Fairbairn, Nicholas   182
Fairlie, Henry, *The Life of Politics*
    123, 145, 147
Falklands crisis (1982)   61, 70, 88, 93,
    94, 182, 240
federal system   217–18, 219, 220
finance   18, 148–9, 155–61; local
    government   203, 204, 210–12; *see
    also* public expenditure; taxation
Finance Bill   148, 159, 160
First World War   26, 27, 28, 236
Foot, Michael   49, 50, 98, 99–100, 232
Foreign Office   80, 89, 147, 181, 182,
    188
foreign policy   30, 42, 68, 70, 80, 87,
    88, 152, 169
Foreign Secretary   68, 70, 79, 181
'Fourth Party'   149
Franks Report (1957)   133, 134–5
Fraser, Tom   70
free trade   26, 31, 235
freedom, personal   129–30
Freud, Clement   117
Friends of the Earth   243
Fulton Report (1968)   28, 34, 180,
    189–90, 191–2, 193, 194, 200, 213,
    226, 231
*The Future Structure of the Health
    Service* (Green Paper)   208

Gaitskell, Hugh   82, 98, 240
'Gang of Four'   239, 240
Gaulle, General Charles de   119
general elections   11, 17, 20, 24, 26,
    50, 53–4, 56, 60, 61, 62, 75, 78, 83, 85,
    91, 103, 104, 109–12, 123, 164, 217,
    220, 233, 240; and opinion polls
    115, 116; party manifestos and
    campaigns   105–9; Prime Minister's

right to choose date of 58, 73–4; *see also* by-elections; European Parliament

George V, King 51–2

Gilbert, W. S. 20

Gilmour, Sir Ian 77; *The Body Politic* 37

Gladstone, William Ewart 16, 32, 42, 147, 148, 179

Gordon-Walker, Patrick, *The Cabinet* 70, 78

government: acceptance by electorate (legitimacy) 125–9; administrative reform 31–2; centralized 179, 203; and civil service 86–9, 179–97; decisions in 37; expenditure 26; history 11–22, 31; and House of Commons 84–6, 142–78, 161–7; income 24; limitations on 177; and mass media 93–6; nineteenth-century political reform 31–2; outside Whitehall 198–224; and Parliament 142–78; power structure 36–40; present style 36–44, 225–46; and pressure groups 89–92; and referenda 118–22; scope 21–2, 25–34, 40; and select committees 168–72; special powers taken by 137–8; votes of confidence 164–5

Government of Ireland Act (1920) 184, 222

Greater London Council (GLC), cheap fares policy of 131

Green Papers 33, 154, 208

Griffith, Professor 151

Habeas Corpus Act (1679) 11

Halifax, Lord 102

Hardie, Keir 25

Hart, Dame Judith 80

Hattersley, Roy 46, 50, 51

Healey, Dennis 50, 100

health services 21, 26, 33, 104, 185, 192, 207, 208, 231; Commissioners 137; National Health Service 27, 125, 206, 230

Heath, Edward 39, 40, 49, 59–60, 63, 68, 69, 72, 73, 76, 77, 83, 86, 100, 101, 115, 118, 120, 124, 160, 238, 244

Heffer, Eric 50

Henderson, Arthur 52

Herbert, Sir Edwin 206

Heseltine, Michael 122, 192

Hogg, Quintin (Lord Hailsham) 76

Home Secretary 139, 140, 166, 188

Hopkins, Sir Anthony 88

Hoskyns, Sir John 88, 195

housing 26, 207; council house rents 210; Housing and Building Construction Bill (1983) 175; Housing Finance Act (1972) 205, 209, 238; Minister of Housing 80; sale of council houses 116

Howe, Sir Geoffrey 78

immigration policy 85, 86, 106–7, 116, 123, 163

incomes policy *see* wages policy

Independent Broadcasting Authority (IBA) 93, 96

Independent Television News (ITN) 95

India Act (1858) 138

India, independence of 70, 235, 236

Industrial Injuries Tribunals 134

Industrial Relations Act (1972) 39, 90, 238

Industrial Relations Bill (1969) 63, 65, 76, 80–2, 91, 176

industry(ies) 21, 25, 26, 112, 123, 146, 169, 236; location of 237; nationalized 27, 199–202

inflation 60, 83, 86, 92, 103, 108, 186, 212, 232, 238, 239

Inland Revenue 136

inner-city areas, rioting in 140

interest groups 243–4; *see also* pressure groups

International Commission of Jurists 135

International Monetary Fund (IMF) 60–1, 79, 211

IRA (Irish Republican Army) 223

Iran, economic sanctions against 176

Ireland 179; Home Rule 32, 105; *see also* Northern Ireland

Iron and Steel Board 199

Italian referendum on divorce 121

Jay, Douglas 70

Jenkins, Roy 50, 69, 77, 81, 117, 120, 232, 239, 240

Johnson, Paul 52

Jones, Creech 227

Jones, Jack 90

judicial review, concept of 130

Kaldor, Professor Nicholas 183

Kavanagh, Professor D. 116

Keynes, John Maynard   230
Kilbrandon Report (1973)   33, 216
Kinnock, Neil   49, 50

Labour Coordinating Committee
  (LCC)   232, 233
Labour Party   24, 25, 26, 41, 53, 135,
  156–7, 215, 227–8, 229–35; Annual
  Conferences   40, 41, 46, 76, 82–3,
  84, 98, 107, 228, 230, 234;
  backbenchers   62–3, 75, 142–3,
  144, 165–7, 169, 177, 217; by-
  elections   117; constituency
  parties   45, 46–7, 49, 98, 227, 228,
  234; constitution   45–7, 107, 229,
  233, 234, 239; and devaluation   60,
  69, 77, 231; and devolution   63, 85,
  118–19, 121, 215–17, 218–20, 221,
  242; dismissal of leaders   97, 98–
  100; doctrines and beliefs   229–35;
  and EEC   83, 108, 118, 120, 121,
  239; election of leader and deputy
  leader   45–6, 49–52, 98–9, 100,
  233; electoral college   45–6, 47, 49,
  51, 98, 100; and electoral system
  109–12; fratricidal strife within
  50–1, 231, 232–5; Industrial
  Relations Bill (1969)   80–2, 91;
  intra-party democracy   46–7, 107;
  Labour governments   26–7, 33, 39,
  57, 58, 62–3, 69–70, 75–82, 83, 85,
  90–1, 164, 165–6, 168–9, 176, 199,
  230, 231, 232, 233, 234, 236, 237–8;
  leadership   40, 45–6, 49–50, 59–61,
  75–82, 97, 98–100, 165–6, 233; Left-
  wing   47, 51, 81, 83, 85, 121–2, 144,
  164, 165, 231, 232, 233, 234, 239;
  Liaison Committee   165; Lib-Lab
  Pact   85, 104, 117, 164, 242; local
  government   33–4, 206, 209–10,
  211; London Labour Party   131,
  234; and Lords   174–6;
  manifestos   83, 106, 107–8, 135,
  175, 230, 233; and mass media   93–
  6; and nationalized industries   199,
  201, 230; NEC (National Executive
  Committee)   24, 41, 66, 69, 82, 83,
  107, 116, 164, 227–8, 233, 234; and
  opinion polls   115–16; as
  Opposition   26, 40, 41, 166, 232;
  party loyalty   62–6, 75–6; 'payroll
  vote'   165; PLP (Parliamentary
  Labour Party)   99, 107, 165–6,
  227–8, 233; policies   26, 27, 39, 56–
  7, 60, 82–3; and pressure groups

90–2; and referenda   118–19, 120,
  121–2, 217, 220; SDP split from
  239, 240; and select committees
  168–9; selection and re-selection of
  candidates   46–7, 227, 233;
  Shadow Cabinet   40, 98, 142, 152,
  153, 165; and trade unions   39, 45–
  7, 56, 61, 69, 75–6, 80–2; 90–1, 98,
  100, 113, 146, 232, 233, 234–5; and
  voters   56–7; whips   63–5, 156,
  165, 166
Labour Solidarity Campaign   232, 233
Laker, Sir Freddie   131
land-use planning   132–3, 209
Lansbury, George   98
law (and order)   115, 139, 238; courts,
  role of   130–2; enforcement   137–
  41; judicial review   130; and local
  government   204; personal
  freedom   129–30; public inquiries
  and tribunals   132–5
Lawson, Nigel   77
Layfield Report (1976)   34, 210–11
Leader of Opposition   39, 40, 57, 60,
  91; sacking of   97–102
League Against Cruel Sports   243
legislation, legislative process   56, 92,
  106, 142, 147–51, 153–5, 168
legitimacy of government   125–9
Liberal Party   20, 24, 41, 42, 53, 98,
  121, 199, 217, 221, 240–2, 245;
  Alliance with SDP   240–2; Annual
  Conferences   24, 228; and by-
  elections   117; community
  politics   242; and electoral
  system   53, 55, 109, 111, 241–2;
  governments   57, 147; Lib-Lab
  Pact   85, 104, 117, 164, 242;
  selection of leader   49; voters   56
Life Peerages Act (1958)   174
Lloyd George, David   25, 28, 59, 61,
  68–9
local government   18, 31, 32, 179, 192,
  196, 202–13, 225–6, 242, 245; block
  grants system (1980)   212;
  boundaries   33, 203; and central
  government   203–5, 209, 211;
  councillors   204; 205; education
  204; elections   205, 215, 241;
  finance   34, 203, 204, 210–12;
  functions   33, 206; Local
  Government Act (1972)   33, 118,
  206, 209; Local Government and
  Planning Act (1980)   212; Local
  Government (Scotland) Act

(1973) 206; Local Government
Bill (1981) 122; management 33;
ombudsman 137; rate support
grant 204, 211, 212; rates 62,
122, 210; referenda 62, 118, 120,
122; reforms 32, 33–5, 202–3, 205–
12; rents 209, 210; reports on
190; services 203, 204, 207, 209;
social services 207; staffing 33,
206–7, 212; structure 203, 206;
taxes 203
Local Government in England (White
Paper) 209
London Government Act (1963) 206
London Passenger Transport Board
(LPTB) 27
London Port Authority 27
Lord President of the Council 79
Lords, House of 19, 39, 106, 131, 174–
6; all-party conference on (1967)
175; hereditary v. life peers 174;
reform of 63, 152, 175–6; relations
with Commons 11, 19, 32, 154,
174–6
Luce, Richard 182

MacDonald, Ramsay 51–2, 59, 75, 98,
239
McKenzie, Professor R. T. 228;
British Political Parties 84
Mackintosh, John 220
Macleod, Iain 48, 162
MacMillan, Harold (Earl) 39, 43, 48,
52, 59, 68, 69, 77, 101
Magna Carta 13
Mallaby Report (1967) 33, 206
Marsh, Richard 80
mass media 93–6, 115; *see also* press;
television
Maud Report (1967) 33, 206
Maudling, Reginald 49, 76
Meacher, Michael 51
Medium Term Economic
Assessment 156, 157
Mellish, Bob 65, 81
Members of Parliament:
backbenchers 16, 29, 33, 34, 41,
49, 62–3, 66, 71–2, 75, 77, 81, 85, 86,
117, 136, 142–5, 151, 154, 158, 162,
163, 165–7, 172, 177–8; and by-
elections 117; career prospects
143–4; constituency work 144;
functions 142, 226; influence
161–7; and ministerial
appointments 65–6; Northern

Irish 110, 223–4; and
ombudsman 136–7; party loyalty
to PM 62–7, 71, 75–6, 85, 86;
power 36; PPS (Parliamentary
Private Secretaries) 194; Prime
Minister's patronage 65–6, 71;
private member's bills 19, 151,
158, 161, 162; prospects 30, 65–6;
relations with constituents 23–4;
and select committees 168–72;
selection of candidates 11, 46–7,
227, 233; support for government
17; and television 93, 94, 162;
whipping system *see* Commons; *see
also* Commons; ministers; Prime
Minister
Militant Tendency 232, 234
Milner, Alfred (later Lord) 28
mineworkers, confrontation with
government 56, 91, 124, 238
ministers: and Cabinet 16–17; and
civil servants 39, 88, 112, 179–83,
186–8, 194–7; collective
responsibility 12, 17–18, 181;
dismissal 16, 77; doctrine of
ministerial responsibility 179–83,
184, 190, 191, 193, 194, 226; and
House of Commons 17, 19, 142,
143, 151; junior ministers 77, 143;
maladministration 135–7; and
nationalized industries 199–200,
201–2; number of 30; and party
manifestos 106–9; and political
advisers 194–7; and Prime
Minister 67–72, 76–82; and public
inquiries and tribunals 132–5; and
quangos 198–9; resignation 77,
181–3; workload 80; *see also*
Cabinet
Mitchell, Austin 172–3
monarchy 11, 13, 14, 48, 65, 126
monetarism 88, 171, 211, 239
Monopolies Commission 82
Moodie, Professor Graeme 51
Morant, Sir Robert 28
Morrison, Herbert 50, 51, 76, 199,
230, 240
Mount, Ferdinand 72, 88
Muir, Ramsay 186

National Audit Act (1983) 158, 201
National Audit Office 158
National Coal Board 201
National Debt 156
National Economic Development

Council (NEDC)   92
National Government   26
National Health Service (NHS)   27,
    125, 230
National Health Service
    Reorganization Act (1973)   206
National Insurance Tribunals   134
National Plan   27
National Union of Conservative
    Associations   48
Nationalist parties *see* Scotland; Wales
nationalization   26, 27, 56, 230, 231,
    233, 240; acts   27; nationalized
    industries   27, 199–202, 236;
    privatization   192, 202, 239; Select
    Committee   168, 170, 200, 201
Northcote–Trevelyan Report (1853)
    183–4
Northern Ireland (Ulster)   77, 129,
    212, 221–4; administration   184,
    214, 222; army in   137–8, 222, 223;
    Commissioner for Complaints
    137; direct rule   222, 223;
    European elections in   111;
    general strike (1975)   125;
    Government of Ireland Act
    (1920)   184, 222; Northern Ireland
    Assembly   223–4; Northern
    Ireland civil service   184; Northern
    Ireland Office   223; number of
    MPs   110, 224; power-sharing
    223; Prevention of Terrorism Act
    (1976)   130; referendum (1973)
    118; riots (1969)   138; Royal Ulster
    Constabulary (RUC)   222; Sinn
    Fein and SDLP   223; Stormont
    184, 222, 223, 224; taxation   222
Norton, Philip   163, 172
nuclear disarmament/weapons   57, 82,
    231, 239

O'Brien, Sir Leslie   183
ombudsman (parliamentary
    commissioner)   135–7, 172, 181
opinion polls   38, 65, 74, 75, 82, 105,
    111, 115–16, 235; *see also* referenda
Opposition (in Commons)   17, 26, 57,
    58, 73, 85, 95, 104, 108, 142–3, 150,
    154, 155, 159, 161, 162, 164, 166,
    167; Leader of   39, 40, 57, 60, 91,
    97–102, 146
Ostrogorski, M. I.   227
Our Changing Democracy (White
    Paper)   217
Owen, Dr David   239, 240

Palmerston, Viscount   146, 147
Parliament: authorizing public
    expenditure and taxation   155–61;
    and civil service   190, 192–4; and
    devolution   218–20; governing
    through   142–78; how executive
    gained control   147–53;
    influence   176–7; legislative
    process   153–5; and nationalized
    industries   200; pressing
    government, methods of   161–7;
    role   103, 142–7; standing and
    select committees   167–72; *see also*
    Commons; Lords; Members of
    Parliament
Parliament Acts: (1911)   11, 32;
    (1949)   11; (No. 2) Bill (1969)   63,
    81, 152
Parliamentary Private Secretaries   65,
    166, 194, 195
Parsons, Sir Anthony   72
party leadership   38–40; character
    57, 58–61; constraints on   82–4;
    dismissal   97–102; limitations on
    power   75–96; and public   103–41;
    selection   45–53, 98–9, 100, 233;
    strength of   62–74; *see also* Prime
    Minister
patronage   30, 40, 61, 65–6, 71, 102,
    174, 197
Peel, Sir Robert   16, 20, 146
Pitt, William, the Younger   31
Plaid Cymru *see* Welsh Nationalist
    Party
Plowden Report   156
pluralism, political   92, 243
police: community policing   140;
    complaints procedure   139–40;
    corruption   139; law
    enforcement   137–41; Police Act
    (1964)   139; Police Bill (1983)   62;
    Police Complaints Board (1977)
    140; public accountability   139,
    140; Scarman Report   140; Willink
    Commission (1959)   138–9
political parties   243; Annual
    Conferences   24, 40, 82–4, 228;
    and by-elections   116–17;
    campaigns   20, 25, 105, 108–9; in
    Commons   161, 163, 165–7, 176–7;
    and the community   227–9;
    constituency parties   227, 228; as a
    constraint on Prime Minister   82–
    4; deputy leader's election   50–1;
    dissolution threat of   65; and

electors 12, 103–41; leadership *see*
party leadership; machinery 20,
24, 25, 227–8; manifestos 83, 105–
9, 135, 175, 229, 233; nationalists
215–17, 220; opinion polls 115–16;
organizations 21, 24; party
loyalty 62–7, 71, 75–6, 161; party
system 67, 227–9; role outside
Parliament 41; selection of
candidates 11, 46–7, 227; two-
party system 14, 20, 38, 53–5; *see
also* Conservative Party; Labour
Party; etc.
political reform, nineteenth-century
31–2
Pompidou, President Georges 68
Powell, Enoch 49, 76–7, 84, 120
press 23–4, 25, 95–6, 162
pressure groups 21, 28–9, 38, 40, 41,
84, 86, 89–92, 113–14, 154, 159, 192,
244; and civil service 193–4;
growth of 243
Prevention of Terrorism (Temporary
Provisions) Act (1976) 130
Prime Minister: and Cabinet 16, 39,
67–72, 76–82; character 45, 57,
58–61; and civil service 38, 67, 72–
3, 86–9, 112–13; and Commons
19, 38, 84–6, 143, 163, 165–6, 173,
176; criticisms of 39, 66; decision-
making 67–8; election date chosen
by 58, 73–4; and electorate 41,
42, 43, 53, 57, 103–41;
expectations 45; and international
diplomacy 68; limitations on
power 75–96; loyalty to 62–7,
71, 75–6, 85, 102; and mass media
93–6; and ministers 30, 39, 65, 67–
72, 76–82; and party 82–4, 107–8;
patronage 30, 65–6, 71, 102, 174;
personal contacts 122; policy
advisers to 72, 88; power 36, 37,
38–40; and pressure groups 89–92;
public relations 39–40, 73–4, 94–5;
sacking of 97–102; selection of
51–3, 53–8; social class 58–9;
staff 72, 73; strain on 59;
strength 62–74; *see also* party
leadership
Prior, James 77
privatization 192, 202, 239
Privy Council, Judicial Committee 218
Profumo affair 60, 101
proportional representation 19–20,
111, 112, 239

Public Accounts Commission 158
Public Accounts Committee 18, 149,
158
public expenditure 42, 87, 104, 124,
196, 238; control of 11, 18, 148–9,
155–61, 185; cuts 87, 88, 164, 192,
211–12, 239; estimates 148, 155–8,
160; five-year planning 40, 156–7;
local government 203, 204, 210–
12; public accounts 148–9, 158
Public Expenditure Scrutiny
Committee (PESC) 156, 157, 185
public inquiries 132–5
Pym, Francis 77, 166

quangos 198–9, 213

racial tension 140
railways: closure 133–4;
nationalization 27
Rank and File Mobilizing Committee
(RFMC) 232
rate support grant 204, 211, 212
rates, local 62, 203, 210; Committee
of Inquiry (1965) 206;
equalization schemes 209
Redcliffe–Maud Commission (1969)
33, 206–7, 208, 209
Rees-Mogg, William 95
referendum (referenda) 118–22, 176;
devolution 63, 85, 118–19, 121,
176, 217, 220; EEC 118, 120, 121;
local authority 62, 122; Northern
Ireland 118
Reform Acts: (1832) 14, 23; (1867)
14, 147; (1884) 14; (1918) 23;
(1928) 23; (1969) 23
regional government, regionalism
184–5, 198, 213–21, 225–6, 231–2,
237
Rent Tribunals 134
*The Reorganisation of Central
Government* (White Paper) 244
Representation of the People Act
(1948) 11
Retail Price Maintenance 146
Rhodesia (now Zimbabwe) 68, 75;
Southern Rhodesia (Sanctions)
Order (1968) 174
riots, inner-city 140
Rodgers, William 239
Ross, Stephen 241
Royal Ulster Constabulary (RUC)
222
Russell, Earl 147

St John Stevas, Norman 77, 158, 201
Salisbury, Lord 29
Samuel, Herbert 52
Scargill, Arthur 92
Scarman Report 140
Scotland 42, 179, 237; civil service
184; devolution 85, 118–19, 164,
215–20, 221, 242; health services
33, 137; local government 33, 202–
3, 212, 213; local government
ombudsman 137; Local
Government (Scotland) Act
(1973) 206; Police Committee
139; Scottish Affairs Committee
169; Scottish Assembly 117, 216,
217, 218, 220; Scottish
Constitutional Committee 216;
Scottish Grand Committee 168;
Scottish Nationalist Party (SNP)
41, 54, 85, 104, 109, 117, 164, 215,
216–17, 220, 228, 242; Scottish
Office 184–5, 213–14, 215;
Secretary of State for 139, 216,
218; Solicitor General for 182;
'West Lothian question' 218–19;
Wheatley Commission 33, 206,
207–8
Second World War 26, 28, 75, 93,
114–15, 236
Sedgemore, Brian, *The Secret
Constitution* 195
Seebohm Report 33
Select Committee(s) of the House of
Commons 19, 145, 147, 151, 153,
154–5, 157–8, 162, 167–72, 180, 193,
201; Agriculture 169;
Broadcasting 172; Corporation
Tax 160; Defence 169, 171;
distinction between standing
committees and 168; Education
169; Estimates 155–6, 157, 169;
European Legislation 169;
Expenditure 157–8, 169, 170, 238;
Home Affairs 171; Nationalized
Industries 168, 170, 200, 201;
ombudsman 172, 181; Overseas
Aid 169; Procedure 34, 156–7,
158, 160–1, 162, 169; Public
Accounts 18, 149, 158, 170, 177;
Public Expenditure Scrutiny 156,
157, 185; Race Relations 169;
Science and Technology 169;
Scottish Affairs 169; Treasury
160, 169, 171; Wealth Tax 160

Selwyn Lloyd, John 101
Shadow Cabinet (Parliamentary
Committee) 40, 98, 142, 152, 153,
165, 166, 227
Shelter 243
Shore, Peter 46, 50, 80
Sinn Fein 223
Smith, Cyril 241
Smith, Ian 68
Soames, Christopher (Lord) 227
'social contract' 39, 56, 232
Social Democratic and Labour Party
(SDLP: Northern Ireland) 223
Social Democratic Party (SDP) 228,
239–41; Alliance with Liberals
240–2; and by-elections 117, 240;
and electoral system 109, 241–2;
and 1983 elections 240, 241;
policies 239–40; selection of
leadership 49
social policies, emergence of 25–8
social services 169, 207, 208; alleged
spongers on 103
Special Policy Unit 68
state ownership *see* nationalization
Steel, David 117
Stokes, Richard *see* Butler, David
Stormont, Northern Ireland 184, 222,
223, 224
Straw, Jack 195
strikes 39, 91, 104, 124–5, 238; civil
service 192; General Strike
(1926) 93; and police behaviour 139
Stuart, J. G. (Viscount Stuart of
Findhorn) 146
student protests 125, 139
Suez crisis (1956) 60, 70, 75, 93, 94,
101, 152–3
supplementary benefits 204
'sus' law, repeal of 171

taxation 12, 13, 25, 56, 103, 104, 116,
123, 148, 153, 158–60, 203, 210–11,
238, 239; corporation tax 159, 160;
and EEC 12; Northern Ireland
222; PAYE 210; rates 62, 203,
210; and social policy 25, 56;
supertax 159; VAT 159, 210;
wealth tax 160
Tebbit, Norman 77
television and radio 25, 94–5, 96; and
Commons 172–4; and MPs 93,
94, 162; political balance on 12,
93, 96; and Prime Minister 94–5

Thatcher, Margaret 30, 40, 49, 50, 56, 59, 60, 61, 77, 78, 80, 87, 88, 90, 92, 94–5, 124, 163, 166, 176, 195, 196, 199, 211, 213, 238, 244, 245
Thorneycroft, Peter 77
Thorpe, Jeremy 120
tobacco industry 244
trade unions 38, 69, 116; and Conservative Party 89–90, 92, 238; and election of Labour leader 45–6, 47, 49, 98; Industrial Relations Bill (1969) 63, 65, 76, 80–2; influence of general secretaries 46, 113; and Labour Party 26, 39, 45–7, 49, 56, 61, 75–6, 80–2, 90, 100, 113, 228, 232, 233, 234–5; protection for 25; reform of 76; social contract with 39, 56, 232; strikes 39, 91, 93, 104, 124–5; *see also* wages policy
trade unions (by name): AUEW 46; NFU 113, 243; NUM 91; TGWU 90
Trades Union Congress (TUC) 25, 39, 76, 81, 90, 125, 243; executive committee 28–9
Transport Act (1962) 133
Transport Users Consultative Committee 133
Treasury 79, 89, 114, 187; criticism of 186; devaluation 40; estimates 156; financial control by 32–3, 148, 160, 185, 214, 231; and local government 34; planning 156–7; role of 18–19; Select Committee 160, 169, 171
tribunals 132–5, 140
Truman, President Harry S. 37
two-party system 14, 20, 38, 53–5, 164

unemployment 25, 26, 56, 60, 61, 86, 104, 124, 140, 233, 235, 237, 238, 239
unilateral nuclear disarmament 57, 82
United Nations Charter of Human Rights 129

United States, Bill of Rights 129, 132

VAT (value added tax) 159, 210
Victoria, Queen 126
Vietnam War 80

wages policy (incomes policy) 25, 39, 40, 60, 61, 76, 83, 91, 104, 108, 201, 237, 238, 239, 244
Wales, Welsh 42, 179, 184; devolution 118, 164, 215–18, 219, 220, 221, 242; Grand Committee 168; health services 33, 137; local government 33, 202, 206, 209, 212, 242; ombudsman 137; referenda 118, 220; Welsh Affairs Committee 169; Welsh language 242; Welsh Nationalist Party (Plaid Cymru) ,41, 54, 117, 164, 215, 216–17, 228, 242; Welsh Office 185, 213, 214, 215
Walker, Peter 77
Walters, Professor Alan 72, 88
Watch Committees 139
welfare benefits 26, 231; cuts 88
'West Lothian question' 218–19
Westminster model 14–15, 16–22, 23, 28, 29, 31, 32, 42, 142, 225–7
Wheatley Commission (1969) 33, 206, 207–8
'Whig theory of history' 14
whips *see* Commons, House of
Whitehouse, Mary 243
Whitelaw, William (Viscount) 50, 78, 106–7, 166
Whyatt Committee 135
Williams, Shirley 117, 239
Willink Commission (1959) 138
Wilson, Harold (Lord) 39, 40, 43, 49, 56, 59, 60, 63, 64–5, 68, 69, 70, 73, 75–6, 77, 78, 79, 80–2, 83, 85, 86, 91, 92, 95, 98, 104, 107, 117, 120, 165, 189, 210, 231, 232
Wrigglesworth, Ian 240